Small

Sacrifices

Small Sacrifices

Religious Change and Cultural Identity among the Ngaju of Indonesia

ANNE SCHILLER

New York   Oxford
OXFORD UNIVERSITY PRESS
1997

Oxford University Press

Oxford   New York
Athens   Auckland   Bangkok   Bogota   Bombay   Buenos Aires
Calcutta   Cape Town   Dar es Salaam   Delhi   Florence   Hong Kong
Istanbul   Karachi   Kuala Lumpur   Madras   Madrid   Melbourne
Mexico City   Nairobi   Paris   Singapore   Taipei   Tokyo   Toronto

and associated companies in
Berlin   Ibadan

Library of Congress Cataloging-in-Publication Data
Schiller, Anne Louise.
Small sacrifices : religious change and cultural identity among
the Ngaju of Indonesia / Anne Schiller.
     p.   cm.
Includes bibliographical references and index.
ISBN 0-19-509557-X (cloth). — ISBN 0-19-509558-8 (paper)
1. Ngaju (Indonesian people)—Religion.   I. Title.
BL2123.N43S35   1997
299'.92—DC20   96-20913

9 8 7 6 5 4 3 2 1

Printed in the United States of America
on acid-free paper

For Poter

Acknowledgments

"If someday you write a poem, then for nine years keep it safely indoors. Making changes is quite allowable, before you publish. Once freed, words can't return." So Horace advised readers of the *Ars Poetica* (Jacob Fuchs, translator). Nine years have passed since the end of my doctoral studies, with which this book began. During those years, my understanding of the relationship between Hindu Kaharingan and identity in Central Kalimantan has deepened, and religious practice in Central Kalimantan has continued to change. I have returned to the field several times to follow those changes and others. In the course of my studies and travels, I have incurred debts to family, to friends, to teachers who became friends, and to friends who became family.

The late Victor Turner was among my first teachers in anthropology. Participation in seminars hosted at his home kindled my interest in the study of ritual when I was an undergraduate at the University of Virginia. I was fortunate to have other fine teachers at that institution as well, including Christopher Crocker and Peter Metcalf. My interest in ritual was nurtured during my graduate work in the Southeast Asia Program at Cornell University. There I was privileged to study with James Boon and A. Thomas Kirsch. Both scholars have had a profound effect on my approach to the study of religion and society, and I am deeply grateful to them. I am also grateful to John Wolff of the Department of Modern Languages at Cornell for teaching me to speak Indonesian.

This manuscript specifically and this project broadly defined have benefited from the advice and scholarship of many friends and colleagues in the United States and abroad. In this regard, I would like to note especially Bernd Lambert, Michael Malley, Molly Mullin, Martin Rouse, Abby Ruddick, Vinson Sutlive,

Chee-Kiong Tong, and Robert Winzeler. George Appell provided a close reading of chapter 4 and made many valuable comments concerning my presentation of data on kinship.

Reid Barbour read the entire manuscript several times with patience and care. I am grateful for his critical readings, cogent suggestions, unflagging support, and more.

I began writing this book when I was a faculty member of the Department of Anthropology at Ithaca College. I thank my former colleagues and friends in that department, as well as Dotty Dekker, manuscript processor at the college. I completed the book at North Carolina State University. I am grateful to the faculty and staff of the Department of Sociology and Anthropology for providing such congenial surroundings in which to write and teach. Exchanges with my colleagues at North Carolina State University have broadened my own horizons in social science.

My parents, Frances Myers Schiller and John Frederick Schiller, have encouraged me wholeheartedly in countless ways for many years. I cannot adequately express my gratitude to them for their love and support, but I welcome this opportunity to say thank you.

The fieldwork upon which this volume is based was carried out between December 1982 and June 1983 and in the summers of 1991, 1995, and 1996. My research has been supported by the Fulbright-Hays Doctoral Dissertation Abroad Program; two grants-in-aid from the Wenner-Gren Foundation for Anthropological Research; a Palmer Award from Wellesley College; a grant-in-aid from the Sigma-Xi Scientific Society; two grants from the Association for Asian Studies in conjunction with the Luce Foundation; National Geographic Television; and a North Carolina State University Faculty Development Fund Award. I acknowledge the assistance of these institutions with gratitude. I would also like to thank the Indonesian Institute of Sciences (LIPI) for permitting me to conduct research in Central Kalimantan.

Cynthia Read and Paula Wald of Oxford University Press have guided me through the process of transforming a manuscript into a book. It has been a pleasure to work with them both.

I am indebted to I Wayan Madu, former counselor to the Hindu-Buddhist congregations in the Office of Religion in Palangka Raya, for unfailing assistance throughout my initial period of fieldwork in Palangka Raya and during later research trips to Bali. He and his family have become dear friends, and I am indebted to them for their many kindnesses.

My initial fieldwork in Central Kalimantan would have been more difficult without the support of the late Johannes Saililah, who befriended me soon after my arrival and generously shared his formidable knowledge of ritual with me. Among my most cherished memories from that period is of a trip we made together to visit a *tiwah* on the Kapuas River and to tour other sites where he had served as head specialist at death rituals in the 1930s. Saililah was an ethnographer in his own right. It was an honor to know him well.

Mantikei R. Hanyi has been a steadfast friend since we met in 1983 at services we both regularly attended at the Hindu Kaharingan meeting hall in Palangka Raya. As a Kaharingan priest, he has shared his understanding of Kaharingan philosophy with me. As my *dampu*, he has also shared his family. For all of this, I am deeply grateful.

Finally, a word of thanks to my other friends in Central Kalimantan. Aku paham hanjak tutu, tuntung manyewut tarimakasih tagal kakare panduhup mama-mina palus pahari samadiai ije atun intu Palangka Raya atawa kea ije atun intu pire-pire lewu hung Sungei Kahayan tuntang Sungai Katingan. Amun jatun panduhup mama-mina, pahari biti, penelitian ije akan mamampa buku tuh, musti dia tau jadi. Awi te aku manyampai tarimakasih akan Kaluarga H. Adis, Kaluarga Retha Ujung, Kaluarga S.T. Dohong, Almarhum Bue Basir Muka, Bue Pa Tilo, Tambi Indu Sem, Bue Pa Bujang, Bue Pa Tin, Kaluarga Lewis KDR, Kaluarga Bajik Simpei, Kaluarga Simal Penyang, Kiwok D. Rampai, Basir Tian Agan, Basir Sidie, I Wayan Karya, Walman Narang, Sahari Andung, Ebeb R. Tandum, Adi Frin, Rusmawardi, Sri Utami, Liberti Hanyi, Wona Tuwan, Trecy D. Sudirman, Putir Madjat, Yerson HB Suling, Bapa Samboyan, Indu Kahaya, Kaluarga Ludie Djangku, Kaluarga Lodewik R. Hanyi. Kea akan kakare pahari beken ije dia tasewut hetuh. Tagal kahanjak atei kea, hung hetuh kea aku manyampai terimakasih umba gagenep pangurus Majelis Besar Agama Hindu Kaharingan ije halajur manduhup aku metuh malalu penelitian intu pire-pire eka. Aku balaku duhup tinai hung pire-pire katika ije akan naharep, tau labih are mandinu panduhup bara tokoh masyarakat, tokoh hadat, tuntang tokoh Agama Kaharingan, uka kakare gawin itah tau mandinu hasil ije bahalap. Keleh itah belum penyang hinje simpei, panjang umur, tau hasundau tinai.

Raleigh, N.C.   A. L. S.
October 1996

Contents

Small

Sacrifices

1 | Introduction

A report on regional criminality featured in the 5 January 1991 issue of Indonesia's premier newsmagazine, *Tempo*, appealed to its national readership's worst fears about the customs of their compatriots deep in the rain forests of Central Kalimantan. According to the report, titled "Gadut, Tumbal Tiwah" (Gadut, spirit offering at *tiwah*), members of the "Dayak Kaharingan tribe" were continuing their ancestral practice of taking human heads as part of their preparations for enacting traditional secondary burial rituals called *tiwah*. Many readers of *Tempo*'s unsettling report would probably have reacted contemptuously to the term "Dayak," which connotes a host of mostly negative images of Borneo's indigenous inhabitants. Presumably some readers would have subscribed to the popular view of Dayaks as ferocious wild men with a passion for hunting heads and possibly also indulging in cannibal feasts. *Tempo*'s writers suggested a parallel between the exaggerated tales of Native American tribes that skinned or scalped their victims and accounts of the practices of contemporary Dayak peoples. They noted the Kalimantan exception, where head-hunting "isn't a fairy tale" (96).[1]

"Kaharingan," a term less familiar to *Tempo*'s audience, refers to the indigenous religion of many Dayaks, in particular those known as the Ngaju. It is the Ngaju, the largest of Central Kalimantan's Dayak groups, who celebrate *tiwah*. According to the article in *Tempo*, *tiwah* is a ritual that leads human souls to a "seventh sky" upon completion of their existence in this world. In fact, *tiwah* is actually the general designation for a host of rituals that together constitute the final treatment for human souls as well as for mortal remains. During *tiwah*, the souls of the deceased are processed by means of lengthy chants so that they may ascend to a celestial abode. Physical remains are likewise subject to extensive ministrations. They are exhumed from the grave, cleaned, anointed, and placed in handsome bone repositories made of ironwood or cement. Throughout the celebration of *tiwah,* sacrificial offerings are rendered to departed souls in order to provision them for their journey to the celestial "Upperworld," as well as to ensure their comfort on arrival in their new home. These offerings include cooked foods and domesticated animals such as chickens, pigs, and cattle. It is widely acknowledged by villagers that in the past, human beings—either captives from other villages or debt slaves—figured among the sacrifices offered by the living at *tiwah* held for dead kin. The men and women sacrificed during *tiwah* were intended to become the servants of the deceased in the afterlife, to attend their master or mistress throughout eternity.

According to the particulars of the criminal case described in *Tempo,* three Dayak men admitted to decapitating a villager named Gadut, claiming to have killed him at the behest of an elementary schoolteacher. The teacher, they alleged, had promised them 1.5 million rupiah in cash (about $750) and 50 grams of gold if they could provide him with a freshly skinned head for his later use at a *tiwah.* The accused obtained the head, but their payment never materialized. They claimed that when the schoolteacher reneged on his promise, they began having second thoughts: "Because [we were] regretful, we buried the head, so that it couldn't be used again in a *tiwah*" (96). One of the ways that heads could apparently be utilized in the context of *tiwah* was suggested by a non-Dayak police officer present at an interrogation. He volunteered to reporters that participants in *tiwah* sometimes drank rice wine from skulls that had been acquired for the occasion. The report closed on a provocative note. According to *Tempo's* reporters, the adherents of Kaharingan religion did not consider head-taking within the context of *tiwah* to be a criminal offense. *Tempo* informed its readers: "Without a 'fresh' head, *tiwah* isn't really authentic."

The noteworthiness of this report does not rest solely in its subject matter, though descriptions of Ngaju death rituals and associated practices of human sacrifice have long held the interest of general readers in Indonesia, as well as of ethnologists around the world. From time to time, similar reports of head-taking and human sacrifice in the context of *tiwah* have appeared in Indonesia's popular press. These accounts are usually featured in glossy magazines published and circulated primarily on the island of Java, where the number of immigrant Dayaks is decidedly small. For example, only a few years before Gadut's demise, in 1987 *Detektif & Romatika* magazine (no. 1233) published a lengthy account titled "Mystery of a Stack of Bones in Kuala Kapuas, Central Kalimantan: Kuni Who Vanished in the Jungle, Is it True That She Has Already Been Decapitated?" *Tempo,* too, had sent a report of this particular alleged head-taking to press, together with a rather dated admonishment from one of

Central Kalimantan's former governors that an unwary visitor should not enter a Dayak village in the midst of *tiwah* lest he or she be earmarked as a sacrifice to the departed.[2]

What made the circumstances surrounding the publication of this latest account of Dayak head-taking so remarkable was not so much the substance of the report itself as the passionate feeling of outrage and the cries for reparation that it evoked when copies of the magazine reached readers in Central Kalimantan. That the most recent depiction of the adherents of Kaharingan as headhunters had not gone unnoticed by those it targeted was evident from a lengthy letter of grievance which appeared in *Tempo*'s "Commentary" column on 22 July 1991. Signed by Lewis K. D. R. B.Sc., "General Chairman of the Supreme Council of Hindu Kaharingan Religion," it ran beneath the caption "Bantahan Hindu Kaharingan" or "Hindu Kaharingan Protest." The letter stated that *Tempo*'s article on Gadut's death "was very damaging to the Hindu Kaharingan congregation." It had "greatly offended the feelings" of the Supreme Council's leadership, as the report "contained within it the degradation and defamation of a religious ritual they themselves regarded as holy and held in high esteem." The author refuted *Tempo*'s claim that a human head is a prerequisite to enacting *tiwah*: "[*Tempo*'s explanation] that without a fresh head *tiwah* is not correct . . . is untrue." He countered that rumors of murders carried out in anticipation of *tiwah* were nothing more than vestiges of a colonial era mentality; that prior to independence, Dutch administrators had invented these fanciful tales to introduce divisiveness into the Kaharingan congregation. "Furthermore," concluded Chairman Lewis, "in the living experience of the Hindu Kaharingan congregation, from early times to the present, the Dayak tribe has generally never drunk rice wine from the skull of human beings."

To scholars who follow developments in Central Kalimantan, and to anyone more generally interested in the relationship between Indonesian minorities and the state, the dispatch and publication of Chairman Lewis's letter had to be counted among the most revealing palpable evidence of the sweeping social and cultural transformations currently taking place in the region—the transformations with which this book is concerned. The letter demonstrated that there were individuals in Central Kalimantan who were concerned with how their way of life was being depicted to their countrymen, and who were willing to speak out publicly on this issue. Their actions suggested that they wanted their local customs to be judged acceptable within the bounds of Indonesian national culture.[3] They have not always been so condoned.

Indeed, Dayak peoples perennially appear to be plagued by "bad press," as I quickly became aware within the first weeks of my initial visit to Indonesia. In 1981 I participated in an advanced intensive Indonesian language training program at Satya Wacana University in Salatiga, Central Java. I recall a parade celebrating traditional Indonesian arts that I attended in nearby Solo shortly after my arrival. A procession of floats, most of them built on the beds of open trucks, streamed by. One of these was manned by a single dancer, apparently ethnically Javanese, wearing only a loincloth and black body paint. He brandished a long sword, which he swung widely about, and grimaced horribly, gnashing his teeth at onlookers. Spectators assembled along the parade route roared with laughter. When I asked a Javanese woman standing next to me what the dancer was representing, she replied without hesitation, "Dayak Kalimantan" (a Dayak from Kalimantan). Shortly afterward, when an article in a teen magazine on the "bloody ritual for God" caught my eye, I read the following account of Kaharingan death rituals:

> Perhaps, according to a *master storyteller* [my italics; a Javanese word was used here], in the past, what was offered in this ceremony was "a human head." Well, this can be imagined. How horrifying. . . . And usually the one who became the target was from an outside tribe. So don't be surprised, in that era, that there were often wars between tribes. Of course this comprises a picture of the Kaharingan Dayak tribe tens of years ago. Now they already know modern culture. Although they still conduct *Tewah [sic]*, no "human head" is chopped off; we witnessed buffaloes, cows, pigs, and other [animals]. . . . Sadistic? Sure. That's the *Tewah* ritual of the Kaharingan Dayak tribe. (Ris Prasetyo 1981, 62–63)

In addition to attempting to counter this kind of damaging reportage, Chairman Lewis in his letter to *Tempo* clearly sought, and presumably won, increased national recognition for both a religion and a religious council previously little known beyond Central Kalimantan. The letter also attested to the apparent authority of the Hindu Kaharingan synod to speak out and act on behalf of the "congregation" or "tribe" whose interests it claimed to represent.

Shortly after *Tempo*'s publication of the "Hindu Kaharingan Protest," I arrived back in Palangka Raya, capital of the province of Central Kalimantan, to begin the second of four visits I have thus far made to the field. I was already well acquainted with Chairman Lewis. I had come to know him and most of the other members of the Supreme Council of the Hindu Kaharingan Religion during the eighteen months of field research I conducted from 1982 to 1984. The Supreme Council is an organization founded in 1971 to provide leadership and religious guidance to adherents of Kalimantan's indigenous religion. In July 1991 its leadership's attention was consumed by their suit against *Tempo*. Friends and contacts on the council were pleased to report that in civil arbitration before the Conference of Regional leaders (Musyawarah Pimpinan Daerah [MUSPIDA]), an informal tribunal composed of local dignitaries, *Tempo* magazine had acceded to their demands for a formal apology and had agreed to publish the general chairman's aforementioned letter of grievance. Present at the arbitration, I was told, were members of the Provincial Legislative Assembly, the Appellate Court, and the Office of Religious Affairs, as well as other important individuals. Reparations did not end there, however. The magazine had also agreed to send representatives from its Jakarta office to join in a ritual that would, as Central Kalimantan's then-Governor Soeparmanto phrased it, "neutralize any problems that might arise as a result of the article" (*Dinamika Pembangunan,* 1991b, 6). That ritual, known in the Ngaju language as *hambai,* is one of adoption or "blood-brotherhood": two men would participate, one from the Supreme Council representing the entire Hindu Kaharingan congregation and one from *Tempo* acting on the magazine's behalf.[4] The publishers pledged, furthermore, to donate 5 million rupiah toward the cost of performing *hambai.* Concerning these anticipated festivities, the general secretary of the Supreme Council, Walter Penyang, was quoted in a local paper as saying, "At the time *hambai* is carried out, we will adopt the *Tempo* magazine party as members of the Hindu Kaharingan family" (ibid., 4). Following *hambai,* the *Tempo* representative would be invited to attend a *tiwah,* which was to be celebrated in a Barito River village.

The "Hindu Kaharingan—*Tempo* Insult Case," as this celebrated dispute came to be known, galvanized a large segment of Palangka Raya's indigenous population. The debates surrounding the incident were most instructive, offering a fresh vantage on the concerns and self-image of the Ngaju during a period of heightened cultural awareness. I had returned to the field at an extraordinary moment. The controversy that surrounded this dispute offered a rare opportunity to develop a better understanding of how Kalimantan's indigenous religion figures in the construction and refashioning of identity in a province widely considered to be among the nation's most isolated and undeveloped regions. It also yielded deeper insight into how the evolving relationship between religion and the state in Indonesia was affecting the cultural systems of that country's minorities more generally.

The aim of the present volume is to contextualize and share my understanding of these processes. My broader theoretical concern is to illuminate how notions of authority and authenticity in the "religious" arena articulate with emerging conceptualizations of identity, including cultural and civic identity. I argue that for the "Ngaju," a term that will be subjected to examination, dismantling, and partial rehabilitation in this study, identity is taking shape largely in response to engagements with religious issues. The terms of "Ngaju identity" come under special scrutiny in the context of celebrating life crisis rituals. I suggest that in their quest to fashion a public persona, Ngaju Dayaks are manifestly rethinking their ritual practices and their various roles in them. Toby Volkman has written that, among the Toraja of Sulawesi, "to some, ritual is a source of renewed dynamism; to others it is the object of a nostalgic romanticism; and to still others it is a burdensome legacy that leads to squandered wealth and energy. Through ritual the Toraja enact, elaborate, and reflect upon images of themselves and their society" (1985, 6). In Central Kalimantan, ritual is all of this and more. It is a vehicle through which a community is gradually coming to be fashioned. Chairman Lewis's letter of grievance to *Tempo* provided a glimpse of this process. In his references to a Hindu Kaharingan congregation, as well as to "living experience of the Dayak tribe," he was invoking conceptualizations of emerging communal identities.

My goals in this volume are varied. First, the book is intended to contribute to an understanding of the institutional restructuring of religion in contemporary Indonesia and its effects. I seek to relate changes in religious ritual and belief to other cultural and social transformations. I use the routinization of Ngaju religion as an example of a larger process of reform with important implications for relationships both within "ethnic groups" and between minority peoples and the state. In this regard, the book focuses attention on the changing form and content of the celebrated rites of secondary burial, *tiwah*. It probes the adaptive capacity of *tiwah*, especially in this current period of accelerated social change, and suggests how the evolution of this particular ritual practice articulates with other aspects of Ngaju experience, past and present. This effort interrelates with the volume's second, broader goal, which is to offer a case study that contributes to contemporary anthropological interest in the interpretation of signifying practices in arenas where various cultural systems— local, national, religious, ideological—interpenetrate. Jean Comaroff has observed that "the social field . . . is the product of the continuous and changing relationship between the 'system' under observation and the 'external' world [J. L. Comaroff 1982]" (1985, 3). A particular challenge here, of course, is that the boundaries of cultural systems are amorphous, influencing one another reciprocally and continually. This book addresses how such penetrations have been, and continue to be, insinuated in the formulation of Ngaju identities. Finally, the volume is intended as a contribution to the ethnographic record on indigenous peoples of Southeast Asia.

Despite my obvious interest in exploring what I perceive as a burgeoning sense of Ngaju identity, it is antithetical to the purpose of this volume to reify the concept of "Ngaju," notwithstanding the best efforts of many Ngaju to do just that. Richard Handler (1988) has noted the tendency of citizens of new nation-states to objectify "tradition" as culture. The objectification of culture entails "seeing culture as a thing: (a natural object) made up of objects and entities ('traits')" (14). Objectified culture can be subjected to manipulation and pressed into service by interested parties (Handler 1985). Handler cautions writers on ethnicity and nationalism to "resist all collective terms and rhetorical strategies that suggest the existence of a bounded cultural object. Since his or her subjects will explain themselves in precisely such terms, the ethnographer's interpretive task must take the form of destructive analysis" (Handler 1985, 178).

In this regard, one of the challenges of writing this book has been to present data in a way that captures the continuous oscillation between the deconstruction and construction of cultural identity. In fashioning my presentation, I return repeatedly to religious belief and practice, particularly as they function in the establishment and demise of types of community. Whereas many anthropologists have treated religion as a phenomenon engendered by social organization, which in turn perpetuates that organization, I explore as well the role of indigenous, introduced, and syncretic religious rituals in the development of "Ngajuness" (a term that I prefer over "Ngaju identity" or "Ngaju ethnicity"). The indigenous peoples of Central Kalimantan now operate in a highly formalized religious arena with a variety of religious options. Most have converted to pan-ethnic religions. And there is much variation in ritual and belief within the community/congregation that has now been designated "Hindu Kaharingan." Rita Kipp has noted that "surprisingly little has been written about the effects of religious pluralism on ethnic identity" (1993, 77). I suggest that religious pluralism operates at two levels in Central Kalimantan—a "macro" one and a "micro" one—and that both levels affect how "Ngajuness" is taking shape today.

With regard to the relationship between pluralism and identity, it is important to point out early on the tremendous influence that living under colonial and neocolonial systems has had on the construction of identity among many Indonesian peoples (George 1996, Hefner 1985, Kipp 1993, Pemberton 1994, Tsing 1993, Volkman 1985). In the case of the Ngaju, it is particularly by means of religion that colonial and modern authorities have made their presence felt. During colonial rule, conversion to Christianity, while not required or even widely promoted, was nevertheless attractive to some locals for the economic and educational advantages it bestowed. The earliest Christian missionaries had little success in terms of sheer numbers of converts won, but by the early twentieth century conversion was proceeding apace. At the same time, an increasingly visible and vocal segment of society sought to proclaim their Dayak identity in religious terms that were inimical to Christianity, and especially to Islam, which was widely embraced by non-Dayak peoples of the coastal areas. Resistance to conversion to pan-ethnic religions became for some Dayaks emblematic of their resistance to co-option into broader cultural systems. Today in Central Kalimantan religious affiliation and participation in ritual practices continue to be means of making powerful political statements.

In 1980 Kaharingan was recognized by the Indonesian Department of Religion as a variety of Hinduism. This recognition constituted a mandate for the Supreme Council to compose and enact an agenda of religious reforms. Council members have also taken an increasingly high profile in provincial affairs; several have been elected to government office. At the same time, the council and its policies do not enjoy universal support among adherents of Hindu Kaharingan. Some object to the council's activities, particularly with regard to standardizing ritual, on the grounds that, as a result, traditional practices may become etiolated. Others feel that what is unique in their culture will be lost as they become "more like the Balinese," who are nearly all Hindu. Still others reject what they consider an intrusion into an essentially private domain.

The relationship between religion and cultural and civic identity remains highly contested in Central Kalimantan and a regular topic of discussion throughout Ngaju society. With regard to my interest in these matters, it should be noted that 1991 was not my first occasion to consider the evolving relationship between religion and identity in the course of my Ngaju research. Certain dimensions of that relationship had been important foci during my earlier period of ethnographic study. Yet, during my first fieldwork, my primary aim was to try to gain access to villagers' notions of identity as these were rooted in conceptualizations of kinship and the family. I hoped to uncover these notions through investigation into the cosmological and supernatural beliefs surrounding major life crisis rituals. As part of my research strategy, I selected death ritual and eschatology as special areas of study.

The Ngaju "Death Cult"

There are several reasons why the investigation of death ritual is an especially appropriate starting point from which to build an understanding of Ngaju identity. First, the most dramatic and complex of Kaharingan rituals are those associated with the mortuary cycle. Nothing else, save marriage and its associated genealogical deliberations, so evokes enthusiastic discussion on the part of upriver villagers. Young and old, ritual specialists and lay practitioners, and even converts to Christianity and Islam eagerly share their comments, experiences, and accounts of *tiwah*. The celebration of *tiwah* is therefore clearly an event of significance in the lives of most of Central Kalimantan's indigenous peoples. Second, the investigation of death ritual serves as an especially dynamic point of departure for a study of identity, as the form and content of the ritual appear to be in flux. Chairman Lewis's letter to *Tempo,* for example, suggests that the meaning of *tiwah* is currently the subject of rather self-conscious analysis on the part of many people. At the same time, it should also be noted that the existence of descriptions of secondary burials dating back more than a hundred years suggests that *tiwah* has long been of significance to Ngaju peoples.

Missionaries and colonial administrators traveling in southern Borneo between the mid-nineteenth and early twentieth centuries penned the earliest description of death ritual in what is now Central Kalimantan.[5] The first Protestant missionaries, representatives of the Barman Mission, reached southern Borneo in 1835 and soon afterward made tentative forays up the Kapuas River from their base in Banjarmasin. Early missions established in the region included Bethabara (1838), Pulau Petak (1840), Pulau Telo (1851), Merutuwu (1851), Penda Alai (1853) and Tanggohan (1855). The outbreak of the Banjar War (1859), however, temporarily curtailed further missionary efforts. Early evangelicals posted to southern Borneo were awestruck and repulsed by the so-called death cults they encountered there. To those missionaries, *tiwah* rituals were frightening, even physically repellent. Regarding the refusal to accept into the faith one local notable who insisted that he still be allowed to *tiwah* his father, a missionary wrote to his superiors that "such a feast was a heathen matter, involving the slaughter of buffaloes and pig, sometimes three or four slaves, not to speak of the activities of the priestesses" (Harrisson 1959, 130). Another described the dances performed around mortuary edifices: "There danced the devil's brides, the *blians,* with men in a circle around an erected skull accompanied by a crazy, dull music. The movements of the dancers, their facial expressions, their bodies, grew almost hellish. I shivered and went away quickly. I had seen enough" (ibid., 125). Michael Perelaer described a Kahayan River *tiwah* of 1863 in similar terms:

> When the fatal day has arrived, a pole is fixed in the ground having at its upper end a rudely-carved human head, with the tongue stretched at full length out of the mouth. This pole, usually made of ironwood, is called *sapoendoe,* and stands out of the ground a little more than the height of a man. At this post is the slave doomed to suffer martyrdom. Opposite him the youths and able-bodied men are drawn up in a row, armed with their lances and in full war attire, and step forward one after another to wound the wretched man, while the *balians* and *bassirs* (priests and priestesses) howl a dismal song. When many slaves are offered their sufferings are relatively short, though never lasting less than one hour. If, however, the giver of the feast is not rich, and only a few slave debtors are killed, each unfortunate victim may stand three, four, or even six hours chained against this fatal pole. His tormentors purposely wound him but slightly, in order to satisfy to the utmost their thirst for blood; and the suffering wretch dies a lingering death, succumbing simply from loss of blood. (Quoted in Bock 1985, 219–20 [1881])

Another visitor remarked, "One cannot imagine a more devilish enterprise than this *tiwa [sic]*" (Ullmann 1868). These authors' biases, religious and otherwise, notwithstanding, such eyewitness reports make clear that for the indigenous inhabitants of the region, the death of a kinsperson constituted an event of immense sociological magnitude that evoked a complex ritual response. Not surprisingly, *tiwah* quickly seized the interest of colonial administrators and ethnographic reports of this practice by Dutch officials soon followed. One of these, published in an anthropological journal in 1889, was F. Grabowsky's article "Der Tod, das Begräbnis, das Tiwah oder Totenfest bei den Dajaken." Grabowsky described an elaborate set of rituals, the goal of which was to transport the souls of one's ancestors to a cosmological Upperworld. Souls could ascend to this place only after a three-stage cycle of ritual had been performed on their behalf by their descendants. Until souls and physical remains were processed completely, both the living and the dead were prey to dangers of supernatural origin. It was the proper performance of death ritual, which entailed dance, ritual ablutions, feasting, sacrifice, and the disinterment and later reinterment of the deceased's remains, that progressively distanced these dangers. Grabowsky included sketches of various mortuary edifices, many of which appear strikingly similar to those erected in upriver villages even today. Other accounts of *tiwah* by colonial administrators and missionaries practiced in ethnography followed, including J. Mallinkrodt's study of mortuary chants (1928).

From these chronicles of *tiwah* past, I was able to procure valuable data about the mechanics of ritual performance. At the same time, I found the bulk of these accounts strangely lacking in important detail concerning the social context in which the rituals were carried out. Questions about the sociological implications of these celebrations continued to puzzle me. Then a brief note was published in the *Borneo Research Bulletin* by a field researcher based among the neighboring Luangan Dayaks of East Kalimantan (Weinstock 1981) that implied that *tiwah* was still being performed in Central Kalimantan. This suggested that an opportunity remained to study the social significance of *tiwah*.

With regard to the social organization of *tiwah*, early writers had largely failed to make explicit exactly who participated in these celebrations or to offer a convincing rationale why certain individuals assumed particular roles. I was likewise troubled by the absence of information concerning the source of the data presented in those accounts. For example, the most celebrated account of *tiwah* to date appears to be based largely on the exegesis of a single individual. Hans Schärer's posthumous volumes, *Die Gottesidee der Ngadju Dajak in Süd-Borneo* (1946), translated into English as *Ngaju Religion* (1963), and *Der Totenkult der Ngadju Dajak in Süd-Borneo* (1966), were based on his seven years' residence as a missionary in southern Borneo prior to World War II. In the preface to *Der Totenkult der Ngadju Dajak,* Schärer describes the format of his interviews with Johannes Saililah, a former Kaharingan ritual specialist, or *basir,* who converted to Christianity while still a young man (1966, 4). Saililah went on to earn much local renown as a *damang,* or expert in customary law.[6] At one point in their association, Saililah came to Schärer's house every evening and discussed the equivalent of thirty-six pages of mortuary chants (Schärer 1966, 4). Saililah was also a gifted artist. He drew two illustrated maps of the cosmological Upperworld and Lowerworld that were included in *Die Gottesidee der Ngadju Dajak.* Although we cannot know precisely the extent of Schärer's debt to Saililah, Saililah himself claimed to be the source of most of what was eventually published. At least that is what he told me. Some forty years after Hans Schärer left Borneo, I arrived at Saililah's door. He had learned from an administrator at the provincial university that yet another anthropologist was coming to study Ngaju religion. Having heard that Saililah was still alive, I hastened to arrange an introduction. As he ushered me into his home, I recall Saililah remarking in a rather offhand way, "It took you a long time to get here. I wasn't sure how much longer I'd be able to wait."

Like Schärer and others, I too had the privilege of coming to know this remarkable cultural broker well.[7] My confidence in Saililah's claims about his influence on Schärer was bolstered by many incidents, including one that occurred quite early in my research. That particular evening we were sitting up late discussing the intricacies of various aspects of ritual observance. From time to time, Saililah would recite parts of the mortuary chants to illustrate a point. One time he lost his train of thought. I sat quietly, helpless as to how I might jog his memory. I was also secretly grateful for the break. We had already been working for five hours, as I tried all the while to scribble down words in a language of which I had absolutely no comprehension. Saililah insisted that I take notes by hand rather than use a tape recorder. This was a laborious exercise for both of us, as at that time I spoke good Indonesian but very little Ngaju. Actually my lack of competency in Ngaju mattered less than it might have. The chants were in a ritual language called *basa sangiang*. As I sat exhausted, Saililah excused himself for a moment. I watched as he went to the study to retrieve his personal copy of a book that I was unaware he owned, *Der Totenkult der Ngadju-Dajak in Süd-Borneo*. After looking up the next line of the chant, he closed the volume and continued to recite.

That evening proved to be a watershed. Saililah's reliance on a text he had, in some capacity, authored long before and its bearing on one he was producing for my benefit alerted me to the problematic relationship between sources of Kaharingan religious knowledge and broader religious understandings that are circulating today. On the one hand, Saililah was convinced that Schärer had mistaken significant aspects of Kaharingan belief. On the other hand, for Saililah, Schärer's volume embodied a fixed standard on which he himself could depend and to which he had greatly contributed. My own reliance on Saililah's authority became more complicated still as my network of contacts came to include *basir* and others who would, or would not, interact with me based on my association with Saililah. It seemed to me that it was not so much the man himself that evoked their strong reaction as his views about religion. Some extolled the knowledge that he shared. Others minimized it. Few were neutral. The ironic note on which that evening in Saililah's front room ended, then, ultimately had a profound impact on my research strategy throughout my initial stay in Central Kalimantan.

Over the course of my fieldwork, my relationship with Saililah deepened, professionally and personally. During those initial months when I was resident in Palangka Raya, we worked together closely and nearly continuously. Given the intensity of my fondness and respect for Saililah, readers can perhaps understand how my determination not to rely on him as my sole informant was sometimes problematic for us both. Regardless of Saililah's eloquence, I was intent on resisting the strategy adopted by some other ethnographers who privilege the accounts of but a few informants, and this informant in particular. It is apparent from elsewhere in Borneo that accounts of ritual specialists differ strikingly, even within the same general region.[8] Might not the esoteric accounts of *basir* concerning the meaning of *tiwah* also diverge considerably? To what extent would a layman's view of *tiwah* vary from that of a *basir?* I reasoned that comparing various vantage points would lead to mutually enriching rather than mutually exclusive interpretations of this important celebration. I therefore persisted with my efforts to speak with a broad range of people. It was in this way, too, that I came rather quickly to sense the political implications of religious practice in Central Kalimantan.

The "Ngaju" People and the Ngaju Region

The Indonesian province of Central Kalimantan, one of four Indonesian provinces on the island, comprises an area of nearly 154,000 square kilometers composed mostly of jungle (82%), swamp (12%), river, and swidden (see map 1). On the flight from the southeastern port city of Banjarmasin to Palangka Raya's Tjilik Riwut Airport in one of the prop planes that serve the interior, a visitor's first impression of Central Kalimantan might be of gnarled brown fingers of river clutching a verdant rain forest gem (albeit one fast becoming less green owing to the ravages of logging and repeated widespread forest fires)(see map 2). Peering intently through the low clouds, one occasionally detects a diesel-powered "river bus" chugging toward a port of call or a speedboat, perhaps transporting a timber executive to his company's barracks. Out of sight, tucked beneath the coconut palms that grow in clumps along the river's edge, are the villages of the Ngaju Dayaks. Swidden horticulturalists, they live along the middle and lower reaches of many of Central Kalimantan's waterways, including the Kapuas, Kahayan, Katingan, Rungan, and Mentaya rivers. They speak a language that, despite dialectical variation, is known generally as Ngaju (Hudson 1967, 7). They share as well a rich system of traditional law *(hadat),* first codified in 1894 during a Dutch-sponsored conference in the village of Tumbang Anoi, where slavery, head-taking, and human sacrifice were originally outlawed (Ilun et al. 1983b). Exact census figures are unavailable. Indonesian censuses are ethnically blind. Some local estimates, however, place the number of Ngaju-speakers at between 500,000 and 800,000 in a province with a total population of only 1,543,179 (1994 estimate), dispersed at an average of a mere three persons per square mile. While some live in the more populated cities of Kuala Kapuas on the Kapuas River, Sampit on the Mentaya River, and Palangka

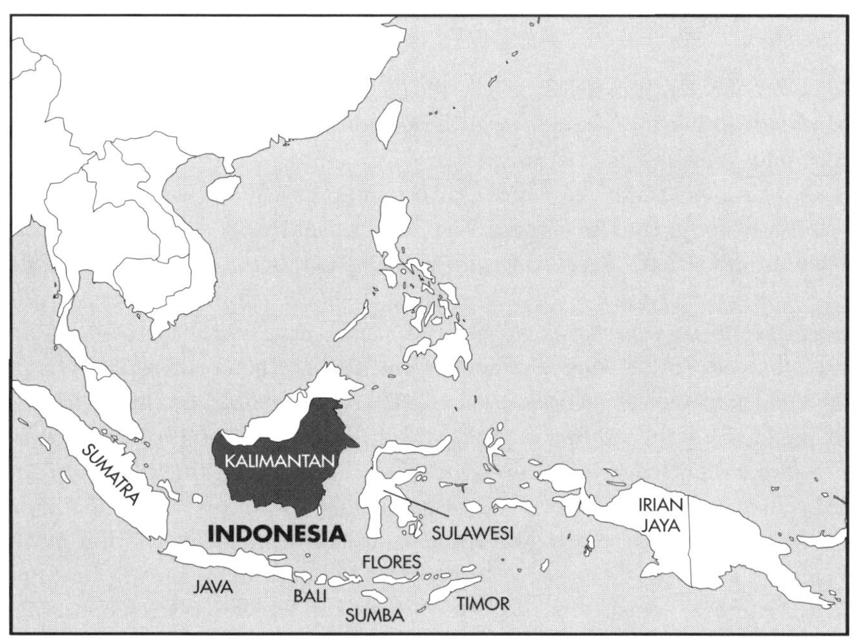

MAP 1. Kalimantan (Indonesian Borneo) in Relation to Other Indonesian Islands

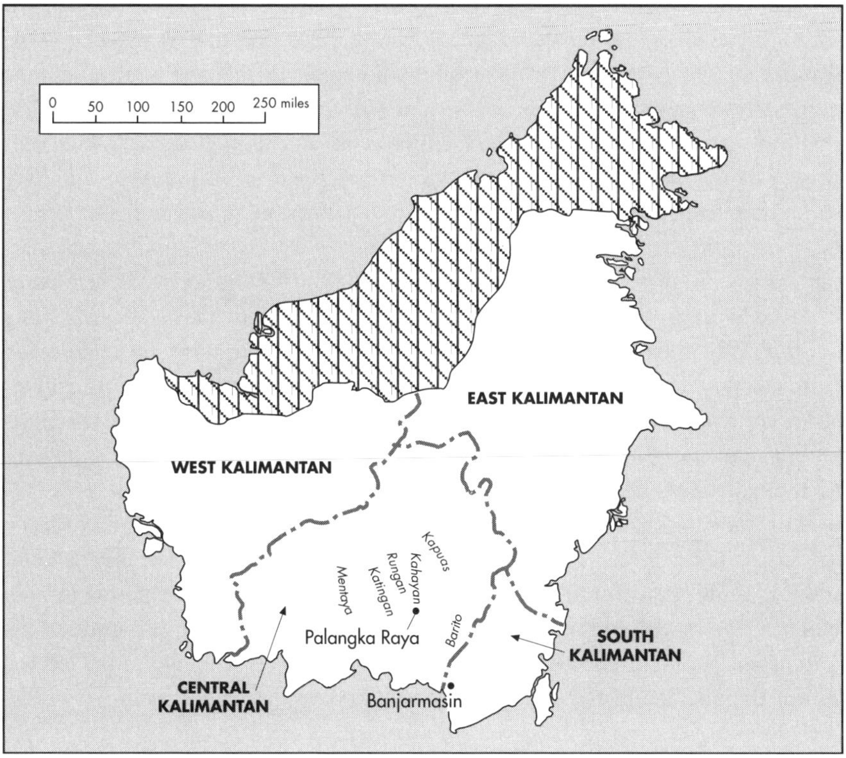

MAP 2. Central Kalimantan

Raya on the Kahayan River, or in towns such as Kasongan and Tumbang Samba, most live in villages of relative isolation, with only a few hundred persons inhabiting any one settlement.

Despite long-anticipated plans for an interprovincial highway, there are as yet few roads in interior Central Kalimantan. Until quite recently, the main road out of Palangka Raya, built with Soviet assistance in the late-1960s, dead-ended at a small town called Tangkiling, about 35 kilometers away. Rusted tractors emblazoned with Soviet insignia abandoned at the side of the road used to be a constant source of amusement. By my second trip to the field in 1991, the tractors had been removed. An 82 kilometer road branched off Tangkiling Road (by then known as Tjilik Riwut Road after a local hero) and connected the capital city with Kasongan. On my third trip to the field, I learned that it was now possible to travel by automobile to Sampit, and that a road between Palangka Raya and Kuala Kapuas would be completed within a few years. For all practical purposes, however, it is still difficult to travel to Palangka Raya by motor vehicle from the coast. Journeys between villages, especially between those on different rivers, remain difficult and sometimes fraught with risk. During the dry season, rivers wither, and travel by foot along jungle paths may become the only mode of transportation available in some areas.

Given the region's sparse population and the sheer physical challenges to travel imposed by the environment, it is not surprising that rivers and other features of the landscape have become landmarks that serve as physical foci around which groups of men and women orient and locate themselves. For example, people usually describe themselves as an "uluh Kahayan" (Kahayan River person) or an "uluh Katingan" (Katingan River person), and so on. They sometimes resist the designation "Ngaju," which in that language means "upriver" and carries pejorative connotations of rusticity and provincialism. Similarly, they may claim to speak "basa Kahayan" (Kahayan River language) or "basa Katingan" (Katingan River language) rather than "basa Ngaju."

Physical boundaries or landmarks are also often coterminous with variations in regional styles in ritual. Hence it is possible to point to a "Kahayan River style" ritual or a "Katingan River style" ritual and to even smaller subdivisions within these categories. On the one hand, such variations in ritual praxis may be thought of as mere variations on a theme. Yet to so characterize them fails to do justice to the significance placed on these differences in format and technique by the celebrants themselves. Variations that to an outsider appear to be nothing more than minor stylistic deviations may assume tremendous importance in the minds of the sponsors of ritual. The significance of these variations is nowhere more apparent than in discussions concerning the ritual observances that are associated with *tiwah*, the climax of the mortuary cycle.

Tiwah and the Issue of Ritual Acceptability

Arriving at a village in the midst of *tiwah,* one would probably have the first impression of a raucous party extending nearly around the clock, a veritable carnival at the jungle's edge. Unwary visitors might be surprised when village hosts welcomed them by daubing dampened pressed powder across their faces, then pausing to be similarly "decorated" in turn. When they are not dancing around the sacrificial cattle tethered to posts, stopping occasionally to fortify themselves with a shot of home brew or of "Old Man" brand whiskey from the single glass making the rounds from hand to hand, celebrants wander up and down the village paths. They stop frequently to chat or to sample snacks prepared by vendors who have traveled from Palangka Raya or elsewhere to set up shop temporarily. Off the main path, tucked away from public view, visitors might come upon groups of men and women occupied in games of chance. The overall impression is of festivity, joviality, and playfulness.

Despite the casual air that seems to pervade *tiwah,* however, these events are actually highly orchestrated. The celebration of *tiwah* is characterized by myriad prescriptions and prohibitions. The entire performance is carefully managed by sponsors and ritual specialists who work in tandem to make certain that each phase of the ritual is carried out "correctly." Yet my discussions with villagers concerning how to enact *tiwah* suggested that much more than mere unbending adherence to a set of rules figured in the construction of these events. I noted that each step in the planning of *tiwah* was surrounded by discussion. Before any specialists were retained, sponsors conferred among themselves over the format their celebration should take. How many days should the festivities last? What foods would be proscribed for the duration of *tiwah?* Of what material should the bone repository be constructed and how should it be decorated? Thus, although the longevity of *tiwah* as a recognizable ritual form demonstrates that its construction is governed by convention, the content of sponsors' deliberations reveals that these rituals are nevertheless dynamic in nature. Within certain general boundaries, the performance of *tiwah* appears to be ever-evolving. This situation recalls Stanley Tambiah's proposition concerning the dual aspects of rituals as performances (Tambiah 1985, 124). On the one hand, public rituals appear to reproduce seemingly invariant and stereotyped sequences. On the other, no two performances are ever precisely alike. As Tambiah reminds us, "It is therefore necessary to bear in mind that festivals, cosmic rituals, and rites of passage, however prescribed they may be, are always linked to status claims and interests of the participants, and therefore are always open to contextual meanings" (125).

The recognition that these celebrations do change over time and that they are historical events gives rise to important questions concerning *tiwah* as it might be employed as a vehicle of adaptation, of resistance, or otherwise. The dynamic potency of *tiwah* was largely overlooked in earlier studies such as Schärer's that emphasized the celebration's role in perpetuating a particular conceptualization of social structure (that is, an ethnographer's). On their own, those accounts might lead us to expect the kind of reliance on set ritual convention that the anthropologist Robert Hefner encountered among the priests of the Tengger people of East Java. The Tengger, who, like the Ngaju, have lately become numbered among Indonesia's Hindu population, are descendants of non-Islamic Javanese who fled to the mountains of the west following the collapse of the Majapahit kingdom in the late thirteenth century (Hefner 1985, 6). Hefner reports that for the Tengger, "the faithful performance of received ritual forms takes precedence over evangelical exhortation or collective effervescence" (20). Authority of established forms, then, at least partly explains the longevity of Tengger priestly traditions.

If we can judge from the accounts of missionaries and others, the traditions of Ngaju-speakers, too, appear long-lived. Yet I failed to discover any unequivocal formula that defines the sole "correct" method to *tiwah* the dead. The relationship between ritual praxis and textual authority is most illustrative in this regard. A crucial part of the celebration of *tiwah* is the recitation of chants intended to transport the souls of the dead to the Upperworld. These chants, performed by *basir* in the ritual language, recall the first *tiwah* enacted by immortal supernatural beings, *sangiang,* on behalf of their mortal human counterparts. Yet even those chants, which describe a primordial "ideal" *tiwah,* fail to make the format of the ritual explicit. They are open to various renderings, renditions, and readings.

Rather than holding celebrations that follow an exhaustively arranged pattern, villagers adopt a different procedure. Throughout the planning and enactment of a mortuary celebration, participants continually assess the "acceptability" of the format that they have chosen. The acceptability of any particular ritual can only be defined negatively; that is, sponsors know that they have correctly performed a ritual only by the absence of signs of "misperformance." Such signs include accidents, sponsors' illness, even the occasional premature death of animals destined for sacrifice. This powerful notion of ritual acceptability originates within a broader concept, that of tradition, which comprehends a supernatural dimension. Tradition, a concept that implies continuity, is in fact itself transformed through the construction of ritual. Today in Central Kalimantan, the transformation and objectification of indigenous ritual traditions have critical implications for the transformation of identity as well.

Kaharingan Ritual and Ngaju Identity

Ngaju rituals are obviously not unique in possessing an adaptive capacity. A growing body of literature continues to grapple with the issue of how public rituals may universally operate as adaptive devices (Comaroff 1985, Kertzer 1988, Knauft 1985, Peacock 1968, Turner 1969). Among the foremost writers to address this aspect of ritual in sustained fashion is Clifford Geertz. In an illuminating discussion that appeared in 1973, Geertz argued that symbols possess the capacity to serve at once the dual roles of "models of" and "models for" behavior" (1973f, 93–94). Symbols, wrote Geertz, "both express the world's climate and shape it" (95). On the one hand, ritual symbols may render the particular social world one inhabits somehow more "graspable" (124). On the other, they may help to inculcate attitudes that may direct a future course of action in that world. For the Ngaju today, *tiwah* and its associated symbols serve as resources that can be drawn on in adapting to a rapidly changing local environment, as well as a changing relationship to other Indonesians.

To treat *tiwah* as models both of and for reality requires an examination of how the celebrations articulate with conceptualizations of kinship. For instance, my own observations in upriver villages led me to recognize that performances of mortuary rituals accentuate important series of differentiations between and within groups of participants. The rituals underscore a differentiation of kin from non-kin and at the same time promulgate a particular conceptualization of kinship. This argument will be elaborated in a subsequent chapter. In the meantime, to phrase the issue a bit differently, I would suggest that celebrations of *tiwah* should be thought of as vehicles of discrimination, pointing out the bounds of one's personal loyalties. Much of this notion of loyalty revolves around cognatic kinship. For example, the solidarity of an extended family is strengthened in the course of focusing attention on its human and material resources during *tiwah*. Everyone who can claim relation to the deceased is ideally expected to participate. Many villagers say that the affective bond that unites the sponsors of *tiwah* is so strong that it cross-cuts even religious boundaries. Indeed, one of the most striking aspects of the many *tiwah* I have observed is that adherents of other religions, both Christians and Muslims, often join their Kaharingan kin in their celebrations. Yet, while the rituals promote solidarity among the members of sponsoring families, they simultaneously accentuate points of differentiation among those same family members. Death rituals pose unrelenting challenges to participants' own idealizations of their family. Thus, on the one hand, the members of extended families like to describe themselves as "all the same." Stressing their common kinship, they insist that they will all enjoy a reunion in the Upperworld. Yet close attention to the ritual symbols employed at *tiwah* reveals that every possible effort may be made to forestall this very possibility; that is, the remains of certain family members must be excluded from the repositories of their spouse or their spouse's parents.

It is important to note that differentiation is not confined to the realm of human social relations. A similar sense is reflected in distinctions made between the varieties of supernatural beings said to take an interest in the processing of the dead. According to sponsors of *tiwah*, participants in the ritual must include supernatural as well as human contingents to ensure its success. Not all types of supernatural beings are welcomed equally, however. This distinction suggests the possibility of parallels between social organization and popular cosmology that have been overlooked or misunderstood by earlier writers. In this regard, I argue that for the Ngaju, the construction of social and cosmological orders has, at some point, indeed been a reciprocal process. Distinctions between men, played out in death ritual, reverberate in associated mythological and cosmological beliefs. Actualized at the level of social interaction, differentiation is idealized in the realm of the supernatural.

At the same time, the perpetuation of a particular reality does not exhaust this vitality of *tiwah*. *Tiwah* acts on participants' worldview as well as reproducing it. The celebration of *tiwah* serves as a heuristic device of adaptation. The power of this adaptive capacity has lately been especially revealed and tested in debates concerning the relationship between ritual and Ngaju cultural identity. It was, in fact, this very relationship that was highlighted by the discussions that surrounded the "Hindu Kaharingan—*Tempo* Insult Case" throughout the summer of 1991.

Yet it did not require the publication of an article of the kind that appeared in *Tempo* to provoke discussion of these issues. During my initial fieldwork, I too had encountered many men and women who were eager to discuss the relationship between this ritual form and identity. Sponsors of the various *tiwah* that I attended at that time told me again and again that "death rituals tell us who we are." Today, more than a decade later, death ritual still seems to be communicating something of significance about who they are to those who carry them out.

In order to understand what these villagers mean by who they are, however, we must move between two levels of discourse. A subtle relationship exists between who someone is in terms of his or her place in a network of kin relations on the one hand, and that person's image of himself or herself as a member of a religious congregation on the other. And how do these identities articulate with the sense of oneself as a "Ngaju Dayak" operating within a larger "Indonesian" community? In order to appreciate the extent to which *tiwah* figures in participants' constructions of the latter identity, in particular, the ritual must be analyzed with respect to how it articulates with historical process, including experiences of colonialism, the founding of the province of Central Kalimantan, confrontations with pan-ethnic religions, and modern religious reform. Much of the contemporary debate concerning Ngaju identity today centers on interpretations of the religious past, in particular past celebrations of *tiwah*, and arguments over its future. Attitudes toward *tiwah* specifically and the traditional religion generally are fast becoming critical to the emergence and reproduction of what might be termed Ngaju cultural identity. In this regard religion is coming to serve as a cultural marker. Yet it is precisely here that the power of the model of/model for paradigm begins to falter. There are many "Ngaju identities," and religion generally and *tiwah* specifically figure differently in all of them.

Some Implications of Religious Change in Central Kalimantan

Change is inherent to every religion. Yet one of the most striking characteristics of Ngaju religion is the rapidity with which it is changing. On 30 March 1980 the Indonesian Ministry of Religion recognized the indigenous religion of the peoples of Central Kalimantan as a variety of Hinduism. This recognition represented the culmination of campaigns for some form of national acknowledgment of the indigenous religion that had been pursued for over forty years. It likewise provided a mandate for religious rationalization, including the standardization of ritual and the codification of belief, under the guidance of an administrative organization known as the Supreme Council of Hindu Kaharingan Religion. Since the official recognition of Hindu Kaharingan, innovations and reformulations aimed at religious rationalization have followed one after the other, led mostly by members of the Supreme Council.

To appreciate the impact that this movement toward rationalization is having on religion in Central Kalimantan, it is instructive to compare it with circumstances elsewhere in Indonesia. Two examples are the "internal conversion" of the Balinese, a process first described by Geertz in his essay by that name (1973d), and the more "external" conversion of the Karo of Sumatra, documented by Rita Kipp (1973).

Among the Balinese, the campaign for governmental recognition of local religious practices began in the late 1950s. That period was characterized by the dissemination of religious literature, the encouragement of wide participation in formal arenas of worship, and the fostering of an atmosphere of quiet reverence in contexts that were deemed religious. There also arose a desire to sort "local tradition" from "religion" in order to get the religion right. Many Balinese argued that religious leadership should no longer rest on hereditary status alone, that priests must also possess knowledge and wisdom. Furthermore, the active role in worship was no longer totally relegated to priests or to a single individual acting on behalf of an entire family. "At least a few ordinary Balinese," wrote Geertz, "are coming to feel that they can get some understanding of what their religion is all about; and more important, that they have need for and a right to such understanding" (1973d, 185).

In 1962 Hinduism, the faith professed by the vast majority of the Balinese, was officially declared one of Indonesia's "great religions," a category that had previously been limited to Catholicism, Protestant Christianity, and Islam. This declaration represented a major success for an important local organization founded twelve years earlier, the Bali Hindu Duty Council, or Parisada Hindu Dharma Bali (PHDB), which had spearheaded the campaign for recognition. After its aim had been achieved, PHDB continued to flourish, becoming even more entrenched. Its sphere of influence soon spread beyond Bali. In 1968 members voted to shorten the name of the organization to the Hindu Duty Council (PHD) to reflect a growing involvement of non-Balinese Hindus in both its own internal affairs and the congregations it served. A final name change occured in 1986, when PHD became the Hindu Duty Council of Indonesia (PHDI), underscoring the national Hindu presence in a country by then reckoned to be about 80 percent Islamic.

PHDI continues to assume the leadership role in all religious matters affecting Hindu congregations throughout the country. It publishes religious tracts and commentaries and supervises religious teaching in schools. Council membership is composed of two tracks, the first made up of clerics *(pasamuan sulinggih)*, and the second composed of lay administrators and educators *(pasamuan walaka)*. In addition to the national-level council, smaller branch councils serve Hindu congregations at the provincial *(propinsi)*, regency *(kabupaten)*, subdistrict *(kecamatan)*, and village *(desa)* levels, as need dictates. PHDI continues to expand its authority and to exercise its power in new directions. It attains added visibility by defending Hindu practices and beliefs from disparagement. For example, in 1991 an Islamic magazine published in East Java overtly denigrated the Hindu Balinese for leaving flower petals scattered about after making their "offerings to statues" and causing the air around Den Pasar to reek. PHDI reportedly waged a successful antidefamation suit.[9] PHDI also pressured a major manufacturer of Indonesian cigarettes to withdraw advertisements that featured the Balinese temple Tanah Lot, claiming that it was inappropriate to use Hindu religious sites to promote commercial ventures. Subsequently PHDI became involved in efforts to prohibit the construction of a luxury residential complex by a Jakarta-based conglomerate within a 2-kilometer radius of the Tanah Lot temple.[10]

The Karo of Sumatra, to a much greater degree than the Balinese, have responded positively to evangelical efforts, both Christian and Muslim. In the past, religious conversion entailed crossing an ethnic boundary. Unlike the case of the Ngaju, however, the move of the Karo was from one marked ethnic category to another. As Kipp points out, in the precolonial period, many Karo resisted Islam, despite the economic and political advantages bestowed by conversion, since adopting that religion may have suggested cultural or political subordination to their Acehnese neighbors (1993, 218). During the colonial period, many Karo were uninterested in converting to Christianity for a similar reason: it was interpreted as a statement of loyalty to the Dutch (ibid., 189).

Today some Karo are Muslim, some are Christian, and some adhere to the traditional religion, Perbegu. The latter are generally split into two categories:

those who ally themselves with a national group organized under the auspices of the Department of Education and Culture (ibid., 244) and those who consider themselves Hindu (246). Kipp notes that, compared to Karo who have converted to Christianity or Islam, traditionalists are generally poor and uneducated. With regard to identity generally, the Karo kinship system, based on five intermarrying clans, remains the essential marker of Karo ethnicity (33). Kipp adds, however, that "the definitive criteria for being Karo and Batak no longer rest on a religious contrast, but the strength and success of the ethnic church show that ethnicity is not totally dissociated from issues of religion either" (212).

The history of the struggle for recognition of local beliefs and the founding of a Kaharingan religious council in Central Kalimantan demonstrates both similarities to and differences from these two cases. First, unlike the Balinese but like the Karo, the inhabitants of Central Kalimantan eventually proved highly receptive to proselytization, in this case by Christians. Whereas most Balinese are Hindus, the majority of the indigenous inhabitants of Central Kalimantan embrace Christianity, and a growing number have converted to Islam. The 1994 census reports that only 15.37 percent of the province's inhabitants claim to be Hindu, the category that now subsumes Kaharingan. Yet even that figure is misleading, as it includes the thousands of Balinese transmigrants who have settled in the area. For comparative purposes, it should be noted that 67.76 percent of the citizens of Central Kalimantan identify themselves as Muslim, 14.31 percent as Protestant, 2.25 percent as Catholic, and 0.31 percent as Buddhist (Departemen Agama 1994/95, 17). According to some local estimates, at best only about 30 percent of the Ngaju continue to embrace the traditional religion openly, though it is rumored that many more than that number observe it surreptitiously.[11] Second, unlike the case of the Balinese and Hinduism, despite a common language and a similar body of custom throughout much of Central Kalimantan, there seems to be little in Kaharinganism that could have lent itself easily to fostering a broad-based sense of community among that region's inhabitants. Nor is there an overarching kinship system comparable to the Karo clans.

Despite the comparatively small number of avowed adherents today, however, a desire on the part of many Ngaju for recognition of their indigenous religion was at one time an important factor in a chain of events that led to the creation of the province itself. Kaharingan, the name by which the indigenous religion had been known informally in southern Borneo for some years, was "officially" adopted by locals during the early 1950s in the course of a series of meetings held at several Kahayan River villages. Fits and starts of religious rationalization followed such meetings, and attempts to develop "Kaharingan Bibles" were carried out at the individual level (Miles 1976, 129). Among the political parties that operated openly beneath the banner of the indigenous religion was the

Sarikat Dayak Kaharingan Indonesia. For some adherents, religious recognition was closely tied to a sense of cultural identity.

In 1957 Central Kalimantan, formerly subsumed by the province of South Kalimantan, was itself declared a province in the wake of attacks on government posts and an alleged threatened revolt of Dayak peoples (Riwut 1963). Nevertheless, official acknowledgment of Kaharingan was not forthcoming. In the early 1970s yet another council, known as the Council of Religious Teachers of Indonesian Kaharingan (Majelis Alim Ulama Kaharingan Indonesia [MAUKI]), was formed to pursue the issue of religious recognition. According to one former member, this organization attempted to steer clear of the "political concerns" that had characterized its predecessor. MAUKI was also self-consciously "Indonesian."

Although Kaharingan was never recognized as a religion in its own right, it was eventually declared a variety of Hinduism by the Ministry of Religion. Following official acknowledgment of Kaharingan, the members of MAUKI renamed their organization the Supreme Council of Hindu Kaharingan Religion (Majelis Besar Agama Hindu Kaharingan [MBAHK]). Significantly, over time MBAHK has become more overtly political. The council aligns itself closely with the national regime's "New Order" policies and has been an extremely outspoken proponent of Indonesia's present administration.

From its headquarters in Palangka Raya, the Supreme Council oversees associated councils at the regency, subdistrict, and village levels. At every level, much of the council members' energies is directed toward the standardization of ritual and to the codification of belief. It would be fair to describe the Supreme Council as intolerant of variation within the faith. In an interview with *Tempo* published in early 1979, for example, Chairman Lewis, head of MAUKI at the time, was asked to comment on the apparent diversity in Kaharingan practice. He responded "with a smile": "Customs can be simplified, right?" (Adicondro 1979, 54). Council members insisted to me, in rhetoric surprisingly reminiscent of Schärer's *Ngaju Religion,* that the variation that characterizes contemporary celebrations, including mortuary rituals, merely reflects villagers' inability to maintain the integrity of traditional ritual forms over time. Harking back to their "Hindu origins," they claim that in the past, Kaharingan beliefs and methods of worship were identical throughout the region. Nevertheless, difficulties in communication and travel resulted in the montage of belief and ritual that characterizes the religion today. Through various programs, the council exposes adherents to particular interpretations of beliefs and encourages specific forms of ritual praxis. Their efforts are cast in terms of restoring the "purity" of their Hindu thought and practice and contributing to regional "development" *(pembangunan).* Chairman Lewis described this agenda to me in the course of an interview in 1983: "We are doing to Hindu Kaharingan what other people do to rattan. Ask someone what rattan is for. Some people tell you it is for weaving a mat, others say making furniture, others say that rattan is for boiling and eating. We must take the aim, not the details, into account. We find a middle way that is acceptable to everyone because we are all really one people with the same beliefs."

Building on their momentum, the Supreme Council hopes to design and popularize "generic" rituals, including generic death rituals, that will be accepted by all adherents of Hindu Kaharingan. Some adherents are clearly eager for these reforms; others are resentful. With regard to the latter, the Supreme Council sometimes encounters overt or surreptitious opposition from other religious "experts," namely, the traditional ritual specialists, or *basir*. During my first visit to Central Kalimantan, I met many older *basir* who resented what they perceived as an effort on the part of the council to usurp their authority. Their discomfort was at least partly related to the aforementioned issue of how to determine "correctness" in ritual. Prior to the recognition of the Supreme Council, no single authority existed that could render pronouncements on whether particular ritual forms were "appropriate." Concerned sponsors might consult the *basir* of their choice on such matters.

At the same time, it should not be assumed that *basir* were formerly the sole arbiters of religious correctness or agents of innovation or religious transformation or that their opinions always went unchallenged. As Franz Boas pointed out as early as 1902, it is likely that esoteric religious doctrines develop among a select group from the current beliefs of the society at large and, having become established, in turn take on the power to influence popular belief. The same argument might well be applied to the evolution of ritual forms.

Regardless of which came first in this case, the esoteric doctrines of *basir* or the understandings of laymen, elaborate cosmological beliefs or complex rituals, the whole issue of the evolving relationship between religious belief and practice in a rapidly changing society is clearly one of significance to anthropologists. Geertz (1973g), for example, described the crisis that occurred in a Javanese community when villagers found themselves without the means to conduct a "proper funeral" (142-69). In that particular case, no religious specialist was available to advise participants on appropriate ritual forms. Geertz demonstrated how, under the circumstances, confusion over the proper format of a ritual arrested its performance. An important realization emerged from this confusion: that differences between participants rendered long-standing ritual forms no longer appropriate. Along similar lines, Douglas Miles described a Mentaya River Ngaju mortuary celebration during which sponsors were in a quandary as to what ritual they should perform. A compromise celebration was finally devised which incorporated elements from several places within the Ngaju region (1976, 80–82). In Geertz's example people who had previously thought of themselves as the same became aware, through want of both a ritual and a ritual specialist, that they were now somehow different. In Miles's example, people who were different became more alike through their creation of a ritual. When the efforts of the Supreme Council to develop a generic death ritual are viewed in this light, it seems that such a ritual might indeed lead Kahayan, Katingan, Kapuas, Rungan, and Mentaya River villagers to think of themselves as "alike."

And yet, though disputes over ritual forms can sometimes be successfully mediated so as to create a new kind of bond, such bonds are not always easily forged. For example, differing conceptualizations of the relationship between religion, indigenous ritual forms, and identity are increasingly evident between sponsors who are adherents of Hindu Kaharingan and those who are not. Many disputes revolve around who has the right to participate in *tiwah*. Some historical factors make this issue particularly problematic. One is slavery and the celebrated practice of sacrificing slaves and captives at *tiwah*. This dimension of local history is dealt with in several ways. Many Christian families emphasize their ancestors' barbarity prior to conversion. Adherents of Hindu Kaharingan are quick to point out in response that the first converts to Christianity were slaves, redeemed by missionaries and allowed to work off their debt. What former slave, they ask, would be foolish enough to return to a village where people had once hoped to sacrifice him or her at a death ritual? With a different frame of reference, civil servants often claim that human sacrifice was not indigenous but rather was a grotesque variation on colonial divide-and-rule politics. That is, either the practice itself or rumor of it was introduced by the Dutch to ensure the collapse of Ngaju unity as part of a plan to gain easier access to the island's resources. This position was adopted by Chairman Lewis throughout the council's dispute with *Tempo*.

"To be human . . . ," wrote Geertz, "is thus not to be Everyman; it is to be a particular kind of man, and of course men differ" (1973b, 53). Although Geertz was referring to cultures generally, societies too are composed of different kinds of people. Debates over common Hindu origins notwithstanding, so long as there is an ethos that emphasizes the relative autonomy of kin groups, the question persists: To what extent are the Ngaju really "one people"? While in some sense the recent developments in Hindu Kaharingan are having the effect of making the Ngaju think of themselves as more "the same," they are also compelling both adherents and non-adherents of Hindu Kaharingan to choose between identities or to create new ones. In the making of such choices conflict seems inescapable. Today in Kalimantan the celebration of death ritual, which involves making many choices, has become increasingly ambiguous. The goal of the present volume is to explore this ambiguity and to tease out its implications.

In her classic study *Purity and Danger*, anthropologist Mary Douglas noted the important role of ritual in the formulation of experience. According to Douglas, "Ritual focusses attention by framing; it enlivens the memory and links the present with the relevant past. In all this it aids perception. Or rather it changes perception because it changes the selective principles" (1966, 64). In exploring the notion of ritual as a perceptual aid, Douglas attended to a key question in the anthropological study of meaning: To what extent does the way the members of a society make sense of their world become accessible to an anthropologist through an examination of ritual forms?

In this regard, it is important to bear in mind that even as rituals focus performers' attention, they may still "make sense" in vastly different ways. Writing in the late 1980s, Maurice Bloch argued that rituals are restrictive: "Ritual is a kind of tunnel into which one plunges, and where, since there is no possibility of turning either to right or left, the only thing to do is to follow" (1989, 41–42). To the contrary, the premise of the present study is that, like the criss-crossing rivers of the Upperworld that souls of the dead traverse to reach their final repose, the meaning of *tiwah* is also convoluted and can be sought in various directions. As Tambiah suggested, rituals may indeed avail the "pragmatic interests of authority." We must not, however, lose sight of the fact that they can simultaneously serve those committed believers who seek to reorder their world and infuse old forms with new meanings (1985, 155).

The descriptive chapters of this volume reveal that the death rituals of the Hindu Kaharingan villagers are rich and complex orchestrations of symbolic codes that include but are not limited to dance, ritual speech, the organization of space and time, and food. They are also lengthy, encompassing three discrete stages. The first two stages in the processing of the dead comprise the rites leading up to primary interment *(mangubur);* the subsequent rituals aim at providing initial processing for the souls of the deceased and cleansing away some of the pollution of death from survivors *(balian tantulak matei mampisik liau).* Both of these stages are described in detail in chapter 2. Chapter 3 focuses on the format and eschatological beliefs specifically associated with the celebration of *tiwah* and explores the dynamic relationship between idealized notions of acceptability and the actual enactment of ritual.

In chapter 4, I present at length an analytical position central to this book, one having to do with conceptualizations of social organization and how these articulate with lay understandings of Kaharingan doctrine. I begin by addressing notions of orderliness and its opposite in death ritual and beyond. The chapter includes a discussion of the concept of tradition *(hadat),* which embraces indigenous understandings of moral and physical order. I explore how the notion of *hadat* is called on to construct and perpetuate a particular vision of society. To this end, I introduce data concerning marriage preferences and conceptualizations of kinship.

In chapter 4, I also suggest that ideas about order in the broadest sense are played out in complementary ways in social interaction and in cosmological beliefs. I situate the notion of ritual acceptability within the broader contexts of popular cosmology and cosmogony and argue that lay understandings of Kaharingan doctrine focus largely on beliefs about two types of supernatural beings. The first, *sangiang,* are Upperworld beings. There are Lowerworld *sangiang* as well, though these figure much less prominently in lay discussions of cosmology. *Sangiang* are like people in that they marry, produce children, live in villages, and so on. In their physical aspect, they are thought to resemble humans. And though the relationship is by now a distant one, *sangiang* are ultimately considered blood kin to humans. Unlike humans, however, they do not die.

Other supernatural beings who figure in local religious understanding are the "Unclean Ones," *(taluh papa).* Unlike people and *sangiang, taluh papa* are promiscuous, amoral, and of inhuman physical aspect. Whereas *sangiang* are well disposed toward the inhabitants of this world, *taluh papa* are supernatural mercenaries and quite frightening. Although some men and women are believed to seek out and propitiate them, *taluh papa* are considered extremely dangerous. One particularly dreadful variety is the *hantuen. Hantuen* can assume human guise. They may do so to effect marriages with humans. The results of these unions are disastrous for the spouse and his or her family. Hence, it is the responsibility of all family members to remain vigilant lest one of their relatives unwittingly initiates an alliance with a *hantuen.* It is not only in this world that one must guard against such contamination. *Hantuen* can follow spouses to the beyond and wreak havoc in the afterlife. Provisions must therefore be made at *tiwah* to ensure that these despised creatures are denied this opportunity.

What is particularly provocative about the distinction I pose between *sangiang* and *taluh papa* is that few villagers make it. Supernatural beings are said to be "all the same." Similarly, one's kin, one's neighbors, and one's compatriots are said to be "all the same." Nevertheless, attitudes about and behaviors toward "others" vis-à-vis one's consanguines belie this encompassing gloss. Chapter 4 suggests that this largely unrecognized homology between the organization of natural and supernatural worlds powerfully affects many social relationships. It may therefore have consequences for the construction of Ngaju cultural identity. Yet precisely how it may eventually affect emerging social forms has yet to become clear. It is important to note that beliefs about *hantuen* and other *taluh papa* have no place in "modern" Kaharinganism.

In chapter 5 I discuss how processes of religious reform in Indonesia have affected this indigenous religion. I suggest that a distinctively Ngaju cultural community is emerging, in part, as a response to the state's deployment of a hegemonic discourse of religion that entails a model of appropriate and orderly practice. At the same time, I point to the fact that, even in an increasingly rationalized religious milieu, resistance to totalizing doctrines, ritual schemata, and identities occurs. The chapter situates the current recasting of the performance of death ritual within this process, examining contesting notions of how to do a ritual correctly and who may participate in the celebration.

Chapter 6 extends the discussion, addressing the relationship between religious adherence and cultural identity, particularly with regard to the burgeoning sense of "Ngajuness" in evidence in Central Kalimantan today. To this end, it focuses on demonstrations held by citizens of Palangka Raya in 1993 and 1994 to protest the central government's decision to appoint yet another individual from outside the province to its governorship.

Chapter 7 offers closing commentary on some of the themes developed in the book. I suggest that beliefs about the "Unclean Ones" may yet be asserting their force, as evidenced in at least one recent episode of mass hysteria incited by rumors of *hantuen* hiding inside a government building. My conclusion recapitulates the tensions and terrors inherent in constructing rituals and identities in this remote region of modern Indonesia. Finally, the discussion relinquishes this larger perspective in order to emphasize the religious understandings of one adherent, Basir Muka. Like many religious specialists, he devoted much of his life to developing his competency in the religious realm. Like others, too, he was called on to accept certain changes in religious beliefs and practices. Late in his life, Basir Muka decided to convey his understanding of his religion through the creation of a work of art that was at once both a sacred artifact and a testament to a specific set of beliefs. In creating this work, Basir Muka claimed to have been guided by supernatural actuation. In light of the changes taking place in his religion and his society, however, he reinterpreted his art as one means of celebrating the immutable relationship he perceived as existing between the integrity of his religious beliefs and his own sense of identity. Although his interpretation may ultimately be labeled idiosyncratic, Basir Muka's quest to articulate the connection between the religious past and the Ngaju present is typical of and pervasive among the indigenous peoples of Central Kalimantan today.

2 | Death Begins

To the adherents of Hindu Kaharingan, death is a journey that culminates at the Village of Gold Sand, known colloquially as the Prosperous Village (Lewu Tatau). The splendor of this heavenly abode is well conveyed by its fuller name, which may be loosely glossed as "Prosperous Village of Gold Sand, of Diamond Beaches, Carpeted with Silk, of Jasper Pebbles, Heaps of Jasper Beads, Grand Place Where Bones Never Decay Carrying the Burden of the Glorious Flesh, Where the Muscles Never Tire."[1] Above the clouds, beyond the stars, the Prosperous Village is separated from earthly villages by the invisible rivers and jungles of a five-layered Upperworld. There, households of ancestors dwell contentedly in splendid surroundings that their children and grandchildren have provided for them. It is said that the relationships villagers find most meaningful in their earthly lives are transposed to this ethereal realm after death: in the next life, as in the present one, villagers turn to the members of their family for companionship and support. Adherents of the indigenous religion regard physical death as a means of reuniting the family throughout eternity. This reunion of the extended family in the afterlife is the nucleus of most villagers' comprehension of eschatology.

Reuniting the family after death is the duty of the living. Three stages of ritual are required to complete the processing of the dead. The complete cycle may extend well beyond the immediate survivors' lifetime. It culminates with the secondary mortuary celebration known as *tiwah*. If for some reason the children of the deceased are unable to sponsor the celebration, the responsibility is passed to future generations.[2] All three stages are necessary to ensure the deceased's ascent to the Prosperous Village.

In the villages of Central Kalimantan, as in many other places, treatment of the dead is a complicated process. The aim of this chapter and the next is to describe Ngaju death rituals in some detail. In offering this account, I mean to help fill the lacuna in precise knowledge of the ritual forms of Bornean peoples, especially their contemporary celebrations. Few extended descriptions of modern death rituals in Borneo are available, except for Peter Metcalf's accounts of the beliefs and practices of the Berawan of Sarawak, Malaysia. Metcalf has documented the indigenous religion of the Long Teru Berawan in three volumes: *Celebrations of Death* (1991), *A Borneo Journey into Death* (1982), and *Where Are You/Spirits* (1989).

In *Celebrations of Death,* Metcalf analyzes the relationship between the performance of secondary treatment of the dead *(nulang)* and the legitimation of status within Berawan communities (133–41). In *A Borneo Journey into Death,* Metcalf offers his most detailed rendering of Berawan ritual practice. Unlike the present study, Metcalf's analysis of *nulang* does not incorporate an explicit discussion of ritual change. He notes that he chose the particular community in which he worked because it was the sole remaining bastion of what he refers to as "traditional" religion (18). Metcalf remarks that, rather than admit the possibility that time and circumstances might alter their practices, the Long Teru Berawan made a conscious decision to suppress key aspects of ritual performance in order to avoid "debasing" their religion (233). In this chapter and the next, I reveal striking differences between Berawan and Ngaju peoples in this regard. The latter exhibit a very different attitude toward absence of ritual elements in the enactment of death ritual. And though they are certainly keen to avoid "debasing" their religion, they are also concerned with preserving it from oblivion.

With respect to literature on the Ngaju specifically, few descriptions of modern death practices have been published. Exceptions are Miles's articles on Mentaya River funerals and secondary mortuary celebrations, published in the 1960s, and two more recent Indonesian-language efforts: Laurentius Dyson and M. Asharini's *Tiwah: Upacara Kematian Pada Masyarakat Dayak Ngaju Di Kalimantan Tengah* (1980/81) and H. Yunus and S. Sastrosuwondo's *Upacara Tradisional (Upacara Kematian) Daerah Kalimantan Tengah* (1985). These authors devise paradigms that will assist individuals interested in comparing Ngaju ritual forms with those of neighboring peoples. Both studies are characterized by serious methodological problems, however, which are evident in the respective authors' discussions of ritual change. Their analyses, cast in the mode of salvage ethnography, force indigenous beliefs and practices into inappropriate categorizations borrowed from other religious traditions (Dyson and Asharini 1980/81) or attribute apparent inconsistencies in the system to confusion resulting from religious rationalization (Yunus and Sastrosuwondo 1985).

The Rituals Today

In chapter 1, I alluded to accounts by missionaries and other travelers to southern Borneo that described elaborate "death feasts" lasting for many days and involving the sacrifice of slaves and animals (Grabowsky 1889). Even today *tiwah* remain the most extravagant and boisterous of celebrations associated with the Hindu Kaharingan religion. In some villages, secondary mortuary rituals may last up to a month and involve expenses equivalent to several thousand dollars or more, as indicated in table 1. Expenses incurred during *tiwah* are particularly high when, as is generally preferred, the remains of more than one individual are treated. Sometimes up to thirty or more deceased persons are processed at a time. Although members of sponsoring families contribute most of the necessary food and goods, some items must be purchased, and a large outlay of cash is required. For example, if the family plans to sacrifice a cow or water buffalo and does not have one on hand, it must be purchased. The price of an average-sized adult water buffalo at the 1995 exchange rate was equivalent to about $430. Ritual specialists are paid partly in cash. Depending on the number of specialists invited to perform, the fee for their services alone can reach nearly $1,000. If the family builds a cement repository for the bones, as has lately become fashionable, the materials may run to more than $100. If a laborer is hired to do the work, the cost quadruples. To put these figures into perspective, the average annual per capita income in Indonesia is approximately $800. For Central Kalimantan villagers, the figure is significantly lower. Thus, although *tiwah* may be held immediately after death if the family can afford it, or if coincidentally the celebration is already in progress, the need to amass sufficient material and financial means to subsidize the ritual may result in its postponement for up to several decades.

More than any other Ngaju celebration, *tiwah* is intensely public. It is a bustling, highly visible, and, as revelers claim, *rami* or (Ind. *ramai*) or "boister-

TABLE 1. Budget of the Committee for Performing the Sacred Ritual of *Tiwah*, Tangkahen Village, Banama Tingang Subdistrict, 7 December 1990–9 January 1991

Cost of preparations through *pamohon gandang* (referred to in this study as *muluh gandang,* a more common term) indicating that *tiwah* has begun	Rp.	550.000
Six water buffaloes	Rp.	5.700.000
Thirteen pigs	Rp.	1.500.000
Eighty-one chickens	Rp.	390.000
Fee for the *hanteran* and nine *basir*	Rp.	1.888.250
One new *sandung*	Rp.	6.150.000
Food and drink for thirty-two days	Rp.	3.150.000
Miscellaneous provisions for the souls	Rp.	300.000
Transportation for *hanteran, basir,* and *sandung* maker	Rp.	1.250.000
Total		Rp. 20.878.250

Note: I am indebted to Sahari Andung for allowing me to include this information.

ous" event. It is not only the immediate family who join in the proceedings. Members of the extended family make a pilgrimage home for *tiwah,* and later guests arrive to share in the excitement and fun. Shortwave radio and word of mouth alert all concerned to the impending celebration. The festivities constitute periods of marked contrast to daily life. No one leaves the village to labor; instead, participants are obliged to remain close to home with family and friends. Entrepreneurs from the provincial capital or elsewhere venture abroad and erect food stalls or open-air shops to cater to celebrants, facilities that do not exist in small villages at any other time. Food and beverages, including steamed cakes, fried rice, and the popular locally produced soft drink "Hollywood," are sold on days and nights preceding key moments in the ritual. Sponsors and guests stroll in animated conversation down the village path, and traders hawk cheaply made clothing and sundries along the makeshift midway or from long, flat boats tied up at the river's edge. If one of the sponsoring families boasts a gasoline-powered electric generator, a string of lights may deck the house fronts. On rare occasions, a video cassette recorder, laboriously transported upriver, may provide a few evenings' entertainment as people congregate before the television screen to enjoy installments of the latest martial arts series to arrive from Hong Kong. As the climax of *tiwah* approaches, more and more visitors arrive and flock to the yard in front of the head sponsor's house. There celebrants perform great circle dances for hours on end, weaving among the temporary mortuary edifices and sacrificial animals tethered to stakes or secured in bamboo pens. An atmosphere of merrymaking prevails as participants gossip, drink, smear one another's faces with wet powder, or cajole a hesitant spectator to join the dance.

The portrait of death ritual presented in these pages derives from spirited exchanges with numerous sponsors over a dozen years, coupled with observation and participation. My village hosts shared my interest in the mechanics of death ritual, particularly *tiwah.* Indeed, little else could so elicit their enthusiastic discussion. With that in mind, what follows is more the ethnography of an enacted ideal than an account of any particular celebration.

There is a great deal of agreement in informants' accounts concerning how *tiwah* ought to be performed. Villagers unanimously agreed that the ideal *tiwah* is one that conforms to tradition *(hadat).* That there is, indeed, much similarity between different celebrations of *tiwah* is reflected in the homogeneity of the present account and earlier writings on the Ngaju. It is clear, for example, that mortuary rituals are informed by a series of complementary oppositions. The extent to which this complementarity pervades villagers' thinking about death and life is evidenced in the way the people describe the ritual and their use of kinetics, dance, music, art, language, and behavioral proscriptions within the context of actual celebrations.

Yet to understand the dynamics of *tiwah,* one's focus must not be limited to ideal rituals; hence, I also discuss celebrations that fell markedly short of the ideal. Nonetheless, rituals that deviate from the format described in this chapter and the next are not necessarily considered unacceptable. In a review article titled "Borneo Death," Tom Harrisson (1962) made some suggestions regarding the interpretation of variations in ritual forms that are worth citing:

> Nevertheless, we . . . have to make Ngaju or Kelabit prisoners in word. That does not mean, though, that while expressing as best we can what is convenient in our writing, we should obliterate what is inconvenient or difficult to simplify in their own ideas. . . . This particularly applies to death rites and their associated beliefs, which can be of the gravest concern to the group and not considered suitable for outside ears at all. It is particularly difficult, in Borneo, to penetrate some of the inner attitudes regarding the spirit and the soul. Further, the incompleteness of death observances is one of their commonest characteristics, for a multitude of reasons. This is not so only among groups who in recent times have not practised secondary elaborate burial in recognisable form. . . . The sort of rites the Berawan-Kenya and Kelabit-Murut tell you they must observe, may in fact only be achieved once in a life time. (16)

In terms reminiscent of Harrisson's admonition, sponsors of *tiwah* insisted that their rituals conformed to the secondary mortuary celebration described in the origin myth, the *panaturan.* That myth, excerpts from which appear in chapter 4, is often recited by a ritual specialist in the context of secondary treatment of the dead. Sponsors' insistence leads one to suppose that the origin myth details the format of an exemplary death ritual. This is not the case however. The origin myth does not make the format of *tiwah* entirely explicit (Simpei and Hanyi 1996, 131–34). Flexibility in the notion of what the ritual should entail allows participants to adapt the format of ritual to the unique circumstances of its performance, to their varying financial means, and to the differing levels of skill of the specialists whose services they have contracted. Thus, although its form speaks to tradition, death ritual, like tradition itself, is eminently transformable and ever transforming.

Despite *tiwah*'s general plasticity, participants consider some *tiwah* incorrect or inadequate and therefore unacceptable *(salah gawi).* In discussing both successful and unsuccessful *tiwah,* I intend not only to illustrate the structural principles that inform the celebration but also to explore the range and limits of the death ritual's adaptive aspect. Although the acceptability of a ritual's format is assessed throughout the planning and implementation of the celebration, the misperformance of *tiwah* or any other stage of the ritual cycle may also be discovered only in retrospect. Misperformance, as I noted earlier, is identified by the appearance of signs such as the illness of a sponsor or the inexplicable death of an animal destined for sacrifice. Even misfortunes that occur many years after the celebration may be attributed to misperformance. The multifaceted problem of ritual misperformance must be understood socioculturally as well as structurally and will be addressed later.

The Three Stages of Mortuary Ritual

Adherents of Hindu Kaharingan claim that the completion of three distinct ritual phases is necessary to process the dead and to ensure souls' arrival in the Upperworld. The cycle commences with primary treatment *(mangubur)*, which includes the wake and primary disposal, usually by interment. The second phase, known as *balian tantulak matei mampisik liau,* primarily consists of chants performed by ritual specialists to "separate" the souls of the dead—that is, to dispatch them to appropriate cosmological locations where they will await further processing—as well as to purge the deceased's home of some of the pollution associated with death. It culminates with a riverine ablution of the bereaved kin who were present at the death, as well as those who were physically involved in primary treatment. The final phase, *tiwah,* completes the processing of the souls and the physical remains. It is followed by rituals to honor and benefit sponsors and their descendants. Were the rituals not performed on the deceased's behalf, his or her soul(s) would be doomed to slumber endlessly in a cosmological limen or to remain mired in the decomposing corpse. Secondary mortuary rituals are performed on behalf of all Hindu Kaharingan villagers, with the exception of some very young children. If descendants have forgotten to *tiwah* bones that are recovered accidentally while plowing a field, for example, not only must the ritual be performed, but also the person who found the remains must be rewarded. In the event that the deceased's physical remains are irretrievable, mortuary rituals are still performed, with appropriate modifications.

Completion of the ritual cycle frees survivors from many dangers of supernatural origin that threaten to beset them if they are remiss in fulfilling the obligations imposed by their bereavement. The kin group as a whole is prey to these dangers, and, theoretically, no one is exempt from participation in a kinsperson's mortuary ritual. Briefly, the dangers include the severe consequences of transgressing proscriptions that surround nonperformance or misperformance of ritual, along with contamination from the pernicious cloud, known as *ambun rutas matei,* which is said to accompany death. The cloud—which clings like a spider web—is believed to be a source of misfortune and illness for those who come in contact with the corpse or with the accoutrements of the dead. The cloud drives away the life essence of plants, so the dead must be kept out of cultivated fields. Soon after completion of primary treatment, the cloud is ritually swept away from people and goods that have been exposed to the corpse; it is "collected," carried to the river, and set adrift. The cloud then floats away, eventually ascending to an Upperworld sea where it no longer poses a threat to mankind. This careful management of death confines the cloud to the deceased's home, thereby decreasing the number of people exposed to its debilitating influence. Heavy fines for the cleansing rituals are levied against those whose relatives inadvertently expire in another family's house or on their land or who tie up a boat carrying a corpse at another family's dock.

Additional dangers are posed by souls awaiting *tiwah*, which are considered capable of vexing or even threatening their kin if the rituals on their behalf are delayed or inadequate. The soul's assault, called *liau nyaranta* or *puji liau*, is recognizable through physical symptoms. The victim may tremble fiercely, run about aimlessly, or mumble incoherently. The victim's children may also be targeted and fall ill. Only the successful and timely completion of secondary mortuary ritual, during which the deceased is "made prosperous" *(inatau)*— that is, given food, animals, and servants for use in the Upperworld—makes the possibility of an attack remote. To understand why souls of the dead are said to have cause to attack the living, it is necessary to examine local beliefs concerning what happens to souls at death and afterward.

Souls and Life Forces

According to adherents of Hindu Kaharingan, everything in the universe—material and immaterial—has an animate essence or sensate life force called *gana*. Humans additionally possess an animate essence of a higher order known as *hambaruan.* In life, the human soul is located in the blood. Accidents or illness are said to make the soul "hot," and attacks on the soul by supernatural beings are frequently cited in the etiology of illness. Prophylactic measures against disease are intended to "cool" the soul and thereby lend it strength. These measures include anointing the body with blood or perfumed water in the context of rituals or upon arrivals and departures. Anointment is often accompanied by chants to cool the soul. Special precautions to keep the soul cool must also be taken when one is near a corpse.

Death ritual is an operation performed on behalf of souls as much as on behalf of bodies. The explicit objective is to emplace the souls of the dead in an Upperworld village and to transfer the animate essence of houses, animals, and servants to meet the souls' conjectural needs in this new abode. Some lay adherents of Hindu Kaharingan espouse the view that humans have but a single soul during their lifetime, though certain ritual specialists suggest that they have up to seven. Most would agree that souls enter the body at the moment of birth. Specialists and laypeople would further concur that at death, or shortly thereafter, the soul trifurcates, or manifests itself in three parts: the soul of the intellect *(salumpuk teras liau* or *panyalumpuk liau),* the soul of the fleshy parts of the body *(liau balawang panjang ganan bereng),* and the soul of bones, nails, and hair *(liau karahang tulang, silu, tuntung balau).* One specialist claimed that the souls of the intellect and of the fleshy parts of the body were the father's contribution to a child, whereas the soul of the hard body parts came from the mother. Another assured me that the soul of the hard parts came from the father, the fleshy parts from the mother, and the intellect from "Almighty God."

The precise moment when trifurcation occurs is unclear. From the moment of physical arrest through completion of primary interment, family members assume that the soul is nearby and able to see and hear them. From the moment shortly after breathing ceases to interment, one relative, usually the spouse or a child of the deceased, takes on a task known as *manunggu hantu,* whereby he or she is required to be in the corpse's vicinity at all times, sharing in its discomfort by sitting upright and abstaining from eating rice. Though free to leave the room whenever necessary, the mourner observing these proscriptions must first inform the deceased of his or her intention either by speaking directly to the corpse or, later, by tapping on the coffin lid. Mourners claim to be unafraid of the souls at this point, believing it unlikely that the deceased is even able to comprehend that he or she is dead. Many assume a markedly playful attitude: on one occasion, a group of men seated near the corpse of a villager who had just died in a hunting accident whiled away the hours taking shots through an open window at the squirrels leaping through nearby trees.

During the second phase of death ritual, souls are directly informed that they have died by means of a chant performed by a chorus of ritual specialists, or *basir.* From the content of the chant, we learn that the deceased's immediate reaction is assumed to be one of disbelief. The deceased is convinced of his or her death only after a particular Upperworld being contacted by the specialist commands the deceased to distinguish between the six cardinal points— upriver, downriver, up, down, sunrise, and sunset—and the deceased finds himself or herself unable to comply. Then the being is said to hand a mirror to the souls. The souls see from their reflection that they have been "touched with gold," that is, that their nails and hair have become golden as a result of being rubbed either with the precious metal itself or with a particular type of plant, an anointment that is required before a corpse can be placed in a coffin. The soul of the intellect is then transported to the Upperworld in a fabulous ship. It is not taken directly to the Prosperous Village but rather is transported to another region, where it will wait weeks, months, or even years to be summoned for *tiwah.* The two remaining souls remain temporarily in the grave pending further treatment.

Even after death, souls are said to stay in contact with the living. Communication between the living and the dead is possible through apparitions or dreams. In dreams, for example, the dead come to their descendants to make requests or even to chide them for having been remiss in their ritual obligations. By way of example, one man related to me his mother's dream, in which she was contacted by her recently deceased father and summoned home to attend to his mortuary rituals:

When my grandfather died, my father was in Java. My mother was ill and staying with the nurse. I was the oldest in the house and didn't know how to cleanse the death of my grandfather. My mother had a dream. She met my grandfather, who told her to come home. "The house is dirty," he said. My mother, in her dream, went home and saw that the house was full of spider webs. Grandfather told her to look at his fingernails. He complained that they weren't golden and that he was walking around like a blind person. Because we didn't know, we hadn't rubbed gold on grandfather's nails before putting him in a coffin. Grandfather told mother to go home. "Not yet," she said. "The nurse will give you permission," he replied. At the moment my grandfather embraced my mother in her dream, the nurse came and embraced my mother. The nurse gave my mother permission to go home. The *balian tantulak matei mampisik liau* was held one week after my grandfather was buried.

The relationship between the living and the dead is not characterized solely by the dead making requests of survivors. As the living hope to acquire gifts and blessings from the dead, the relationship can be characterized as one of exchange. Drawing on the work of Marcel Mauss (1967) and Pierre Bourdieu (1971), Chee-Kiong Tong (1993) has argued with regard to Southeast Asia generally that death rituals must be understood within the framework of all the transactions in a society, including those between the living and the dead. The idea of a reciprocal relationship involving the giving of gifts and countergifts, even when one of the parties to the exchange is no longer alive, is vital as it functions to provide corporateness to the group and to maintain continuity over time. Among the Ngaju, offerings of food and tobacco or areca nuts for chewing are often left on coffins or graves to curry favor with the dead. Providing elaborate funerals or *tiwah* is also said to please the dead, and survivors anxiously await subsequent signs of favor. For example, I was present on one occasion when a stone seemed to leap into the air from a grave that was being filled with earth. The deceased's children seized the stone and decided to keep it, interpreting the episode as proof of their mother's satisfaction with how her burial was carried out. Similarly, survivors who can boast of prosperity in years following *tiwah,* of large harvests and of debts paid, attribute their good fortune to their deceased kin. Villagers are not obligated to "worship" the dead, however, in the sense that it is not incumbent on them to prepare offerings for ancestors either before or after *tiwah,* though they may do so by choice. I know one Palangka Raya Muslim family who leaves offerings of tobacco on the bone repository of a deceased grandfather every Friday.

The treatment of souls is said to be complete when they have been transported to the Prosperous Village. Hindu Kaharingan villagers generally do not espouse a belief in reincarnation into this world, although they do claim that the dead are reborn into another existence. Some villagers hold the theory that stillborn children, as well as children who have died at a very young age, can be reincarnated within the same nuclear family. Burying a child below the edge of the roof where rainwater will strike the grave is said to make it easier for the child's soul, in this case its *panyalumpuk liau,* to return. Like the souls of the dead who wish to contact the living, the child may make people aware of its intention through dreams. Sometimes another soul conveys the information. For example, when an acquaintance of mine died in Palangka Raya late in her pregnancy, the child, too, was lost. One month later, a friend's wife gave birth to a son. That evening the deceased visited the new mother in a dream and announced, "Your child is my child." Shortly thereafter, the newborn's parents held a *hambai* to allow the child to be adopted by the deceased woman's husband. These adoptions are considered a means to add parents rather than replace them. The biological parents' rights and responsibilities toward the child remain intact, and the adoptive parent is expected to assume responsibility too.

When a family has lost a child and a subsequent birth is thought to be the reincarnation of the deceased, a special ritual is performed. Afterward a male infant is given an earring and a female child is given a silver anklet. I observed children up to the age of nine or ten years still wearing these items. I encountered only one reference to the reincarnation of adults into this world from a ritual specialist who told me that souls are reborn in the Upperworld, complete seven cycles of rebirth there, and then are reincarnated into the world of the living. Ritual specialists, unlike lay adherents who usually emphasize the reunion of the family in the Prosperous Village, often hold that the dead are given an entirely new identity in the Upperworld, where they are reborn as beautiful young men and women.

Ritual Specialists

Performance of the second and third stages of death ritual is the domain of the *basir.* These ritual specialists have long been of interest to Borneanists and to wider anthropological audiences as well. The literature on specialists suggests that they defy typification. According to one scholar, "uncertainty and contradiction" surround these "so-called priests" (Wulff 1960, 121). Diversity in specialists' portrayal is due partly to scholars' disregard of how local peoples envision the roles of religious functionaries. Local characterizations of specialists are also enigmatic, however.

Contemporary Kahayan specialists claim that they are recognized for their skillful and efficacious performance of ritual rather than their dress, origin, or sex. According to an important myth, the first ritual specialists were trained by 177 female Upperworld beings, the *bawi ayah,* who descended to villages along the Kahayan River. Today there are few, if any, female *basir.*[3] In early accounts of the activities of these religious functionaries, they were generally depicted as the veritable dregs of society. For example, Carl Bock, paraphrasing descriptions of *basir* and *balian* from the works of Schwaner and Perelaer, characterized them as follows in *The Head-Hunters of Borneo:*

> Dr. Schwaner and Mr. Perelaer both refer to these functionaries as being employed. . . on the occasion of a funeral to recite the virtues of the dead and make a request that he may be received into heaven. There are two classes of them, the *Bassirs,* who are men dressed as women, and the *Bilians* or *Balians,* who are women, the last named as being the more influential of the two. Their chief functions are to make as much noise as possible. Dr. Schwaner and Mr. Perelaer state that these people, both men and women, are ordinarily occupied in various disgusting and immoral practices when not specially engaged at feasts, funerals, &c. (1985, 219–20)

Hans Schärer proposed that *basir* are nearly exclusively hermaphroditic or impotent (1963, 57), a suggestion strikingly unlike the reputation that many specialists enjoy today. Contemporary specialists acknowledge the existence of transvestite *basir* but suggest that these have always been uncommon. I recall quite vividly the good-natured laughter that my question whether all *basir* used to be transvestites evoked early in my fieldwork. In any case, several *basir* explained to me that whether a specialist is male, female, or transvestite is indicated in his or her ritual title, or *tandak.* The *tandak* is either chosen by the *basir* (male or female) or bestowed by another specialist at the start of his or her career. For example, one celebrated *basir* of the past, Kuri, bore the *tandak* "Sambang Bapa Laut, Garun Mama Burong." From this *tandak,* specifically the words *bapa* (father) and *mama* (uncle), we see that Kuri was a male who performed as a male. A female *basir,* Sanun, who lived earlier in this century, bore the *tandak* "Sambang Indu Bulau Balemu, Garun Mina Rabia Natai." *Indu* and *mina* mean "mother" and "aunt," respectively, so Sanun was a female who performed as such. The *basir* Dahiyang, however, was a transvestite. His *tandak,* "Sambang Indu Nampa, Garun Mina Ujan," reveals that he consistently performed as a female. In fact, Dahiyang's pride at the profoundness of his transvestism was legendary. He reportedly became irritated with those who referred to him as "Bapa" rather than "Indu Nampa." One *basir* who had known Dahiyang well related the following anecdote. After the conclusion of a particular ceremony, all of the *basir* involved walked down to the river to relieve themselves. One *basir,* annoyed to discover urine on the logs on which he was standing, shouted, "Who is it that has urinated all over and made this mess?" This angry outburst pleased the culprit, Dahiyang, whose purported response was, "I did it. Women, not men, always make a mess when they urinate."

Among the Ngaju, it is the degree rather than the kind of knowledge that distinguishes specialists from lay adherents of the indigenous religion and enables them to assume featured roles in the performance of certain types of ritual. Their role is legitimated by their competency in ritual language styles, knowledge of cosmology, and presumed access to supernatural sources of power. Beyond this, specialists resist categorization. Some deprecate their expertise or even deny that they are specialists.

Their humility notwithstanding, *basir* are the most cosmologically sophisticated adherents of Hindu Kaharingan, though they are not the sole type of ritual specialist (Schiller 1989, Jay 1993). They acquire extensive knowledge of cosmology and cosmogony during a lengthy apprenticeship. The religious understandings of *basir* are highly personalistic, reflecting the influence of teachers coupled with experience. Much of their training involves mastery of ascetic practices, which enable them to maintain and utilize arcane knowledge *(kaji)* as personal sources of power. All adult adherents of the indigenous religion attempt to attain some control of this knowledge, which can take the form of mantras, physical actions, oils, charms, and so forth, but specialists are said to be exceptionally adept. Apprenticeship also involves memorization of chants delivered in a ritual language style rich with cosmologic imagery (Fox 1971a).[4] By using chants, specialists transpose the animate essence of their voices and words to other realms in order to request aid from supernatural beings. The specialist's own soul is not generally thought to travel to these realms.

Recitations of chants in the context of ritual are known as *balian.* During *balian,* an odd number of specialists seat themselves on a long bench *(katil).* Their feet straddle gongs, a roof of cloth hangs above their heads, and each holds a ritual drum. Chants are led by the most skilled specialist, the *basir upu* or *upu balian,* who sings in exquisite metaphors charting journeys through other realms of existence. The remaining specialists respond in unison, and all accompany the chants on their drums. Expertise can be determined by where each specialist sits in relation to the head *basir,* who sits at the center of the bench. *Basir* positioned to the immediate right or left of the *basir upu* are referred to as *pangapit sambil* and *pangapit gantau,* respectively. *Basir* seated at the ends of the bench farthest from the *upu* are the *lawin katil.*

At the most abstract level, then, *basir* are simply individuals who take part in *balian.* Commencement of the specialist's training may or may not be associated with unusual psychic experiences, although among certain other Dayak groups, the role of religious functionary is legitimated specifically through such experiences. In describing the experience of the Iban *manang,* for example, Vinson Sutlive notes that the "calling" takes the form of the appearance of a supernatural familiar in a dream. The familiar informs the dreamer where to locate certain magical quartz crystals and how to use them in diagnosing future patients (1976, 67). The familiar returns to the *manang* during episodes of possession. Among villagers in Central Kalimantan, it is often lay adherents rather than specialists who are subject to this kind of possession by supernatural beings, though ritual specialists do claim to be entered by supernatural beings during rituals. In their performance, they describe the course of their possession, singing of the being's descent into their own body. One specialist explained the experience in a parallel drawn from modern telecommunications: "When a radio announcer reports events, he is doing only that, nothing more. He cannot make events happen simply by talking about them. So it is with us. If we were not entered by other beings, we could do nothing. We would speak but nothing would happen. The presence of the other beings makes us effective."

Today any villager so inclined may apprentice to become a *basir*. Unless that person acquires the requisite level of skill to serve as head specialist, no public initiation marks achievement of proficiency. Before a specialist may officiate at a *balian* for the first time, however, he or she must hold a ceremony to establish a "bridge" to other cosmological realms for use throughout his or her career. An exception are *basir* who have inherited the use of such a bridge from a deceased relative. Individuals who participate in *balian* irregularly or who have achieved only rudimentary skill often say that they can "join a *balian*" rather than that they "are *basir*."

An especially arduous role in the specialist's repertoire is that of serving as head specialist at a secondary mortuary ritual, during which he is responsible for emplacing the deceased's souls in the Upperworld. Not all specialists are equipped to assume this awesome responsibility. The hierarchy that obtains among ritual specialists is most apparent here. The ideal *tiwah* involves participation of a particular kind of ritual specialist who can sing the course of the deceased's journey to the Upperworld and whose performance involves recitation of the origin myth. This specialist is called the *tukang hanteran* or *magah liau*. Not all *basir upu* have the ability to serve as *tukang hanteran*. The *tukang hanteran*'s chant escorts the soul of the intellect to its Upperworld abode. The origin myth, which is recited as part of this chant, is said to re-create a purified cosmos. Before a *tukang hanteran* may officiate at *tiwah* for the first time, he may perform a chant to escort the animate essence of a fruit tree to the Upperworld. If the fruit tree withers and dies shortly after the chant, the specialist is said to have demonstrated the level of skill necessary to perform at *tiwah*. It is this kind of skill that earmarks the *tukang hanteran* as a potentially dangerous individual, one who hypothetically possesses the ability to dispatch the souls of living men and women to other cosmological realms, causing these individuals to sicken and die. On the evening following a *tukang hanteran*'s performance, the remaining souls are processed by a chorus of specialists in a *balian* of a few hours' duration. The alternative *tiwah* format is to hold a single *balian* to process all three souls at once without performance of the origin myth or participation of a *tukang hanteran*. Factors influencing the choice of format are discussed in chapter 3.

The Mortuary Cycle: Death and Primary Treatment

Death ideally occurs at home, with the dying person surrounded by as many members of the extended family as possible. To facilitate dying in this setting, those for whom death seems imminent are rushed to their homes, even from public health clinics and hospitals. Their kin are summoned by means of death-watch announcements broadcast daily throughout the region via shortwave radio.

When no trace of a pulse remains, a gong is struck in a series of staccato bursts *(titih)* to announce the death and bid all within hearing distance to come to the deceased's home. The gong is struck repeatedly, seven times in a row for men, five times for women, three times for children. Survivors ethno-semantically distinguish their deceased kin from other dead persons. From this moment on, mourners speak of the deceased as having "vanished" *(nihau)*. Only animals, slaves, and sometimes members of other people's families are referred to as "dead" *(matei)*. The remainder of the ritual cycle is largely di-rected toward re-placing vanished kin, relocating them in the Upperworld.

After a death, five gongs are brought into the front room of the deceased's house and placed at the downriver end of the room. Guests arrive carrying gifts of sugar or tobacco; their donations are said to ease survivors' burdens and to ward off misfortune *(sial-kawe)*. Most of the guests seat themselves in the front room near the corpse, though some of the women go to the back of the house to assist in the kitchen. Any of the bereaved kin may wash and dress the deceased, which is also done in the front room. While some lay out the corpse, others disassemble the deathbed and carry it out of the house, and still others erect devices on the downriver side of the house to fend off unwelcome supernatural beings.[5] Five protective devices are commonly prepared against them. The first is a miniature fence *(tarinting dawen sawang)* of withered *sa-wang* leaves *(Cordyline terminalis)* strung on a rope between a downward-pointed spear and a branch from which all living matter has been scraped. The second device, a bamboo container full of water *(tampulak humbang)*, creates a sea that the unwelcome beings cannot cross. Third, a sharpening stone *(batu asa)* is set out to create a wall beyond which the beings cannot see. A fourth device, consisting of a bunch of leaves and vials of potent oil *(panulak)* is usually hung in the doorway of the house to dissuade unwelcome beings from entering. In the past a crocodile egg *(tanteluh bajai)* might be hung in the window on the downriver side of the house for the same purpose.

In the center of the front room, a bamboo plank *(talatai)* supported by a row of gongs is readied for display of the corpse. The corpse is dressed in everyday clothing that has been turned inside out, and the jaws of the deceased are tied shut. The body is arranged *(mahujur hantu)* on the plank with the face exposed, hair loose. Women are displayed with their feet pointed upriver, men the reverse. This arrangement is explained by the association of women with panning for gold at the headwaters and men with wandering the length of the rivers toward the coast. More examples of differentiation according to the sex of the deceased arise throughout the mortuary cycle.

Silver coins are placed on the corpse's eyes or cheeks, and a cup filled with the blood of a freshly slaughtered chicken is placed on the deceased's chest above his or her folded arms. A triangular roof of wooden poles and cloth *(tingkap tingang)* is hung about four feet above the platform. Gongs are struck loudly and repeatedly during these emotionally charged moments. Thus arranged, the corpse may remain from two days to a week on the platform or in its coffin. Survivors usually attempt to schedule interment to guarantee participation by the maximum number of extended family members.

The bereaved spouse and children position themselves near the head of the corpse, speaking to it or caressing it. The deceased is addressed with the expectation that he or she is capable of hearing and culpable for the suffering that the death has brought upon the family. One distraught young woman remonstrated with her deceased husband, who had accidentally shot himself while cleaning a hunting rifle. His kin had not known how to staunch the flow of blood, and the man himself had refused to be transported to a nearby public clinic for medical treatment since it was illegal for him to have owned the rifle in the first place. His wife cried out: "The emptiness, the emptiness. How will your children live? We have four children and we will soon have another. My parents are poor, my father is old and ill. Now your soul *[liau]* must watch over us. We have so many debts, nearly 20,000 rupiah. How can I pay them without making a slave *[jipen]* of myself?"

Outbursts of grief are neither condemned nor encouraged. Seemingly little heed is paid to the spouse, as mourners busy themselves arranging food and goods near the displayed corpse. These are intended for the souls' use. Cigarettes, oil lamps or flashlights, and suitcases full of clothing and personal effects are set out, as are tools appropriate to the sex of the deceased. (One man was laid out with a briefcase full of business papers at his side.) An egg placed below the platform is said to keep the corpse from rapidly decomposing. Heirloom jars are brought out, and more gongs are hung in a corner of the room. Death is the only occasion when the family displays these treasured possessions, perhaps with the hope that the deceased will be pleased to see them or will augment them. The valued goods are arranged in full view of the guests, providing a rare glimpse of a family's wealth.

Plans for *tiwah* begin within hours of death. During an interlude known as "becoming a widower/widow" *(mambuyu/mambalu),* a blood relative of the deceased, ideally a sibling, gives a token amount of money to the spouse and announces whether the minimally acceptable beast to be sacrificed at *tiwah* will be a water buffalo, a cow, or a pig. That person will usually be the first to stab the animal at *tiwah.* The second, often a first cousin to the deceased, ties a strip from the shroud around the bereaved spouse's head. At *tiwah,* this cousin will eat the animal's hind leg, sharing it with the deceased's sibling. The third to stab the beast, preferably the deceased's second cousin, is often appointed later.[6] Should the spouse remarry before sponsoring *tiwah,* the number of animals to be sacrificed is supposed to double.

Throughout the night following the death and on all succeeding evenings while the corpse or coffin is displayed, neither family members nor visitors in the house may sleep. The assembled family and visitors wait up with the corpse. They entertain themselves, and presumably the deceased, with "souls' games." Most characteristic is a game known as *hapuar* or *sepak sawut.* The game is played with a husked coconut that has been immersed in a flammable liquid for several hours. At nightfall, the coconut is set ablaze, and barefoot men and boys spend hours engaged in a furious game of fiery soccer. Meanwhile, inside the house, red ants' nests, animal excrement, and scorching rice may be tossed back and forth. Lizards or pigs covered with excrement may be set loose and chased among the mourners. If burial is delayed for several days, the decomposition liquids are sometimes collected on cloths and stealthily placed over the mouths and noses of unwary sleepers. I was told that, in the past, ritual specialists would use their knowledge to make the corpse rise up and walk around the room to amuse the guests further.

As the nights wear on, participants take turns playing gongs. The particular tattoo played on these occasions is said to provoke shivers of fear in those who hear it. According to villagers, dangerous supernatural beings, or *hantuen,* try to locate the source of the music and come to dance at the doorway and on the windowsills. Jasper bracelets worn by the deceased's kin are thought to protect them from these beings. Some people take further precautions. In Katingan River villages, masked dancers *(habukung)* perform around the corpse, hoping to deceive any unwelcome beings that may be in the vicinity into believing that others of their ilk have beaten them to the remains (Miles 1964, 332).

On the morning of the second or third day, a black cow or pig provided by the bereaved spouse or children is sacrificed by the deceased's opposite-sex sibling or first cousin. Some of the cooked meat from the animal is added to the foods already arranged near the corpse; the rest is consumed by mourners. Blood from the beast is used to anoint the seven, nine, or eleven men who will spend the rest of the day constructing the coffin *(raung).* The blood is said to cool the men's souls and to protect them from injury in their work.

According to Kahayan villagers, coffins should be carved from living trees, preferably ironwood or fruit trees. Before the tree is felled, a chant is sung, accompanied by a scattering of rice mixed with the blood of a chicken, to inform the tree's animate essence of the purpose to which it will be put. Before commencing to build the coffin, workers carve small figurines to represent and protect themselves. If one of the men is injured and bleeds while constructing the coffin, it is said that his soul will become the deceased's servant in the Upperworld. Should an accident occur, the victim must prepare a remedial sacrifice soon afterward. The coffin builders observe other proscriptions as well. They must cook their own foods, be careful not to step over the coffin, and be watchful lest some animal pass over it.

Traditional coffins from the region are elaborate works of great beauty. These include women's coffins carved in the shape of a particular type of bird, men's coffins carved with the head and tail of a water snake, and a third type, suitable for either sex, with the head of a water snake and the tail of a bird. Most decorated coffins depict particular Upperworld beings said to assist the deceased on the journey to the Upperworld. Villagers may also construct smooth, undecorated coffins with upturned edges or simple plank coffins.

When the coffin is completed, it is brought back to the house. Before the corpse is placed in it, the family performs a brief ritual during which the widow, widower, or children apply yellow juice produced by crushing the leaves of a particular plant to the hair and nails of the deceased or touch the corpse's hair and nails with gold. Gold is touched five times to women, seven times to men. Only then may the corpse be placed in the coffin. Traditional coffins are narrow. The corpse is placed on its left side if female, its right if male. Finally,

Woman's coffin *(raung basangkuwai)*. Kahayan River, 1983. Photo by author.

the coffin is secured with rattan bands. Five bands stretched over twenty-one wooden wedges secure a woman's coffin; seven bands over twenty-three wedges secure a man's. If the coffin is not otherwise decorated, it is usually painted with scenes from the deceased's life at this time.

At least four methods of primary storage are practiced. Remains may be cremated and the ashes placed in a Chinese jar inside a roofed hut, suspended in a hanging coffin beneath a roof made from an overturned canoe, sealed inside a wooden or cement crypt, or buried in the earth. Of these four options, burial is the most common.

Bodies are laid to rest according to certain geographic and cosmologic rules. Sunrise and upriver are associated with life, sunset and downriver with death. Most houses are built facing the rising sun, and the dead are buried with their feet pointing in the direction of the setting sun. Graveyards are usually located

Removing a coffin from a house. The deceased's son is sitting astride the coffin. Kahayan River, 1983. Photo by author.

on the downriver side of the village, and interment begins well after dawn, when the sun has nearly reached the midpoint of the sky. Such acts underscore complementary oppositions in the realms of death and life. Family and friends who will escort the deceased to the graveyard gather early in the day to help remove the coffin from the house. A long pole slipped beneath three strips of wood fastened by rattan bands on top of the coffin is used to lift and carry it. A tiny basket of cooked meat is tied to the head of the coffin as a gift for the first Upperworld being the deceased encounters on the journey.

The coffin is first moved to the doorway of the house, where it is swept with leaves waved from the direction of sunrise to sunset, from upriver to downriver. A wand of burning bamboo is likewise passed over the coffin. Before the coffin is lifted, a direct descendant of the deceased sits atop it, facing the back of the house. This action is said to provide a temporary escort for the souls and to demonstrate the esteem in which descendants hold the deceased. It also underscores the opposition between the living and the dead. A house where death has occurred is thought to be in a special geographic relationship to the Upperworld. It is believed that the area is elevated and that just beyond the house awning lies a sea that the soul is assisted in crossing by a supernatural being. After lifting the coffin, the bearers begin a halting march, advancing and retreating. They walk, one step forward, one back, two steps forward, two back, until they reach the doorway in seven steps. Then the mourner straddling the coffin quickly climbs down, and the bearers carry their burden briskly out of the house. Other mourners, usually weeping and sometimes sobbing loudly, pause or are restrained for a moment at the doorway. Reaching the bottom of the steps, the bearers slightly damage the stair railings, a sign for the souls that they will not be returning to the house in the normal manner.

A large procession follows the coffin to the river's edge, where canoes await. There the coffin is loaded on a canoe and taken to the graveyard. Gongs to be played during the wake and cooked foods prepared for the souls are also taken aboard. A particular tattoo is played on the gongs throughout the journey. The canoes that carry mourners are packed nearly to the point of capsizing. The lone exception is the canoe bearing the coffin and the grieving spouse, who is accompanied by only one or two oarsmen.

Locating a place to dig the grave usually involves crashing through the scrub. Hindu Kaharingan villagers do not clear graveyards and rarely visit them unless they are burying the dead or recovering bones for a secondary mortuary ritual. As they search for a site, mourners carefully sidestep gaping holes in the earth, evidence of earlier *tiwah*. A small fire is lit, and some of the deceased's tools and baskets are relegated to the flames. Red and yellow rice along with bits of cooked food are scattered over the coffin as offerings for supernatural beings. Mourners scatter these offerings with their left hand. The rattan bands securing the coffin are slowly loosened, and the coffin is lowered gently into the earth.

The mourners then move to one side of the coffin, the side of the setting sun, and in unison pull out the bands, afterward intoning a chant for the protection of their own souls and the souls of their children and grandchildren. Everyone helps to fill the grave with handfuls or shovelfuls of earth. A branch scraped clean of leaves and bark so that it cannot take root is stuck into the earth at the head of the grave. Atop the branch, a piece of the shroud is tied like a small flag above a basket of uncooked rice. Another branch, without the strip of shroud, is left at the river's edge nearest the graveyard as a sign that a funeral has taken place. On the upriver side of the grave, an oil lamp is lit and extinguished three times before being abandoned. With each smothering of the flames, the assembled shout, "Belep sial kawe!" (Dampen all misfortune). Survivors may erect a wooden statue, carved to resemble a human being and representing a figure of the same sex as the deceased, near the head of the grave.

The mood of participants departing from the gravesite changes drastically from the somber mien of the preceding hours. Now there is laughter, pushing, and racing, particularly among the young people, as mourners hurry back to the boats. Their merriment is said to be controlled by the personality of the deceased. If the deceased was personable and well liked, the scene will be raucous and exciting. When the canoes arrive at the village, the gongs, the implements for digging the grave, and the participants themselves must be immersed in the water and soaked thoroughly before they can return to land.

Once home, the family prepares for a final sleepless night. Implements used to prepare the grave are assembled in a corner of the room and covered with a fishnet. At sunrise the net is removed, and rice is scattered for supernatural beings believed to be present.

The Mortuary Cycle: Informing the Deceased

The second stage of death ritual cleanses away still more of the pollution of death and sends the deceased's souls out of the village. This ritual, *balian tantulak matei mampisik liau,* ideally falls on the seventh day following death, two days after burial. In practice, it may be delayed a month or longer, especially if the bereaved family is hard-pressed to amass goods and cash to fund it and pay for the participation of ritual specialists. The ritual begins in the early evening, shortly after sunset, and continues until nearly sunrise. Chants are performed by an odd number of specialists, usually five but never fewer than three. The chant series has nine parts, with rest periods in between. The first five parts of the series are intended to dispose of the cloud said to accompany death; the remaining four provide initial treatment for the souls.

The ritual begins inside the front room of the house. The specialists seat themselves on their long bench. A roof of colorful cloth hangs above their heads.

From the cloths cascade shredded strips of bamboo on which supernatural beings summoned to the house are said to sit. Behind the specialists is another wall of cloths. A variety of cooked foods, including whole chickens and cakes, as well as raw rice in brass bowls that contain a hornbill feather, are arranged before the bench. The essence of the food is intended for the souls of the deceased. Later the foods will be carried outside the house and left in a shrine for the village's supernatural guardian. Other ritual paraphernalia include an uprooted *sawang* plant covered with a black cloth and tied to a downward-pointing spear. The spear stands in a bowl of uncooked rice, which also contains an unhusked coconut. A bowl of water is placed amid the branches of the plant. A wreath made of bamboo and black cloth is hung from the spear, as are seven bamboo tubes bound together and covered with a black cloth. These articles are used in the latter part of the ritual, when specialists help prepare souls to depart on their journey. Tools used to dig the grave and gongs struck at the wake are placed together in a downriver corner of the room.

The ritual commences when the head specialist lights a smoldering fire of odoriferous resin. Chanting a mantra, he passes a bottle filled with red and yellow rice, areca nuts, and tobacco or cigarettes through the smoke. The bottle is touched to the head of each person in the room, then shattered against the stairs leading into the house. Participants claim that the contents of the bottle are for the dangerous supernatural beings that will converge on the deceased's house. They hope that having received the gift of the bottle's contents, the beings will not attempt to disturb the rest of the proceedings.

The chants of ritual specialists are accompanied by drumming. But chanting and drumming are not sufficient to remove the pernicious cloud of death from the deceased's home, from the tools used to dig the grave, and from the vicinity of the survivors. Rodney Needham (1967) has pointed out the association between noise and transition in many cultures. In the Ngaju case, loud noises are thought to startle the cloud and drive it out. Thus, during the fifth set of the evening's chants, the head specialist arises and seizes heated sections of bamboo sawn apart at the joints. Other ritual specialists follow him in a procession through the house. They comb the various rooms, from the kitchen in the back to the sleeping quarters in the middle to the large front room, sweeping the air with handfuls of *sawang* leaves and waving the bamboo vessels. These vessels burst with a loud noise when struck sharply against the windowsills and doorways. The specialists continue their procession until they arrive at the front room once again. There the head specialist anoints the assembled family members with a silver coin dipped in the blood of a chicken slaughtered earlier. Blood applied to the throats, heads, and shoulders of the assembled mourners is said to strengthen their souls. Other specialists scatter uncooked rice and sprinkle water on the remaining participants. Finally, the ruptured sections of bamboo and the *sawang* leaves used to clean the house are tied to small wooden figurines representing the deceased's family. A chant is performed at the doorway, then the leaves, bamboo, and figurines are carried to the river's edge by the specialists and set adrift on a miniature raft. Foods arranged near the specialists' bench are then taken to the shrine of the village guardian. A brief rest period follows, during which specialists, guests, and mourners consume beverages and cakes of sticky rice.

The chants resume shortly past midnight. Before the specialists return to the bench, the paraphernalia arranged in front of it are altered and augmented. The black cloth covering the *sawang* is parted to reveal the tiny bowl of water where the souls are said to bathe. A miniature house of sticks is placed in a bowl of rice and added to the goods before the bench. The animate essence of this house is said to provide a temporary home in the Upperworld for the soul until *tiwah* is carried out on its behalf, and the wreath covered in black cloth previously hung on the spear is said to mark the soul's doorway. It is hoped that Upperworld beings, later called to assist with *tiwah,* will not overlook a soul whose house has been so clearly marked. The deceased's personal effects are set out, including a comb, perfume, and powder, so the souls may freshen themselves for their journey. Participants ready themselves as well, fastening strips of bast fiber from a particular vine around their wrists. As the vine acquires strength from wrapping around trees, so too will the mourners grow strong through interdependence.

The head specialist performs a chant accompanied by a scattering of rice, the animate essence of which is said to become transformed into seven messengers to the Upperworld. The rice must strike all of the deceased's kin who are present, as the specialist is petitioning on their joint behalf. The messengers are believed to contact a supernatural being named Raja Duhung Mama Tandang Langkah Sawang Apang Bungai Sangiang, and to request his help in processing the souls. He is said first to approach the village's supernatural guardian and request his permission to inform the souls that they have died and to carry one of the souls out of the village and to the Upperworld.

The manner in which Raja Duhung Mama Tandang is said to approach and contact souls is contingent on how the deceased met his or her fate. In instances where the body is missing and the person is presumed dead, Raja Duhung Mama Tandang sends the hornbill named Tingang Entas Talamba to locate the souls. In the case of accidental death, the animate essence of some natural force is blamed. Specific types of rituals and chants are necessary to retrieve the souls and to exact revenge, adding to the elaborateness of the mortuary observances. Some of these include the rituals for revenge against the Lowerworld being Mama Sangiang Bungai for the death of an individual killed by a crocodile; against Pantuh Ganan Kayu Hai for the death of those who fall from trees; against Nyaring Ganan Humbang Rendeng Tingang, the animate essence of a wild animal trap; against Karang Tatu Peres, the animate essence of disease; and against Karihing Ganan Danum, the animate essence of water, for a death by drowning. Also at this time human parties held responsible for or associated in some way with the death may be asked to make partial restitution to the victim's kin. Earlier accounts described the frightening supernatural consequences of "unripe deaths," and reported victims of accidents or illness were said to become evil spirits (Schärer 1963, 62). Today that particular notion seems to be absent, though there is concern that the animate essence of spilt blood demands its own vengeance. As Kahayan villagers put it, "Blood screams."

After the souls are convinced of their death, mourners strain to catch a glimpse of the deceased admiring his or her golden hair and nails in the mirror placed among the personal effects. Then the souls are said to bathe three times in the bowl of water amid the branches of the *sawang*. As the souls prepare to leave, they request a final opportunity to speak to their bereaved kin. An affective change seems to sweep over the mourners and onlookers. A hush settles, and many of the bereaved weep softly. Sputtering pressure lanterns illuminating the room are dimmed, and doors and windows are fastened. Someone goes to

Balian tantulak matei mampisik liau. The souls bid farewell. Kahayan River, 1983. Photo by author.

the kitchen to fetch the wooden pans used to sift the rivers for gold. These are filled with kitchen ashes and placed just inside the front door and beside a window in the room where the deceased expired. Then family and guests sit, immersed in near-total darkness, their attention fixed upon the specialists.

Covering their heads with cloth so that their faces are no longer visible, the specialists proceed to beat a slow tattoo on their drums. With the head specialist acting as mouthpiece, the souls speak once more to their assembled kin. Souls advise and admonish the bereaved, comfort them in their distress, and bestow blessings. One by one, family members approach the bench and line up before the specialists, who intone a dolorous chant. Reaching beneath the cloth that shrouds the head specialist's face, survivors lovingly comb the "souls'" hair, using their left hand. They anoint the specialist's head with perfumed oil. Then the living and the dead clasp hands a final time before the deceased's departure.

As the final mourners pass before the head specialist, the deceased announces that he or she is ready to leave. The specialists abruptly cast down the cloths that have momentarily extinguished their identity. Lanterns are relit, and doors and windows are thrown open again. Gold pans are scrupulously examined for traces of the departing souls' footprints. When the tension becomes acute, almost invariably a young person steps squarely in the pan, leaving a more apparent if less eagerly sought-after print. As the somber atmosphere dissolves into peals of laughter, the specialists commence the closing sequence of their chant. The soul of the intellect is sent to the place of the Upperworld being Balu Indu Rangkang Sulan Mina Perang Matanandau. As in other types of *balian,* different routes can be taken depending on the specialist's expertise and the sponsors' wishes. The souls of the fleshy parts of the body and of the hair and bones are sent to wait in the grave. Finally, the black cloth that wrapped the seven bamboo tubes hung in front of the specialists' bench is parted. The tubes are said to become a stone that separates the world of the living from that of the dead. On the following morning, the bereaved kin accompany the specialists to the river's edge for an ablution, similar to the one that follows *tiwah,* described in the next chapter. Years may pass before the next stage in processing the dead commences. But though the actual celebration may be far in the future, it is rarely distant from anyone's thoughts.

3 | Journey to the Village of Souls

Ritual specialists often draw parallels between the ritual processing of the dead and the nesting habits of rhinoceros hornbills, extraordinary birds that figure prominently in local mythology. As naturalists have observed repeatedly, when a female hornbill is ready to lay her eggs, she prepares a nest inside the trunk of a dead tree. Her mate follows. He entombs her inside, alone behind a thick wall of resins and mud. If abandoned or forgotten, the female would remain in the tiny chamber forever. Day after day, however, the male hornbill returns. He brings food, which he passes through an opening in the mud wall. Her ordeal continues even after the hatchlings appear. According to local lore, the female may not emerge until seven more days pass. On the thirty-third day of entombment, the male hornbill frees his mate, smashing open the entrance to the nest with his massive beak. Remarkably, if the male has died, other hornbills arrive to take his place. Like their metaphorical alter egos, the hornbills, men and women are also dependent on their spouses and others to break open their tombs. Only in this way can souls begin the journey to the Prosperous Village. *Tiwah* is the mechanism by means of which this relocation and transmutation occurs.

Preparations for *Tiwah*

Adherents of Hindu Kaharingan make a distinction between two general varieties of ritual. The first, *gawi belum,* is associated with protecting life and enhancing the prosperity of the living. These rituals include weddings, name-giving ceremonies, and so on. The second, *gawi matei,* comprises the three stages of mortuary observances. Yet even mortuary rituals incorporate life-enhancing dimensions. A death ritual such as *tiwah* comprehends a "life" component in that it is concerned with removing pollution from surviving kin, as well as with the final processing of the deceased's souls and physical remains. One ritual specialist outlined for me seven goals of *tiwah* that bear on the treatment of souls: to summon the souls from their temporary Upperworld repose and from the grave; to bathe them; to provide them with clothing that will never tear; to provision them with foods that will never spoil; to give them the opportunity to bid their kin farewell; to escort them to the Prosperous Village together with the animate essence of creatures sacrificed on their behalf; and, finally, to reunite the souls of the intellect, the bones, and the fleshy parts of the body. The second phase of *tiwah* expressly benefits the living, as sponsors receive honorific titles and ritual specialists ask supernatural beings for generalized blessings on behalf of survivors.

In preparation for *tiwah*, the participants decide, in the course of several informal discussions, who will serve as head sponsor *(upu gawi* or *bakas tiwah)*. Whoever is chosen, usually the most affluent of the bereaved, must at least possess a residence large enough to accommodate the *basir*, who may eat and sleep there throughout the celebration. At some point in the preparations, the head sponsor invites a ritual specialist to apprise the village guardian and other supernatural beings, such as the *jinn* (Ng. *ijin*) of the river, that *tiwah* is being planned. The *basir* attempts to secure their cooperation. At one of these *nenung* I attended in 1995, the officiating *basir* was delighted to report to sponsors that five tutelaries had offered to lend their support to festivities planned for 1996. Later that evening sponsors were further reassured when a visitor from another village, a *tukang sangiang*, slipped into a trance. Although he had not been present at the *nenung*, and had not spoken with the *basir*, he was possessed by three of the five beings. Speaking through the *tukang sangiang*, each being assured the sponsors of *tiwah* that they "had seen" the *basir*'s work earlier that day. They asked to be remembered with gifts of food throughout the celebration.

On a date agreed upon by extended family members, the head sponsor invites his kinspeople to help gather raw materials that will later be used in the construction of mortuary edifices. Before departing on their assignment, participants are anointed with the blood of a chicken to protect them against accidents. The logic here is clear: as with the coffin makers, should one have the misfortune of shedding one's own blood in the course of preparing mortuary edifices, one's souls will be seized as offerings to the deceased. As they collect wood, bamboo, and other materials, participants are obliged to travel in a single direction. For example, should the head sponsor decide that most of the materials are to be found downriver, no one may venture upriver. One sponsor explained the practice by comparing it to clearing land for a swidden field; just as anyone who cleared a swath of land for planting between areas already under cultivation by other people would risk being "closed off" by those people, so too would the living be "closed off" by the dead if sponsors collected materials for *tiwah* from both ends of a village.

After sufficient building materials have been gathered, the sponsors, known as "orphans" *(anak nule)* or "children of *tiwah*" *(anak tiwah)*, sacrifice a chicken and use its blood to anoint the wood. The blood is said to be an offering to the animate essence *(gana)* contained within the materials. Once this sacrifice is made, building may commence.

Twelve required or optional edifices are erected at secondary mortuary rituals:

1. *Balai nyahu:* A hall where gongs are kept.
2. *Sangkaraya:* Bamboo structure, approximately twelve feet tall, where participants dance.
3. *Pasah Pali:* A shrine to supernatural beings *(pali)* who oversee the ritual to ascertain that it is correctly performed.
4. *Balai garantung eka pakanan patahu:* A shrine consisting of an inverted gong filled with foodstuffs, in honor of the village guardian.
5. *Bara-bara* or *hantar bajang:* A bamboo fence decorated with flags to represent souls being processed at *tiwah*. It is erected along the river, its gateway located opposite the head sponsor's house.
6. *Balai kanihi:* A cooking and storage area for the preparation of tubes of rice that the souls of the deceased will carry for sustenance on their journey.
7. *Pandung bawui:* Pens for sacrificial pigs.
8. *Hampatung sapundu* or *sapundu:* Sacrificial poles.
9. *Tihang bandera:* Flagpole.
10. *Pantar sanggaran:* A pole decorated with a Chinese jar, said to have been erected in former times to mark the bone repository of an important individual (uncommon).
11. *Pantar panjang:* A very tall pole, often decorated with a representation of a hornbill or phallus, said to have been erected in former times on behalf of renowned individuals (uncommon).
12. *Sababulu:* Fringed bamboo poles, some erected in the graveyard and beside sponsors' homes, others secured to the *sangkaraya*.

Of these twelve edifices, only the *pantar sanggaran* and *pantar panjang* are optional.

The Start of *Tiwah*

The first structure to be erected is the *balai nyahu* or *balai tiwah*, a "hall" or hut where gongs are played almost nightly and *basir* sometimes sleep. Jars full of rice wine are stored in the hut, as may be branches used as firewood to cook food for souls. The hall also serves as a temporary residence for souls and supernatural beings invited to the village to participate in *tiwah.*

Although extenuating circumstances may require participants to postpone further preparations, a ritual to mark the start of *tiwah, muluh gandang garantung,* is generally held soon after the hall is finished but before the other structures have been erected. A male pig is sacrificed and its blood used to anoint the pillars, window, door, and roof of the hall. At midnight on a specified evening, usually three or five days after the appearance of a full moon, the head sponsor, assisted by several other participants, brings drums *(katambung)* and gongs from home and arranges them in the *balai nyahu.* The head sponsor, ideally working with a *basir,* stands inside the doorway of the hall and raises a ritual drum high in the air. He strikes the drum six times. Each time he points the head at one of the six cardinal directions, moving from the "side of life" (sunrise) to that of death (sunset). The sound constitutes an invitation for the inhabitants of the supernatural world to descend and join him in the hall. The gongs are then pounded in unison, the resultant cacophony greeted by cheers and a characteristic shout known as *malahap.* Today this haunting ululation is uttered almost only within the context of death, though in the "age of head-taking" *(jaman kayau),* it also denoted a victorious engagement with an enemy. Seven times the sponsors cry out "Lu-lu-lu-lu-luuuuu-ueehhh huie," as loudly as they can. The head sponsor cuts the throat of a chicken, collects its blood, and mixes it with rice. He scatters this rice in the cardinal directions, all the while reciting a protective chant. The remaining blood from the chicken is used to anoint the hall and the gongs once more.

The second and third structures to be erected are two "shrines" *(pasah,* or small huts), located close to the *tiwah* hall. The first, *pasah pali,* contains offerings for particular supernatural beings, the *pali,* who are said to oversee the proper performance of the ritual. In scrutinizing these goings-on, the *pali's* primary intent is to discover mistakes in the ritual's enactment. These beings, and the punishments that they may mete out to the sponsors of *tiwah,* are discussed in chapter 4. The *pasah pali* itself resembles a small, open-sided hut on stilts. It is usually decorated with a carved and/or painted representation of a water snake with its head pointing downriver. A red banner or the red and white flag of the Republic of Indonesia waves atop the shrine—red being the color associated with the *pali.* The second shrine, *pasah patahu,* contains offerings for the village guardian, the *patahu.* The structure consists of an inverted gong atop a bamboo tripod, topped with a wide-brimmed woman's hat or an open umbrella. White and yellow are colors usually associated with a village patahu, although neither banners nor flags adorn this particular *pasah.*[1]

When the shrines are completed, participants ready the centerpiece of their celebration, the *sangkaraya*—a twelve-foot high bamboo structure resembling an inverted umbrella. The core of the *sangkaraya* consists of a pole topped by a small box or bamboo basket containing a coconut. Several sponsors I spoke to claimed that in the past, the box contained the head of a freeman, harvested for the occasion from among neighboring enemies. Participants offered two interpretations of the symbolism of the box and its contents. Many lay adherents of Hindu Kaharingan emphasized that the soul of the decapitated victim would become a slave to the deceased in the afterlife. At the same time, several ritual specialists proposed that the coconut/skull also represented the transfiguration of a particular supernatural being who could be called on to protect the deceased.

Radiating from the base of the *sangkaraya* are numerous bamboo poles decorated with bamboo streamers and topped with a flag. The poles represent deceased family members whose souls are to be processed. Extra poles are included too, and whenever necessary, a pole is added to bring the total to an odd number. The poles are secured with folded crosses of palm frond *(sampalak)*. Sponsors were unclear as to whether the color of the flags on the poles is of any significance. For example, Indonesian flags are used today. When I inquired as to the color of the flags used immediately before independence, I was told that they, too, were red and white, specifically, white with a red circle in the center. After a moment's reflection, I realized that my informants were referring to Japanese flags during the years of the occupation. Photographs of *tiwah* taken prior to World War II reveal that Dutch flags, too, once waved above mortuary edifices.

After the *sangkaraya* is complete, it is anointed with the blood of a chicken and a pig, and participants prepare to dance. Women drape long shawls over their shoulders and grasp the ends of the shawls in their fists. Only kin of the souls on whose behalf *tiwah* is being performed are permitted to join in at this time. To the accompaniment of a tattoo that will be beaten again and again throughout the weeks of *tiwah*, mourners execute a dance called *kanjan*, which is restricted to the occasion of secondary treatment of the dead. To commence, dancers form two concentric circles around the *sangkaraya*. Men dance on the outside, women on the inside. Seven times these two parallel rings of participants circumambulate the *sangkaraya* counterclockwise. Suddenly there is a pause in the music. The dancers halt, their arms outstretched at their sides at shoulder level, their fists clenched. Slowly bending their knees until they are nearly squatting on the earth with their legs together, the dancers lower their arms to their sides. When they have nearly reached the ground, they suddenly spring upright and emit the cry known as *malahap*. They repeat their ululations three times before the music of the gongs recommences and their circumambulations resume.

After the dance, sponsors turn their attention to the other structures and monuments they must prepare. Construction may occupy much of the participants' time for several days. The first "permanent" edifices to be readied are sacrificial posts *(sapundu)*. These were traditionally made of ironwood, though lighter, more common woods are increasingly being used. The types of sacrificial posts seen in Kahayan villages include:

1. *Sapundu hatue:* Resembles a man, often a ritual specialist, carrying a traditional iron dagger *(duhung)*.
2. *Sapundu bawi:* Resembles a woman, usually carrying materials used in preparing betel leaves for chewing.
3. *Sapundu embak bakas:* Resembles a man carrying a container of uncooked rice around his neck.
4. *Sapundu sambali:* Resembles various types of animals including a male tiger, a dog, or a crocodile.
5. *Sapundu haramaung:* Resembles a female tiger carrying a snake in her mouth.
6. *Sapundu rahu nyampang:* Carvings depict two persons, husband and wife.

If the deceased was female, a sacrificial post representing a man is usually prepared for her *tiwah,* and vice versa. Contemporary *sapundu* display a high degree of artistic license. Among the carved posts I have seen was one from a 1984 *tiwah* depicting a young woman in blue jeans and a sleeveless T-shirt wearing a Sony Walkman. Another one, from a 1993 *tiwah,* represented a man and a woman with the legend "Eternal Birth Control" *(KB lestari)* carved near their feet. Some *sapundu* have English inscriptions: "*Tiwah* Party," "Memory Day," "God Save Our Soul." Notches *(tetek janet)* incised on the post are intended to serve as reminders to the souls of the animals, rice, and other goods donated by survivors to ensure the deceased's comfort in the afterlife.

In addition to sacrificial posts, participants must also fashion an ossuary to house the deceased's remains if a suitable repository is not otherwise available. Like *sapundu,* bone repositories are ideally made of ironwood. There is much variety in the types of bone repositories that one might encounter in the region. Those found in Kahayan villages include:

1. *Sandung buwuk:* A repository made from a tree trunk and carved with a single opening (uncommon).
2. *Sandung tunggal:* A repository that stands on a single pole.
3. *Kariring* or *sandung kariring:* A long repository supported by two poles.
4. *Sandung keratun:* A repository on four poles.
5. *Sandung samburup:* A Chinese jar in a small, open-sided hut (uncommon).
6. *Sandung munduk:* A repository built directly on the ground.
7. *Sandung tingang:* A brass container placed in an open-sided hut with a roof carved to resemble a hornbill. This type of repository was described to me only once and was the deceased's own design.

8. *Pambak:* Resembles a stone or wooden crypt. These are seldom used by Kahayan peoples but are common on the Katingan.

Since the mid-1960s, with the increasing availability of cement, cement repositories have become widely popular. These are usually of the *sandung munduk* type. Fragments of tile and mirror are pressed into the drying cement. Repositories also vary in height and in size: some stand four feet from the ground, others up to twenty feet or more; some are built for the bones of a single individual, others for the remains of fifty or more persons. In general, Kahayan peoples prefer large ossuaries capable of storing the remains of dozens of kin, whereas Katingan peoples appear to favor much smaller repositories. Reasons why some individuals' remains are placed alone seem to vary. Some informants suggested that repositories of the *sandung tunggal* type were built primarily for persons who had died a "bad" or unnatural death. Others implied that this type of ossuary was constructed for individuals of repute as a means of honoring them while at the same time ensuring that their remains were not stolen. Still others claimed that single-person repositories were usually erected when it was somehow "inappropriate" to inter an individual's remains with those of other family members. The reason behind choosing this option is explored in chapter 4.

At a glance, *sandung* appear to resemble spirit houses found elsewhere in Southeast Asia. Most repositories resemble a miniature house, complete with a traditional-style roof, a tiny door, and windows. Like houses for the living, houses for the dead are constructed facing the sunrise. Representations of a small bird, a type of wild chicken, are often placed on the roof of the repository. Villagers claim that this bird, called *piak liau,* becomes the deceased's possession in the afterlife and can be raised for food. The moon and stars are often painted or carved on the downriver side of the ossuary, and the sun is depicted on the upriver side. It is said that souls must pass all of these cosmological landmarks on their way to the Prosperous Village.

On both sides of the miniature door at the front of the repository are figurines, one male, the other female. These are said to marry and produce children who will eventually assist their parents in guarding the repository. Tiny steps are carved on the posts supporting the ossuary. It is said that the souls of the dead travel in the opposite direction from the living, so these steps are "reversed" to enable them to descend and walk about. Also carved on many posts are ferocious faces with bulging eyes and distended tongues. These represent the animate essence of the bone repository *(ganan sandung),* said to be capable of defending the ossuary's inhabitants from potential assailants.[2] In some places, wooden or stone phalli are erected alongside bone repositories. These range from about a foot in height in the central Kahayan River region to several meters high along stretches of the Katingan River. Unlike graves, which are usually located some distance downriver from villages and avoided scrupulously, ossuaries and *sapundu* are generally placed in prominent places throughout the village. They remain standing for hundreds of years, reminders of the glories of *tiwah* past, of ancestors processed, and of duties discharged.

During the period when bone repositories are under construction, the sponsors of *tiwah* have the right to ask for gifts or small amounts of money from all boats that happen to pass their village. A decorated canoe bearing a sponsor may be sent to meet a boat, and the sponsor subsequently climbs aboard to make a request. Although the passengers decide what to offer, they cannot refuse to make at least a token donation lest they incur a fine.

After most of the mortuary edifices are completed, sponsors observe a full day of nonactivity. On the following morning, a canoe is decorated, and several participants leave the village to fetch the ritual specialists who have previously agreed to perform at *tiwah*. The specialists must all arrive on the same day. Furthermore, all specialists should ideally live either upriver or downriver from the village where *tiwah* is being celebrated, and the men who escort them should live on the same side of the village as the direction in which they will travel to meet the specialists. These proscriptions echo those associated with collecting building materials for use at *tiwah*, which I have already described.

Ritual Specialists at *Tiwah*

The performances of two types of specialists may be utilized in enactments of Kahayan River *tiwah*. One format involves chants led by a head specialist *(basir upu)*, accompanied by a chorus of six or eight other specialists. Their performance is referred to as a *balian basir munduk*. If sponsors elect this option, all three souls of the deceased are processed on a single evening in a chant of a few hours' duration. Another format utilizes an additional specialist, the *tukang hanteran* or *magah liau*, who recites the origin myth in describing the souls' journey to the Upperworld. Unlike the *basir upu*, this specialist performs alone and without percussive accompaniment. During the course of his performance, which lasts about thirteen hours, he calls on particular supernatural beings for help in processing the soul of the intellect and in inviting the soul back to the house for a final farewell to its kin before it leaves for the Prosperous Village. On the following evening, a *balian basir munduk* is performed to escort the two remaining souls and reunite them with the first.

Although many secondary mortuary rituals are performed without *tukang hanteran*, participants usually acknowledge that it is preferable to utilize both types of specialists. Cost was usually the factor cited for the decision not to include performances of both types, for to incorporate both into the celebration of *tiwah* nearly doubles the specialists' total recompense. Other reasons given were family tradition and prior requests of the deceased. Sometimes a *tukang hanteran* is simply unavailable. On the Katingan River, especially, *basir* are scarce, and it is not uncommon to find abbreviated death rituals at which only a lesser Kaharingan functionary, a *pisur,* officiates.

During their journey to the village where *tiwah* will be held, specialists perform chants to inform supernatural beings that a ritual is in progress. As their canoe approaches the village, the head sponsor descends to the river's edge to meet the specialists. As they prepare to disembark, he "sweeps" them with *sawang* leaves to clear away any unwelcome supernatural beings that may have accompanied them. He anoints them with water and rice to cool their souls and ensure their well-being throughout the duration of the celebration. Only then may the specialists climb up onto the bank and enter the sponsor's house. Each begins to observe various proscriptions, including idiosyncratic and highly secretive ones, intended to guarantee the quality of their voices and to protect themselves from harm. After they have eaten and rested, specialists and sponsors hold a meeting to determine the schedule for the remainder of the celebration. Sponsors contribute actively to these discussions, and a sponsor's wishes concerning how long the celebration should last and how many days of ritual nonactivity should be incorporated into its format may override a specialist's.

During this meeting, the head specialist collects critical particulars about the souls to be processed. This information includes the total number of the dead, who among the deceased was the eldest, where the deceased lived throughout the course of his or her life, how many animals are to be sacrificed and in honor of whose souls, whether any new repositories have been erected, how many guests are expected, and whether other families plan to send goods on behalf of the souls. Much of this information will be reiterated later by the specialist as he performs chants on the deceased's behalf. Sponsors must also elicit information from *basir.* For example, sponsors must pay fines to specialists who have recently experienced a bereavement if they were asked to perform *tiwah* before having had the opportunity to attend to their own kin. No ritual activity may take place on the day following the specialists' arrival in honor of the specialists' and sponsors' supernatural guardians, some of whom, it is believed, may already be residing in the *tiwah* hut.

The Cosmos Unlocked: Souls and Remains Are Treated

On the evening they begin their chants, the *basir,* with the exception of the *tukang hanteran,* arrange themselves on a bench in the front room of the head sponsor's house. Beginning with the *basir upu,* the head sponsor fastens a jasper bead or silver coin around each *basir's* wrist. A bead or coin is also tied to each one's drum. The head sponsor then touches an egg to the specialists' foreheads and afterward invites them one by one to spit onto a plate. The plate and the egg are tossed out the window. According to sponsors, this action protects the specialists from any minor, mysterious discomforts that might plague them during the performance. A specialist skilled in making predictions then performs *nenung* to locate any additional supernatural beings that might be willing to participate, followed by chants to invite the village guardian as well as the animate essence of the village itself to the ritual. Specialists may also perform praise songs *(karunya)* to honor the sponsors at this time. The most important of these, however, are reserved for performance pending the completion of *tiwah.*

The next day specialists perform the *mampunduk sahur,* as they recite chants to invite the Upperworld being Raja Duhung Mama Tandang Langkah Sawang Apang Bungai Sangiang and forty of his assistants to take up residence in the *tiwah* hall. Raja Duhung Mama Tandang, as previously noted, is the Upperworld being who informs the deceased of his or her death during the *balian tantulak matei mampisik liau.* It is said that he travels from the Upperworld in a fabulous ship that he exchanges for a smaller vessel as he approaches the village. Some of my more widely traveled informants compared this to the size of the planes they had seen flying into Banjarmasin, the capital of the province of South Kalimantan, as opposed to those that arrive in Palangka Raya.

Having disembarked, Raja Duhung Mama Tandang and his helpers assist their human hosts with cleaning the village and completing the mortuary edifices with wood that they bring with them from the primordial village in the Upperworld. Raja Duhung Mama Tandang himself, conveying his message through the *basir upu,* calls on sponsors to erect festooned bamboo poles on the graves of the ancestors who are about to receive final treatment. This act initiates a cycle of mutuality between humans and the inhabitants of supernatural realms that is repeated throughout the course of *tiwah.* Supernatural beings are said to perform the tasks described in chants on the day before or after their human counterparts enact them; the cooperation of both parties is held to be indispensable to the successful completion of the ritual.

The following morning, sponsors travel to graveyards and erect the bamboo poles. They generally take this opportunity to exhume physical remains, an act called *nalampas.* They begin with the skull and continue to collect bones in as orderly a manner as possible until the entire skeleton is complete. The recovered bones, to which flesh might yet cohere, are cleaned by lustration or by being passed briefly through a small fire or both. Although it is preferable to exhume dry bones, the recently dead may be included, too. One *basir* related the story of a Kahayan River woman who died on the first day of a *tiwah* at which he officiated in 1994. Her children decided to wait and hold her *tiwah* at some later date, yet to be determined. At the graveside, during the *nalampas* a few days later, the newly deceased woman's daughter suddenly became pos-

Nalampas. Remains are exhumed and prepared for further treatment. Katingan River, 1996. Photo by author.

sessed by her mother's soul as she exhumed her long-dead father's bones. "Why are you ignoring me?" the mother's soul cried out. Both husband and wife were exhumed that day. Sometimes, in an attempt to forestall the jealousy of souls who must wait for *tiwah*, kinspeople pour rice wine libations on graves. I overheard one woman cajoling her deceased husband's soul and offering wine while another grave was opened nearby. "Don't be angry," she said, "never mind. Your turn will come very soon."

After they are cleaned, the bones are wrapped in white cloth and placed at the graveside inside a small box or gong arranged on a bamboo tripod. An umbrella or wide-brimmed hat is placed above the container. Then the participants return to the village, leaving the bones behind temporarily. Later that afternoon, in the head sponsor's house, specialists perform a chant that narrates Raja Duhung Mama Tandang's own efforts to free the souls. To open the coffin, Raja Duhung Mama Tandang uses an iron dagger, *duhung papan beteng*. Having freed the souls, he extends to them an invitation to accompany him to an Upperworld hall to await further instruction. Thus, whereas human beings can free the deceased's body from the grave, they are dependent on supernatural beings to liberate an ancestor's souls.

While guests watch the specialists' performance, the sponsors prepare bamboo tubes *(kanihi)* filled with rice and sealed with a leaf. Souls are said to carry these tubes with them for nourishment on their arduous journey to the Prosperous Village. At least one tube of rice is readied for each soul: women prepare the rice, and men oversee its cooking. To begin, the men sacrifice a cock, mixing its blood with raw rice, which they scatter over the onlookers. While the tubes roast, the men dance on the cooking platform, as the women stand behind them shouting encouragement, sometimes spraying the men with perfume or rushing up to powder their faces. When the tubes have finished cooking, the men tie them into bundles and set them aside. The men drink heavily throughout the afternoon. Their merriment continues far into the night as they travel the length of the village "stealing" any loose pigs and chickens and "raiding" nearby vegetable gardens. This booty is later cooked and shared by all the men in the *tiwah* hall.

Men and women who are not involved in cooking busy themselves throughout the day with the erection of sacrificial posts. The men dig the post holes. Before the posts are lowered into the earth, the women scatter rice and rub oil on each post's base. Then water buffaloes and cows earmarked for later sacrifice are paraded through the village to everyone's amusement. Afterward they are bathed and caressed before being secured to the posts with a thick leash of heavy woven vines. Their eyelashes are plucked; these will be saved to be mixed later with bits of wood from mortuary edifices and scattered by specialists during invocations. Finally, the creatures' horns and tails are adorned with ornaments made from plaited bamboo and chicken feathers. After the large animals are secured, the pigs to be sacrificed are placed in individual cages at the base of the *sangkaraya*.

Throughout the night, participants dance around these tethered beasts. The dancers powder one another's faces *(hakasai)* and drink alcoholic beverages from a glass passed from person to person. Out of sight, hidden in the jungle foliage, gambling tents offer celebrants other forms of amusement.

One of the most spectacular aspects of *tiwah* is the arrival of a ship or ships full of offerings *(lanting laluhan* or *kapal laluhan)*. These goods are intended for the deceased's enjoyment in the Prosperous Village. Although the arrival of such a ship is not required in order to carry out secondary mortuary rituals, it is considered eminently desirable. If a ship is scheduled, it should arrive on the morning following preparation of the largest sacrificial animals. These ships are festooned with dozens of banners and cloths and laden with animals, rice, and coconuts. An areca palm, heavy with fruit, is affixed prominently to the bow.[3] A miniature *sangkaraya* is also secured on board. These ships are usually sent between unrelated families from different villages. The practice is part of a recurring cycle of exchange; whatever is given by one family is later reciprocated when the senders themselves perform *tiwah*. Hand-delivered, smaller displays of offerings may also be dispatched. In explaining the origin of these gifts, *basir* often go beyond lay interpretations, suggesting that, although most people are unaware of it, the ship is actually sent by the unprocessed dead of other villages in anticipation of their own *tiwah.*

More fantastic than the ship itself is its crew. These men and women arrive in filthy, ragged array. The crew sometimes wear banana leaf garments, which they part to reveal enormous wooden phalluses or halved coconut shells representing female genitalia.[4] They dance, gesticulating obscenely and mimicking coitus. Many disguise their faces with horrific masks *(sababuka)* that depict long, curved noses, wild eyes, and lips turned back in a terrible grimace.[5] Even from a distance, their taunts, intended to intimidate and infuriate sponsors, can be heard. They cry out that the sponsors of *tiwah* are nothing more than cowards and the descendants of slaves; they dare them to swim out and copulate with them aboard ship. As the sponsors converge at the riverbank to face their tormentors, the crew take up dulled spears made from the stems of an aromatic plant that they hurl toward the land. The *tiwah* sponsors quickly open a return barrage. The ship circles seven times in the river, while the opposed groups exchange threats and fire on each other. Finally, the crew's ammunition is exhausted.

After the ship is tied up, the head dancer, wearing a hornbill feather in his hair, descends to a specially constructed platform at the river's edge. This platform is carried up to the *tiwah* gate without the dancer ever directly setting foot on the earth. Alternatively, the dancer is carried on a sponsor's back. Beneath the gate, the dancer comes face to face with a ritual specialist, likewise wearing a hornbill feather. A wooden pole placed lengthwise across the entrance prevents him from crossing to the side where the specialist stands. The dancer is interrogated by the *basir* as to why the ship has come and what it contains. When the specialist is satisfied with the results of the interrogation, the dancer is handed a sword and invited to destroy the barrier *(pantan)* and enter the village. Ther rest of the crew disembarks, and sponsors bathe them in tumeric-infused water. Only then are the newcomers permitted to ascend to the village gate. The crew and the sponsors then dance together beneath the *sangkaraya.* As the dance progresses, both parties cry out in victory. The senders of the ship claim that they are victorious because they have either repaid a debt by avenging a previous "attack" or because they have put another family in their debt. The recipients celebrate because they have acquired additional goods to increase the splendor of their ancestor's *tiwah* at another family's expense. The areca palm is then removed from the ship and erected alongside the *sangkaraya* in front of the head sponsor's house. The miniature *sangkaraya* aboard the ship is moved to the front room of the sponsor's house and placed before the bench where the ritual specialists perform. Finally, the remaining contents of the ship are noted and unloaded and the ship itself is dismantled.

The ritual slaughter of sacrificial beasts, called *tabuh,* usually follows without

Dismantling a *lanting laluhan*. Kahayan River, 1983. Photo by author.

delay. Participants dance around the *sangkaraya* and the animals. Water is sometimes poured near the base of sacrificial poles to increase the chances of the beasts' slipping, for their struggles to regain their footing add to the crowd's merriment. First the pigs are killed, stabbed repeatedly through the open bars of their cages. Then the larger animals are stabbed, while members of the crowd roar out their approval. Dozens of thrusts may be necessary to make a beast fall. Only during mortuary celebrations are animals killed in this intentionally prolonged manner, designed to heighten the spectacle of blood. We might recall, in this regard, Schwaner's and Perelaer's description of the slaves sacrificed during *tiwah* past, for whom the immediate cause of death was loss of blood. Even today some participants identify the animals with slaves. At a *tiwah* I attended in 1996, a teenaged girl whispered to me as we watched one beast being stabbed, "That is really a slave, you know. God transformed him into a water buffalo."

Animal sacrifice *(tabuh)* at *tiwah*. Kahayan River, 1983. Photo by author.

When the animal finally sinks to its knees, its throat is cut to ensure that all present, including Muslims, may partake of its flesh. The sponsors kick the carcass with their left foot, slip their left hand into the gaping neck wound, then kneel nearby and wait for a ritual specialist to anoint them with the animal's blood. The sponsors are anointed four times, each time facing a different direction.

Before they go home to cook the meat, women sometimes insert roots or vines into the animal's mouth. Wearing an adornment such as a bracelet made from these roots is said to provide protection from supernatural reprisal for mistakes made in the sacrifices. The heads of the animals are severed then hung facing skyward on the sacrificial posts. This action is said to constitute proof to the inhabitants of the Upperworld that the sacrifice has been properly enacted. While sponsors cut up the carcasses, the *tukang hanteran* or the head *basir*, wearing a hornbill feather in his hair, anoints the sponsors' homes with blood. He then removes the heads from the poles and carries them to the shrine erected to the *pali*. The specialist dances, circumambulating the shrine seven times, and scatters an offering of blood and rice to atone for mistakes in the ritual.

Throughout the remainder of the day, mourners travel to the graveyard to bring back the bones of the deceased. They transport them in gongs that they secure by tying a cloth diagonally over one shoulder and across their chest, in the manner used to carry infants. The kinspeople who carry the bones must

Heads of sacrificed cattle displayed on the *pasah pali;* the *pasah patahu* is in the foreground. Kahayan River, 1983. Photo by author.

wear wide-brimmed hats or walk beneath open umbrellas. Upon their return to the village, the gongs containing the bones are arranged on tripods alongside the ossuary.

Toward sunset of the same day, the *tukang hanteran,* if one has been employed, commences the chant that escorts the first of the deceased's souls to the Upperworld. Seated on a gong in the center of the main room of the sponsor's house, an iron dagger grasped in his left hand, the *tukang hanteran* is resplendent in his distinctive attire. The costume consists of the following:

1. *Sampulau dare:* A headpiece decorated with hornbill feathers.
2. *Ewah bumbun:* A loincloth. (Most *tukang hanteran* wear the loincloth over trousers.)
3. *Karungkung sulau:* A red vest decorated with rounded bits of shell the size of small coins.

Tukang hanteran. Kahayan River, 1983. Photo by author.

    4. *Lawah:* Shell bracelets.
    5. *Kalumit:* Anklets made of metal beads.
    6. *Penyang:* An amulet belt worn about the waist.
    7. *Duhung:* An iron dagger.

Above the specialist's head may hang a mural depicting a ship, with the head and tail of a water snake, that pulls a second ship filled with representations of the village and of the goods sacrificed on the deceased's behalf.[6] The *tukang hanteran* begins by scattering rice, the animate essence of which is said to accompany the animate essence of his voice *(bahing timang)* to the Upperworld. All of the gongs in the room are sounded simultaneously, and participants may cover their heads with cloth. Moments later they throw off the cloths and seven times emit the ululation associated with *tiwah.* The *tukang hanteran* then turns over the cup of rice that he holds in his hand, whispers a powerful phrase said to "unlock" the cosmos and set it into motion, and commences his chant. Other cups of rice, one for each soul receiving *tiwah,* are emptied too. This rice is thrown about the room, creating the effect of a white rainstorm.

The mood that characterizes the specialist's audience ranges from rapt to listless, depending on what point his recitation has reached. As the night wears on, some participants become restless. They may throw cigarettes or candies at other sponsors and sometimes at the specialist himself. Should the specialist stumble over a word, audience members may correct him. Stumblings may or may not be interpreted as negatively affecting the overall performance of the chant. Some participants simply sleep until the moment of the soul's visit is imminent.

In the Upperworld, it is said, the specialist's voice encounters a female *sangiang*, Kameluh Mandalan Bulan, who commands the voice to identify itself. She also demands to know the identity of the animate essence of the dagger that accompanies the voice. To prove their identity, she commands the voice to recite the origin myth, the story of the founding of the primordial village and the creation of the grandparents of mankind. Only after the story has been told is the animate essence of the voice permitted to continue its journey to the village of the supernatural being whom it seeks, Rawing Tempun Telun.

Rawing Tempun Telun, together with his assistants Telun Mama Tambun Bungai and Hamparung Mama Kandayu Lanting, agree to go to the village that is sponsoring *tiwah*. They board a ship together with the animate essence of the *tukang hanteran*'s voice. First, the ship travels to the lower region of the Upperworld, where the soul is eagerly awaiting its arrival. The deceased asks to visit his or her family a final time before being transported to the Prosperous Village. Rawing Tempun Telun agrees and invites the soul to board a smaller ship that carries it to the village. The soul speaks to its bereaved kin through the *tukang hanteran*. The interlude is similar to the soul's visit during the second phase of the mortuary cycle, although the *tukang hanteran* does not cover his face. The specialist removes his headpiece, and sponsors line up to rub his head with oil and shake his left hand. Then the soul departs, revisiting on its journey places that it frequented during life. It boards a ship that carries it safely past two mountains of fire. The soul bathes in a pool, the waters of which are said to restore youth and beauty. Some specialists propose that at this point the soul is given a fruit that causes the deceased to forget everything associated with its former life. Finally the soul passes over a bridge and enters the Prosperous Village, where its ancestors await its arrival.

On the morning following the *tukang hanteran*'s performance, several short rituals are carried out. Men sever the bands that secure the tubes of cooked rice and carry them to the head sponsor's house. Then the men proceed to the *tiwah* hall, where they drink fermented beverages from the horn of a water buffalo, previously hung on the upriver side of the hut. In the past, it is widely claimed, the skull of a freeman was used for this purpose. The remainder of the drink is poured through the floorboards as the "soul's share." Later in the afternoon, the men move some of the tubes of rice to the shrines near the *sangkaraya*; then, wearing hornbill feathers in their hair, they dance around them. That night the other specialists perform chants to escort the remaining two souls to the Prosperous Village, where they are reunited with the soul of the intellect by being transformed into a hornbill egg placed atop the first soul's head.

The final processing of the remains takes place the next day. The roof of the repository is removed and ladders are erected on either side. The specialists sit on a bench beside the repository and perform a chant that alerts the ossuary's inhabitants to make room for a new arrival.

The bones of the dead are unwrapped, powdered, and anointed with perfumed oil; then they are rewrapped in a white cloth and replaced inside the gongs. Sometimes small coins are tucked into the folds of fabric. Many family members burst into tears as they view the bones or strain to touch them as they are passed overhead. Again, carrying the bones as if they were children, participants circumambulate the repository seven times. As the sponsors dance, they are watched for signs of untoward behavior that might indicate supernatural displeasure. One by one the men and women carrying the bones climb the ladder that rests against the repository on the side of the setting sun. They step on the ladder left foot first. The oldest bones are placed first, arranged on the

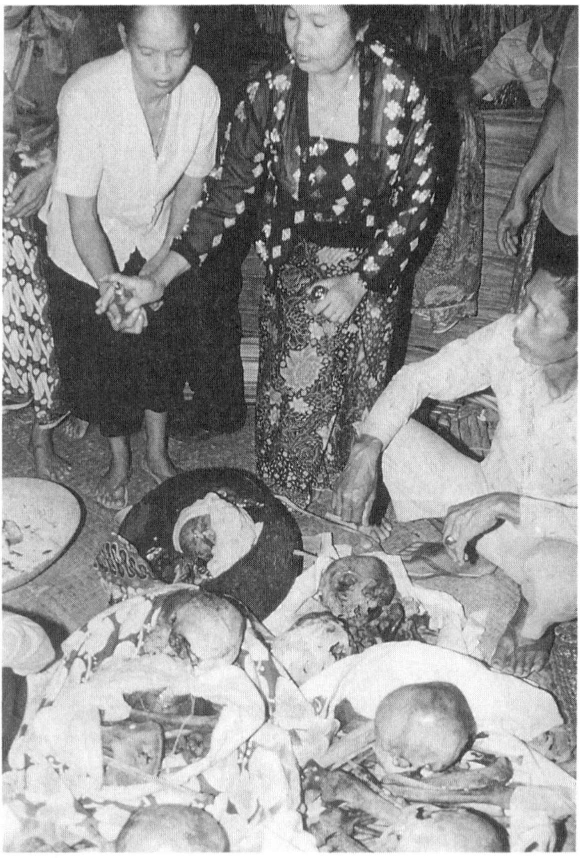

Anointing the bones of the dead. Kahayan River, 1983.
Photo by author.

Emplacing bones in a *sandung*. Rungan River, 1983. Photo by author.

downriver side of the repository. If the remains are irretrievable, handfuls of earth may be placed inside to substitute for the bones. Each time the bones are about to be lowered into the ossuary, sponsors ask loudly, "En kuntep?" (Is it full?). Participants and onlookers always shout back in the affirmative, even if the ossuary is nearly empty. Having deposited the remains, the participants climb down from the repository via the ladder placed on the side of the rising sun. They circumambulate the ossuary seven times, each time pausing to kick the ladder with their left foot. Then those kin who did not personally place bones in the repository may scramble up the ladder and over the roof to show respect for the dead and earn their blessing.

Meanwhile other groups await their turn to emplace bones. While waiting, they may drink heavily, smear powder on one another, or spray one another with perfume. Just before the repository is resealed, a scene of apparent chaos ensues. Seemingly without regard for age, sex, or social standing, participants hurl filth and spoiled foods at one another and across the ossuary. Later that night, ritual specialists perform a chant to cleanse away the animate essence of the spoiled foods and another chant to escort the Upperworld beings involved in the processing of the dead back to their homes.

The next morning, participants are cleansed of all remaining pollution by an ablution at the river's edge, *kangkahem*. The sponsors of *tiwah* climb into canoes. Bereaved spouses wear the clothing that they wore to the funeral. The specialists sweep the participants with *sawang* leaves and flaming areca buds to chase away the "heat" of *tiwah*. Heated bamboo tubes are exploded against the sides of the canoes. Then the head specialist seizes a ritual spear, or the spear previously used to kill the sacrificial animals, and uses it to capsize the canoes three times. Twice the participants tumble into the water in the direction of sunset, then once toward sunrise. As they emerge from the water, the clothes of the widows and widowers are removed by the specialists, cut with knives from their very backs. These garments are set adrift in a wide-brimmed hat. Then the bereaved spouses dress themselves in their most brightly colored clothing and climb up the riverbank to rejoin the others.

The participants immediately seat themselves on the ground near the *sangkaraya*. A ritual specialist anoints them on the head and chest with flour dampened by the blood of a chick. Another chicken is carried from person to person,

Kangkahem. The *basir upu* capsizes mourners' canoes. Kahayan River, 1983. Photo by author.

Mourners "sacrificing" mortuary edifices following *kangkahem*. Kahayan River, 1983. Photo by author.

encouraged to pick rice off participants' heads so that any remaining pollution is transferred to the bird. Its tail feathers are clipped, and the bird is thrown to its freedom in the direction of the rising sun. Widows and widowers, led by the head specialist, proceed to "kill" the temporary mortuary edifices, the animate essence of which has already been dispatched to the Upperworld as part of the deceased's riches. The spouses circumambulate the edifices, stabbing each one seven times, each thrust higher than the last. Assembling once more at the *tiwah* hall, participants may dance around a representation of a fish *(lauk pahi)* made from rice, plates, and beads. The fish is speared by the three relatives of the deceased who were the first to stab the animals during sacrifice.[7] Then the *tukang hanteran* and/or the head specialist proceeds to strike a drum in the *tiwah* hall, in the reverse direction from that struck at the start of *tiwah*. The processing of the dead is now considered complete. The temporary mortuary edifices are dismantled and used to decorate the bone repositories that are found throughout the village. The sacrificial posts are also moved to the side of the ossuaries.

Although the rituals in honor of the dead are finished, rituals to honor and benefit the living continue. One is the bestowal of honorific titles *(patandak)*. Key sponsors, wearing hornbill feathers in their hair, are given praise names by the head specialist. Three by three, the sponsors sit on gongs across from a specialist, the sponsor in the center connected to the specialist by a band of white cloth, the ends of which are tucked into the waist of the recipient's pants or skirt. The title bestowed by the specialist may not be more splendid than the person deserves; standing up denotes acceptance. If the recipient does not deserve the title, it is said that he or she will defecate, faint, or die on the spot when rising to stand. Participants compare it to a chicken loose in the house, oblivious to where it relieves itself. Depending on the number of sponsors involved, this part of the celebration may last for many days. Later, the specialists go from door to door carrying a brass bowl filled with rice and a hornbill feather. As they pass each house, they ask for small offerings, the animate essence of which will be sent to the Upperworld during a chant in honor of a supernatural being associated with life rituals, Mantir Mama Luhing Bungai Salutan Raja Ngalawung Bulau. Their request is known as *basarah*. When the *basarah* is completed, the specialists are paid and escorted home. Visiting kin are also free to leave. Ideally, thirty-three days have elapsed from the beginning to the end of the celebration, the amount of time that a hornbill needs to emerge from her nest.

The preceding description of the eschatological beliefs and
mortuary celebrations of Hindu Kaharingan villagers, in particular those living
along the upper-middle reaches of the Kahayan River, is the product not only
of observation but also of long discussions with many celebrants. As we re-
viewed the format of these celebrations, I was struck by their insistence that
the rituals were "correct": "Jetuh hadat itah uluh Kahayan nah" (This is the
way of us Kahayan people). This notion of the proper way is not restricted to
death ritual only. From birth to death and even beyond, every aspect of existence is said to be governed by rules and expectations constituting the right
way to live. These guidelines are known generally as *hadat*, usually glossed into
the Indonesian language as *adat*. At the same time, the term *adat* (customary
law) fails to communicate fully the many dimensions and complexities of the
Ngaju-language term. *Hadat* is broadly applied, referring to custom, to kinship,
to ideas about order, and to a sense of tradition. This breadth of usage is not
unusual among cognates of the word in other Dayak languages. In a study of
the East Kalimantan Kenyah, for example, Herbert Whittier proposed that it is
often inappropriate to treat *adat* as an analytical category distinct from beliefs
about the supernatural (1973, 135–37). Peter Metcalf, in his study of Berawan
death rituals, raises a similar point about Berawan *adèd*:

> The Berawan language contains no word that could be translated as "religion."
> The general category of things under which the usages of religion are subsumed is
> called *adèd*, but *adèd* involves much more than religion. Table manners, or the
> Borneo equivalent, are *adèd*; so are rules concerning who may fish where, and who
> may wear what kinds of beads, and how fruit trees are inherited, and a thousand
> other things besides. *Adèd* is everything from etiquette to law, everything, in short,

> that is governed by explicit rules or prescriptions, including ritual. *Adèd* is variable from one community to another, but as a concept, it is something that is widely shared by the societies of the whole Indonesian area. (1982, 4)

What Metcalf has suggested for the Berawan pertains equally here, with the notable exception that among the Ngaju *hadat* is broader in scope. Even where *hadat* is not explicitly known to humans, as in the case of the conduct of supernatural beings, the code is nevertheless presumed to exist.

For upriver villagers of Central Kalimantan, *hadat* can be said to constitute a vital point of articulation between natural and supernatural worlds. My aim in this chapter is to subject the notion of *hadat* to close examination and tease out its implications in this regard. I argue that the concept of *hadat* offers access to a nexus between social reality and cosmology that obtains for many people. I explore how myriad social constraints and possibilities that fall under the rubric of *hadat* play themselves out in relations between groups of people and between humans and supernatural beings. With respect to the former, I address conceptualizations of kinship and marriage, in particular attitudes toward cousin marriage. With respect to the latter, my discussion focuses largely on belief in two types of supernatural beings. The first, *sangiang*, are the inhabitants of the Upperworld and the Lowerworld. In affect and demeanor, *sangiang* are much like humans. According to the origin myth, they are, in fact, distant kin to humankind. The second type of supernatural beings are *taluh papa,* or "Unclean Ones." *Taluh papa* exist in this world. They infiltrate humanity by disguising themselves as humans to effect marriages that will ultimately destroy families. I demonstrate in this chapter how the notion of *hadat* provides a means by which we can apprehend an unstated yet intensely significant homology between villagers' cosmological beliefs and their conceptualizations of society.

In order to grasp this relationship fully, it is first necessary to recognize how suffusive the concept of *hadat* actually is. According to the adherents of Hindu Kaharingan, all that there is in the cosmos, material and immaterial, and in Western terms "animate" or "inanimate," has a sensate, conscious essence. Everything, therefore, has a moral obligation to act in accordance with its unique *hadat*. The dead have a *hadat* that requires souls to do things in a manner opposite from the living. In accordance with the *hadat* of the dead, for instance, corpses are displayed with their clothing turned inside out. Sponsors and ritual specialists clasp left hands, rather than right hands, when souls bid farewell to their bereaved kin through the agency of a *tukang hanteran* or *upu balian*. The steps carved on bone repositories are reversed to accommodate the fact that the dead walk backward. Supernatural beings, too, have their own *hadat*. Thus it is, villagers say, that humans and supernatural beings are compelled to behave in specific ways and to adopt particular kinds of relationships toward each other.

Who are these supernatural beings? There is no simple, or even single, answer to this question. Many hundreds, perhaps many thousands, of supernatural beings are said to inhabit the various regions of the cosmos. As the concept of a supreme being or creator figures only marginally in the religious beliefs of most villagers, it is primarily other kinds of beings who are said to influence peoples' lives in various ways. Given their ubiquity and the significance accorded to supernatural beings, it is rather striking that villagers often claim to be unable to differentiate between them. Supernatural beings are usually said to be "all the same" *(uras'a sama ih)*. Yet, to the contrary, they are not. Villagers actually do distinguish between at least two types of supernatural beings—the *utus sangiang* and *taluh papa*—but these distinctions do not generally correspond to an explicit conceptual model.

One very important characteristic that seems to place supernaturals into one or the other of these two categories is that these beings are imagined to be differently disposed toward humans. Villagers pursue relationships with supernatural beings of both categories with an eye to achieving different ends. At the same time, it is apparent that the rudimentary distinction between the realm of human beings and that of supernatural beings is not absolute. Under certain circumstances, the latter may infiltrate the former, confusing or collapsing the distinction between human and nonhuman. This infiltration has the potential to plunge the cosmos into chaos, with dire consequences for individuals, families, and even entire villages.

Collapse of the distinction between human and supernatural spheres originates with the practice of exogamous marriage, or marriage between persons who are not cognatically related. Exogamous marriages, although common, are said to be contrary to *hadat* and as such are flirtations with cosmological disaster. As it is mankind's responsibility to do everything possible to maintain the larger cosmic order, keeping close checks on genealogies and guarding one's interactions with non-kin are considered an integral part of obeying *hadat*. These axioms apply to the next life as well as to the present one. The successful completion of mortuary rituals on a family member's behalf should also be understood as the ultimate means of distancing one's ancestors from the distressing natural and supernatural consequences of a marriage misalliance. This particular aspect of the relationship between eschatological beliefs and conceptualizations of kinship becomes clearer when the definition of *hadat* is expanded to acknowledge as well its opposite—namely, a sense of that which is forbidden and ideas concerning "anti-order."

Transgression of *Hadat*

According to villagers' explanations, all thoughts, behaviors, and speech that are not in accordance with *hadat* are forbidden. The word used to refer to all that which is forbidden is *pali*—the same word used to describe certain super-natural beings. To behave in a *pali* manner risks supernatural sanction as well as social opprobrium. And as is also the case with *hadat,* this sense of the forbidden extends to every sphere of human and nonhuman endeavor. Some *pali* may be observed only by specific individuals or families; some are unique to particular villages; still others are found widely throughout the region. Many common *pali* can be grouped into general categories: *pali panyakit,* which concern foods that cause illness if consumed; *pali tatamba,* which concern foods that cannot be eaten for a proscribed period following a cure for an illness; *pali tatamba taluh nggaduh/parei,* which concern animal husbandry or the cultivation of land; *pali panyampah,* which concern foods that must be avoided in order to guarantee the success of one's children or the prosperity of one's household; and *pali pahuni,* which concern the misfortune that follows when one refuses an offer of food or drink and subsequently fails to *minjuk* (touch the plate), *japai* (lick the palm of one's right hand), or at least lick one's lips as if one had in fact eaten. In a case of *pali kambaen,* a man promises to go hunting or fishing with a friend but then fails to arrive for their appointment. As a result of this transgression, the friend will be unable to catch animals or fish despite his best efforts. *Pali luas* are associated with childbirth. During pregnancy, for example, neither future parent may wrap a towel around his or her neck or cut the limb off of an animal lest the child be stillborn or malformed. Similarly, when pounding rice, prospective mothers must be careful to sift the rice on the bottom of the mortar to the top before removing it lest their children be born deaf.

A possible consequence of a serious transgression of *hadat* is that the transgressor may be brought before a customary law expert, the *damang* (Ind. *demang),* who may levy a fine *(singer). Damang* often seek the counsel of *basir* when settling suits. Not surprisingly, many weighty rules govern treatment of the dead. The following two examples are quoted from a manuscript prepared by Johannes Saililah, followed by my translation.[1]

Singer tapian tenden tulang
Eweh bewei mahapan arut mimbit tulang ulon, awi ewen mindah sarangan tulang bara eka beken, atawa bara kubur, tau kea awi handak tiwah akan eka beken, metuh ewen magun benteng jalanae hajukung, te ewen ije mimbit tulang hajukung palus tende intu batang talian lewun oloh atawa intu tapian tanan oloh. Te oloh ije mimbit tulang tende tapian oloh, buah hukum singer adat, kahaie: Jipen 1 (Rp. 30.—), paling hai jipen 2. Awi jete dia tau patende "pali." Pambayar te akan oloh huma ije tempon batang-talian, hapa ewen akan ungkus mamapas, manyaki kare batang tapian ewen.

(The fine for pausing with bones at the edge of a river
Anyone who uses a boat to carry human bones because they want to bring the

bones to the graveyard, or for any reason, or for a tiwah at some other place: when they are making the journey, if the boat carrying the bones stops at the dock of someone else's village, or at the dock of someone's field, the person who carries the bones and stops at someone else's dock is fined one or at most two slaves. Because to do this is not allowed, *pali.* The payment is made to the person who owns the dock and is used to pay for sweeping *[pali]*, anointing the dock.)

Singer palanggar balo-buyo
Eweh bewei sala malanggar, dosa habandung dengan balu, dengan buyo, maka hindai jadi barasih gawin pampatei bana atawa gawin pampatei sawae, ie ije sala buah hukum singer adat kahaie: Jipen 2 sampai jipen 3.

(*The fine for trespassing a widow/widower*
Anyone who has an illicit affair with a widow or widower before the work of the death of the wife/husband is clean: the person is fined 2 to 3 slaves.)

In the latter case, the fine would usually be earmarked for application to the expenses of the deceased spouse's *tiwah.*

As is evident from these examples, the settlement of these types of transgressions sometimes requires monetary restitution. Citing values in effect during the colonial period, Saililah set the price of a slave at 30 rupiah. This, in fact, was the rate along the Kahayan and Kapuas rivers only. Along the Barito, the price of a slave was 60 rupiah, and along the Katingan and Sambas rivers, the price was 40 rupiah. Today the price is 15,000–25,000 rupiah. Yet money can resolve only some of the problems created by transgressions. Payment of fines notwithstanding, supernatural pollution clings to sites of transgressions of *hadat.* In many cases, it is therefore also deemed necessary to perform rituals to cleanse or "sweep" away the pollution (that is, the animate essence or *gana* thereof) generated by the improper act. Until ritual restitution is made, the transgressor, his or her kin, and sometimes the entire village are prey to supernatural reprisal.

It is impossible to predict who will be targeted. For this reason, participants in mortuary ritual are concerned that unintentional transgressions caused by carelessness or ignorance may eventually bring harm to their descendants. A ritual specialist described a case to me in which the effects of one transgression of *hadat* became apparent only after many years. According to the specialist's account, on one particular afternoon, a young woman in his village inexplicably climbed a fruit tree near her home. She ignored her parents' anxious pleas to come down. With her clothes in disarray, she shouted incoherently at the people assembled below her. Her distraught family consulted a *basir.* After contacting an Upperworld being for guidance, the ritual specialist announced that the woman was being punished for her grandfather's improper performance of a *tiwah* carried out long before her birth on her great-grandfather's behalf. According to the specialist, the victim's grandfather had failed to place the heads of sacrificed water buffaloes on the shrine to the *pali* before taking them home to cook. "It is *pali*," the specialist explained, "to take the heads for ourselves before exhibiting them to our supernatural guests." He instructed the woman's family to prepare offerings for the *pali* and to leave these in the branches of the tree. When they were ready, the specialist performed a chant to dedicate the offerings. At the end of the chant, the woman in the tree suddenly became aware of her surroundings. She asked for help in descending and later claimed to be unable to recall what had transpired at any point in the unfortunate episode.

In this case, amends were made for the transgression of *hadat*. Some transgressions, however, are nearly beyond reparation. One of these is sexual relations between siblings or between two individuals of different generations within the same family *(pali kawin salah hurui)*. Another is cursing or violence against a parent or against some other relative in an ascendant generation. Thus, whereas most common transgressions thrust the perpetrator into an unfortunate but usually not fatal condition called *kicas,* more serious offenses are said to result in a dangerous condition known as *tulah,* during which any sort of disaster is considered likely to befall the guilty parties or their family. The most dreaded is that the transgressors or their village will be struck by lightning and consequently turned into stone *(baseluh).* In such cases, both kin and non-kin of the transgressor would be affected.

One anecdote related to me by a Kahayan River ritual specialist lends particular insight into the extent to which one must guard against transgressions of *hadat* in order to avoid the possibility of causing *baseluh.* One evening as we walked together along the village path to his son's home, Basir Muka, among the most senior and most important ritual specialists of the Bara Dia region, pointed out a large piece of ironwood that stood like a minor megalith at the foot of a very large durian tree. He remarked that the ironwood was once a beautiful woman, a former *bawi kuwu* (sequestered maiden) of long ago. In the past, he explained, many wealthy families, in response to a kinsperson's dream, would sequester one of their daughters for up to seven years prior to her marriage. These *bawi kuwu* were usually confined to a single room in the family home, where they would pass their time learning fine handwork such as sewing and weaving. This particular woman, a relative of the village's founder, unthinkingly ventured just outside the house to give food to a pig. The pig was suddenly bitten by a ferocious "blood fly," which refused to leave and continued to suck greedily at the animal's blood. The woman became angry and cried out, "Ah, blood fly! You can only suck the blood of a pig! You cannot raise a pig yourself!" She then struck at the fly with a bamboo stick, screaming, "You act as if it was your pig!" Basir Muka interrupted his narrative at this point in order to emphasize that the problem here was not simply that the woman had spoken improperly to an animal, in this case a fly, but that she had spoken and acted "without thinking" *(mantap manyau).* Within moments, said Basir Muka, thick clouds gathered overhead and lightning blazed across the skies. The rain poured down, and many trees were blown over or split in two by the lightning. Villagers rushed home to seek security behind the protective ironwood fence that stood like a fortress around the village. But there was no quarter for the transgressor herself: she was struck by lightning and transformed into the massive piece of ironwood that was wedged tightly among the roots of the durian tree that we stepped around in the evening shadows.

How are punishments such as the one that was handed down to this unfortunate maiden meted out? When asked to explain how the consequences of a transgression of *hadat* come about, villagers generally recall the notion that even one's actions and speech have an animate component and that transgressions themselves take on a separate existence. Many claim that offenders are "eaten by their own *pali*" and become perpetually "unlucky" (*kicas*) or worse. Ritual specialists offer more cosmologically sophisticated explanations. They cite an additional dimension to the concept of *pali*. According to some *basir,* a number of Upperworld beings, specifically a "king," his family, and his minions, are also referred to as *pali.* The king is known colloquially as "Raja Pali," though his full title is Raja Nyahu Erang Matan Andau Kilat Panjang Dimpah Ruang Langit. When enacting rituals, sponsors and specialists must not only observe proscriptions referred to as *pali* but also prepare offerings for watchful supernatural beings called the *pali.* Many of Raja Pali's descendants are said to dwell in the world of men, attentive to transgressions of *hadat,* which they immediately report. Punishment, whether swift, as in the case of lightning striking the village, or delayed, as in the case of the woman whose ancestors performed *tiwah* incorrectly, is handed down by the king himself. Hence, on nearly every ritual occasion, offerings are made to appease the *pali* for transgressions committed during the course of the event.

The ubiquitous nature of the *pali* and *pali* (future references to the dual concept will be cited as the *pali*) was made explicit by one *damang,* himself a former ritual specialist:

Nyahu Erang Matan Andau Kilat Panjang Dimpah Ruang Langit had as his descendants Pali Bujuh Apang Panjung and Samulang Amai Belang; his descendants went on and on down to Tatun Tapang, Belang Lehe, Kikir Petak, Garut Langit. They live in clouds, at the ends of palm branches, at the end of *sawang* leaves. Suak Suek lives in the upper part of holes in the ground, Belas appears everywhere, Lambak is in the inside of trees that wrap around other trees, Merap lives in the leaves that have already fallen, Sangkalilik-Sangkalalak in the beams below the house floor. They are everywhere investigating works that are *pali.* . . . If someone does something that is not in accordance with *hadat,* they will be plagued by misfortune and cannot live happily.

To recapitulate, then, *pali* has a double referent. First, it is the generic name of a host of supernatural beings descended from or associated with an Upperworld king. Second, it refers to all that is forbidden. Through its dual dimensions, the notion of the *pali* provides powerful enforcement for the maintenance of *hadat* and at the same time insinuates itself as a means of change within local tradition. Most important, the *pali*, as I will show, demarcates, reinforces, and creates distinctions between groups of human beings, and between humans and supernatural beings.

The Origin of *Hadat*

According to villagers, *hadat* has existed since the beginning of time, when the grandparents of humankind still dwelt in the "primeval village." Fraternal rivalry, filial disobedience, and accidental sororicide—serious transgressions all—brought an abrupt end to harmony in the village called Batu Nindan Tarung Liang Angkar Bantilung Nyaring. These events are described in the origin myth, which is often recited by a *tukang hanteran* during the performance of *tiwah* as part of the process by which souls are said to reach the Upperworld.[2] The abridged version of the myth that follows was collected from a Kahayan ritual specialist in his explication of the origin of *hadat*.

The dual creator(s) of all that there is in the universe, Ranying Hatalla Langit Raja Tuntung Matan Andau Kanaruhan Tambing Kabanteran Bulan–Jata Balawang Bulau Kanaruhan Bapager Hintan, unleashed awesome powers. Hatalla-Jata brought the cosmos to fruition, creating mountains and seas, jungles and rivers. These were placed throughout the seven-layered universe. Hatalla-Jata sculpted the five layers of the Upperworld, the Underworld, and the earth in between. Forty-three layers of clouds separate the earth from the Upperworld. With the water of life procured from the trunk of a powerful tree, Hatalla-Jata sprinkled the peaks of the Gold and Jewel mountains located in the Upperworld. The mountains crashed together, and the grandparents of humankind emerged from the resulting thunder and smoke. The name of the grandfather of humankind was Manyamei Tunggul Garing Jajahunan Laut. The grandmother of humankind was Kameluh Putak Bulau Janjulen Karangan Limut Batu Kamasan Tambun.

The pair stayed together in a long boat. Although they lived as one, Manyamei Tunggul Garing Jajahunan Laut and Kameluh Putak Bulau could not produce children because they had never been properly wed. Instead of the offspring they so desperately desired, their union spawned strange and terrible beasts. Hatalla-Jata's power created seven Upperworld beings to wed the pair. After the union was sanctified, the couple produced three sons. The eldest boy was named Maharaja Sangen, the middle boy was Maharaja Sangiang, and the youngest son was Maharaja Bunu.

When the boys were small, they often swam in a river that flowed in front of their house. Once when they were bathing, Maharaja Sangen and Maharaja Sangiang discovered "rising iron" *(sanaman lampang)* in a deep bend of the river. Maharaja Bunu was unable to locate any iron in the water, though he later found "sinking iron" *(sanaman leteng)* on the land amid a clump of *sawang* bushes. After carrying the pieces home, the three boys asked their father to fashion weapons from the iron.[3]

Not long afterward, the boys realized that their weapons were differently "charged." Whenever Maharaja Bunu's weapon struck an animal, the beast would surely die. Yet when wounds made with the other brothers' weapons were clasped with an open palm, the animal would survive. The two older boys could therefore play with animals as if they were toys, stabbing them and later healing the wounds. After this discovery, Maharaja Sangen and Maharaja Sangiang seldom traveled anywhere with their brother, for they were frightened of the weapon he possessed.

One day Maharaja Sangen and Maharaja Sangiang decided to visit a mountain located behind their house, even though their father had forbidden them to go there. Atop the mountain, they encountered a magnificent elephant whose hide gleamed in its whiteness. Unbeknownst to the boys, the elephant was actually their sister, born before their parents had been properly wed by the seven kings. They began to "play" with the elephant, stabbing her over and over. The blood that spilled from her body was transformed into pearls, diamonds, and gold. When Maharaja Sangen and Maharaja Sangiang tired of their game, they simply clasped her wounds with their hands and went home, promising each other that they would return another day.

The two began visiting the elephant regularly. On one occasion, Maharaja Bunu secretly followed his brothers and watched them from afar. Eventually he, too, approached. Then, like his brothers, Maharaja Bunu stabbed the elephant. Blood spurted out, but when the wound was clasped, it did not heal. The elephant ran and ran until it died. Its veins and bones became the treasured wood that holds up the world and is said to have golden roots spreading everywhere.

Hatalla-Jata, enraged at Maharaja Bunu's disregard for his father's admonitions and at the slaying of the elephant, declared Maharaja Bunu unfit to dwell in the primeval village. He was banished to the rivers and jungles that are home to the people of our age. As further punishment, Maharaja Bunu lost his immortality, and a marriage was arranged for him with a woman who was similarly mortal. Like Maharaja Bunu and his wife, all humankind, the descendants of this unfortunate couple, are doomed to labor and eventually to die. These grievous events transpired as a result of ignoring the *pali* and performing acts contrary to *hadat*. Thus, even the grandparents of humankind can be said to have been "eaten by their own *pali*," namely, their illicit acts of premarital intercourse. The punishment for these transgressions was the introduction of death into the cosmos. Death destroyed the primordial homology between humans and the supernatural, and yet, when humankind's ancestor found his way to this world, death itself became a part of *hadat.*

Hadat and the Inhabitants of Upper- and Lowerworlds

The common genesis of humans and Upperworld and Lowerworld beings is made explicit in the origin myth. To summarize briefly, as the first mortal, Maharaja Bunu is considered the founder of humankind *(utus kalunen).* His brothers Maharaja Sangen and Maharaja Sangiang and their descendants, as well as other inhabitants of the Upperworld and Lowerworld who are known as the *utus sangiang,* enjoy a distinct yet complementary relationship to humans. Leaving their Upper- or Lowerworld homes, they travel to the River of Mankind (Batang Danum Kalunen), described in ritual contexts as the "village borrowed by the hornbill" *(lewu injam tingang).*[4] It is striking that villagers' remarks concerning the emotional qualities and even the physical characteristics of many of these Upperworld and Lowerworld beings depict them as having much in common with humankind. Like humans, the inhabitants of the Upper- and Lowerworlds live in villages along rivers. They marry and produce children, who in turn grow up and have children of their own. There are already thousands of these beings; and over time, more and more are born or reveal themselves to humans. So great are their numbers that even the most competent ritual specialist can never aspire to learn the names of more than a few hundred. Unlike Maharaja Bunu's descendants, Upperworld and Lowerworld beings age but do not die.

The inhabitants of the Upper- and Lowerworlds assume crucial roles in all rituals associated with the indigenous religion. Contacted by ritual specialists, and in some contexts by lay practitioners, they are said to board ships and travel to villages to offer their assistance to humans. Diverse abilities and powers are ascribed to particular beings; those who care for the dead during a secondary mortuary celebration, for example, are not the same as those who heal the sick. Even in nonritual contexts, Upperworld and Lowerworld beings influence human lives: for instance, as we have seen, Raja Pali and his army of descendants are said to surround us at every moment.

Although ritual specialists possess sophisticated knowledge of the inhabitants of other cosmic realms, even lay adherents of Hindu Kaharingan are familiar with the names and characteristics of at least some beings to whom they turn in times of need or distress. Many of these can be contacted without specialists' intercession. Indeed, an essential characteristic of the indigenous religion is its practitioners' belief in personal, ongoing relationships between Upper- and Lowerworld beings and human individuals or families.

Covenants between humans and Upperworld or Lowerworld beings generally begin with the human attempting to contact one or more beings by making an offering and uttering his or her petition. The animate essence of rice that is scattered is said to travel to the Upperworld or Lowerworld. Individuals who regularly provide offerings to specific beings make direct supplication to that particular being, for example, to protect travelers on difficult journeys, to make barren women fertile, or to reveal the outcome of future events. If a supernatural being is thought to have interceded on a human's behalf, a large celebration is held in its honor, and subsequent requests, accompanied by the promise of another celebration, are made at that time.

In these kinds of cases, the supernatural being in question becomes a tutelary guardian, a *sahur parapah* or *sahur* for the villager. It may also serve as guardian for an entire family or even an entire village. Often the humans involved with such a guardian must observe particular proscriptions, known as *pali sahur parapah*. Some tutelaries are very well known. Nearly every village, for example, is said to be protected by its own village guardian, the *patahu*. Particular *patahu* often demand that villagers observe unique proscriptions on their behalf. In Basir Muka's village, for instance, it was *pali* to drag the stalk of a coconut palm leaf along the ground, as this sound annoyed the *patahu*. According to some of my informants in that village who claimed to have received assistance from that *patahu* in times of distress, their *patahu* would always make a loud clicking noise to let them know that he was nearby and that they would be safe. The *patahu* is often said to manifest itself in the guise of a strong old man in warrior dress or as small stones that appear or disappear at will in various places in the village. The village guardian occupies a prominent place in most conceptualizations of humans' relation to the supernatural. Men and women turn to him for protection from their natural and supernatural enemies. Miniature huts on stilts *(pasah patahu)* are erected as a home for the village guardian. There villagers leave gifts of rice, tobacco, areca nuts, even bottled soft drinks or coins.[5] Many villagers attempt to negotiate mutually beneficial agreements *(hajat)* with the village guardian. One woman related her own such encounter as follows:

People in this village have many experiences [with the village guardian]. Once when I went to leave some food for him I saw a curled-up vine on top of the rock inside the guardian's house. The vine was swarming with black ants. In front of the guardian's house I saw many poisonous caterpillars. I was very surprised because I had never seen anything like that. When I left the food in the house I made a promise to the guardian. I told him that my son would soon leave the village to search for diamonds. If my child found the diamonds, I would prepare a huge celebration [in the guardian's honor]. After I went home, I had a dream that the vine and the ants were actually riches intended for me. The village guardian came to me in the dream and said, "These are your treasures. I will return your gifts because you did not bother me. The rock that you saw was merely my clothing." One year later my son returned to the village with 2 million rupiah. He purchased a boat and has now become a successful trader.

Although specific *pali* are associated with particular village guardians, some prohibitions are common to all. One is the prohibition against moving stones that may be associated with the guardian. Reprisals are said to be most severe, as is apparent from a case related by a ritual specialist about his own grandchild:

Many years ago there was no house for the guardian of this village. It was difficult to distinguish the rocks belonging to the guardian from other rocks scattered along the river's edge. My grandson was walking along the riverbank searching for ironwood that could be used to build steps leading up from the river. When he shifted one particular piece of wood, he saw a large rock underneath. He thought that the rock would be good for securing his fishing net, so he carried it away. He sank the rock in the river. Not long afterward he began to demonstrate symptoms of being crazy. He did things that we thought were very funny and that made us laugh. Evenings he would play music on empty oil drums. Mornings he would tell us that he was going fishing, but when he reached the river's edge he would jump into the water and scare the fish away. Once he ran into my house to tell me that he wanted to shoot a bird perched in the top of a tree, then he grabbed a broom and pretended to fire out the window. Finally, his mother dreamed that she saw her son tied up in a bamboo cage. The men who surrounded him in her dream said that he was being held because he had tied them up at the bottom of the river. That was a sign. We realized what had to be done in order to make my grandson well. We prepared to perform a ritual and sponsor a sacrifice in honor of the guardian. The boy's father, who was Christian, cautioned us against it. He said that his son was ill with malaria, that he had a fever. He wanted us to send him to the coast for treatment. When we held our ritual and built a house for the village guardian, my grandson's father remained inside his own house and mocked us. Not long afterward my grandson returned to normal. His father died of a fever.

In addition to having the ability to communicate with men and women through dreams, village guardians, like other Upperworld and Lowerworld beings, are able to possess human beings. Possession *(manyangiang)* is usually short-lived and ecstatic, and it may or may not recur. It may be serial or limited to visits by a single being. Possession by the village guardian or by other inhabitants of the Upper- or Lowerworld is not usually considered dangerous or even particularly frightening. Some people, known as *tukang sangiang*, are often solicited by their neighbors to go into a trance.[6] The first symptoms of possession are trembling or convulsions. The medium appears disoriented, and his or her eyes often roll back in their sockets. The medium may introduce himself or herself as a particular being and request specific foods or comforts, then proceed to advise or chastise the people in the audience.

More women than men experience this form of possession. Furthermore, few ritual specialists are subject to it. Three phenomena, each related to the use of language, distinguish *manyangiang* from the experiences of ritual specialists. First, the possessed speaks in everyday language rather than in the ritual language style invoked by specialists. The daily language uses a different vocabulary and does not hinge on metaphor and parallel construction (Fox 1971). Although the remarks of the medium are often bawdy, scatological references in the ritual language are couched in figurative speech. Second, the medium banters with the audience. Spectators joke with supernatural beings, share cigarettes with them, and invite them to dance. "Oh, Grandmother," or "Oh, Grandfather," villagers often shout, "What have you brought me?" Mediums respond to these attentions "in character," moaning, laughing, or sobbing as appropriate. Dialogue between ritual specialists and spectators is generally inappropriate, however, and mediums rarely exhibit the *basir*'s usual quiet dignity. Finally, lay villagers subject to possession often claim to be unable to remember what they said or did during the episode. They cannot usually predict when possession will recur. By contrast, specialists easily recall chant sequences when they are not performing. The specialist controls his or her own experience in terms of beginning or ending chants and when summoning beings or sending them back to other realms. Unlike most villagers who experience possession, specialists continue to be able to converse normally while resting "between sets," while the beings are still said to be within their bodies. One *basir*, in answer to the question I posed, responded that he felt "perfectly usual" *(biasa ih)* when his body was occupied in this way. He knew the spirits were in him, but their presence did not affect the way he saw, heard, or moved.

From this description, it is clear that the *hadat* of Upperworld and Lowerworld beings allows them to travel to and from the world of mortals. Humankind's *hadat*, however, prevents men and women from accompanying supernatural beings to the other realms. Exceptions are those few individuals, culture heroes in particular, who are said never to have died but instead to have ascended to the Upperworld in glorious apotheosis.

And yet, although the realms of Upper- and Lowerworld beings are clearly demarcated from the world of humans, a reunion of sorts remains possible. The key to this reunion lies in the origin myth. After detailing Maharaja Bunu's exile to the fifth level of the cosmos and his eventual marriage to a mortal woman, the myth goes on to explain that even after Maharaja Bunu lost his immortality, the three sons of the grandparents of humankind were eventually reunited. Upon Maharaja Bunu's death, his two older, immortal brothers were overcome with grief and pleaded with Hatalla-Jata to restore their younger brother to their midst. Hatalla-Jata relented and instructed Maharaja Sangen and Maharaja Sangiang in the performance of secondary mortuary ritual. The brothers in turn taught elements of *tiwah* to their own descendants. Maharaja

Sangen instructed Raja Duhung Mama Tandang in the method of freeing souls of the dead from the grave. Maharaja Sangiang taught Rawing Tempun Telun how to reunite the three souls of the deceased. Thus it is that, even today, Upperworld beings travel to and from the earth in fabulous ships to assist Maharaja Bunu's descendants in processing their dead. Secondary mortuary rituals reunite the descendants of the three original brothers, just as extended family members are reunited through their duties and privileges as the sponsors of *tiwah.*

Hadat and Jungle-Dwelling Beings

Inhabitants of the Upper- and Lowerworlds are not the only supernatural beings said to occupy the cosmos. Humankind coexists with members of yet another category of supernaturals, known generically as "Unclean Ones" *(taluh papa).* Unlike Upper- and Lowerworld beings who reside mostly elsewhere in the universe, Unclean Ones reside directly in the natural world.

As is the case with Upperworld and Lowerworld beings, the origin of this second category of beings can also be traced to the creation of the cosmos. The same specialist who offered the account of the origin myth also insisted that among the original Upperworld beings was one who claimed to be "the creator" rather than "the created." He refused to accept his *hadat* and, as a result, was cast from the Upperworld. Since that time, Angui Bungai Mama Lengai Tingang, known colloquially as Angui Bungai, dwells with his wife and children in a remote corner of the cosmos. Through his minions, he orchestrates his evil works in the world of mortals. On one infamous occasion celebrated in Kahayan mythology, Angui Bungai deceived Maharaja Bunu and thereby condemned Maharaja Bunu's wife to mortality.

Although Angui Bungai himself is not as well known among villagers as he is among ritual specialists, his minions, the Unclean Ones, certainly are. These constitute the animate essence of particular creatures, pseudo-beasts, and some jinn. Unlike the inhabitants of the Upper- and Lowerworlds, Unclean Ones are more mercenaries than guardians. Humans initiate relationships with particular Unclean Ones, who then become supernatural allies *(sahabat).* Those Unclean Ones include, among others, a ferocious supernatural dog *(bahutai),* an enormous supernatural snake *(hanjaliwan),* and the animate essence of banyan fig trees *(nyaring pampahilep).* Also unlike Upper- and Lowerworld beings, Unclean Ones are said to be of inhuman or feral aspect. Most live in the jungle, particularly in uncleared, specially demarcated patches of scrub *(pukung pahewan)* that stretch between villages.

As mercenaries of the supernatural world, Unclean Ones can be sent to attack the enemies of whoever propitiates them. They are said to cause death and disease. Potent talismans and oils, affixed to doorways or carried on one's person, provide some protection against them, as do secret kinds of knowledge. Unclean Ones also have an ability to possess humans *(nyarung taluh papa)*. The man or woman possessed may take on the attributes of this ally so that, for example, the person who has entered into a relationship with a supernatural snake writhes on the floor when possessed. Possession by an Unclean One is feared, or at least usually not considered a suitable public spectacle. For instance, on the one occasion when I saw a *tukang sangiang* possessed by a snake, she first sent everyone except her daughters and me out of the house.

Unclean Ones are more demanding of those who petition them than are the inhabitants of the Upper- and Lowerworlds. In addition to celebrations in their honor—secret events that sponsors generally deny ever took place—Unclean Ones must be remembered with bits of food at every meal. Dissatisfied with these gifts, they may select a member of the petitioner's family, usually the spouse or a child, and cause his or her death by "feeding on their blood." Thus, Unclean Ones are conceptualized as dangerous, undependable, and difficult to control.

An especially feared Unclean One is a being with the ability to detach its head and fly about in search of blood. Such beings are known as *hantuen* (or *hantuen baruwut)*. *Hantuen* are said to have an ability to transform themselves *(pangoloh)* into jungle beasts. More dangerous still, they can assume human guise. It is difficult to recognize *hantuen* except by the absence of one physical characteristic: the indentation of flesh between the nose and the lips. It is said that humans can also become *hantuen,* either intentionally or inadvertently, by ingesting a certain potion. In such cases, the humans lose their souls. It is suspected, furthermore, that the condition runs in families. *Hantuen* may be of either sex. If the *hantuen* is a woman, she is thought to be exceptionally beautiful and seductive. She appears naked to men traveling in the jungle and kills them after having had sexual intercourse with them. *Hantuen* are said to be particularly fond of the blood of the newly dead or of women in childbirth. Detaching their heads from their bodies, *hantuen* pursue the scent of blood. The unfortunate victims of their assault usually die. *Hantuen* are thus especially feared, as they have the potential to dwell both outside and inside human society.

Tales of personal confrontations with *hantuen* are rampant. One friend told me of a chance meeting in a marketplace with a woman who grabbed her arm. For more than an hour afterward, blood seeped from the spot where she had been touched. That, and the fact that the unknown woman wore heavy makeup around her throat (to cover the seam where the head comes loose), convinced my friend that she had encountered a *hantuen.* A man described his grandfather's experience. A young *hantuen,* just a child, boasted to the old man that he could turn himself into a deer. He asked that an enclosure be built, and he secluded himself within it. After a few minutes the old man heard hoofbeats, and when he peeked over the fence, he saw that the boy had transformed himself into an animal. "Look at me, Grandfather," he cried naively. "I told you I could do it." Another woman described a funeral she had attended in her village. When the deceased's coffin had been lowered into the earth, a teenage boy tried to throw himself into the hole. Restrained by onlookers, the young man parted his lips. His tongue, which she claimed was more than a meter long, darted toward the coffin lid. He was forcibly returned to his parents in the next village, who merely laughed when they were informed of his horrific seizure. This, she claimed, proved that theirs was a family of *hantuen*. She expressed surprise that the crowd had not killed them on the spot.

Earlier ethnographic studies also include data on *hantuen*. Hans Schärer placed their origins within the bounds of humankind. According to Schärer, *hantuen* make up a distinct social group: witches.

> The fate of witches is by no means easy to bear. They are continually subject to the contempt and mistrust of their fellow men. Neither have modern times and the numerous administrative regulations been able to change any of this. Formerly the murder of witches was common. Short work was made of them. They were tortured in a frightful fashion and beaten to death like mad dogs. I myself have seen such cases in recent times. In the case of an undecided issue at law, or of suspicions and insinuations, the defendant or suspect had to undergo an ordeal and perform the well-known dance around the *sandong* (a little house for the dead). The deities and ancestors decided on his guilt or innocence, and also his fate, and the community carried out the sentence. (1963, 52)

Once identified, the *hantuen* would be put to death. As it had no soul, no death rituals would be held on its behalf.

A particular dread of many villagers is that of inadvertently having *hantuen* introduced into otherwise normal families through marriage. The consequences of such misalliances are recounted in legends. An especially well known one is that of Angkes and Tahuman. There are many versions of this story (Schärer 1966, 55–62; Danandjaya 1971b, 269–71). The following tale was related by a ritual specialist who lived but a short distance from one of the villages mentioned in the account. He told the legend in the course of an explanation of the *hadat* associated with arranging marriages.

> Tapih lived with her family in the village of Barasmanyang on the Rungan River. One day while she was bathing in the river, the wind blew away her hat. At that very moment, in the Kahayan village of Sepang Simin, a man named Antang Taui was trying to obtain an omen concerning the success of his upcoming journey. The hat floated to earth at his feet. He decided to locate the hat's owner, and he left his village without waiting for the omen he had previously sought.
>
> After a long search, he arrived at Tapih's village. The two married. Soon after

their marriage, Antang Taui went fishing. Among the many fish he caught was one of a large variety known as the *tahuman*. Because the fish was heavy, he decided to leave it in his boat until the next morning. When he returned, he saw that the fish had been transformed into a baby girl. Antang Taui and his wife Tapih decided to raise the child as their daughter. They named their new daughter Tahuman.

Antang decided to take Tapih to visit his home on the Kahayan River. He began to clear a path through the jungle that would lead to his village. One day while he worked he noticed a squirrel, known as the *angkes,* stealing his provisions. He caught the animal and watched as it was transformed into a boy. He and his wife named the boy Angkes and raised him as their son.

After the children grew up, they were married to each other. Tahuman gave birth to a child that died when it was only a few days old. At about that time Tapih, too, gave birth, in this case to a stillborn child. While the two couples were making preparations to hold *tiwah* for the dead children, Angkes and Tahuman suddenly became very competitive toward their adoptive parents. If Antang Taui located a tree for a sacrificial post, Angkes searched hard to find a taller tree. When Antang Taui asked to borrow a water buffalo to sacrifice during the celebration, Angkes refused to lend him one. Finally, Antang Taui cried out in anger, "You should be ashamed of how you have treated your parents! You aren't like other people. Angkes is just a jungle animal, Tahuman is just a fish. Look at the bones of your child!" When they exhumed the remains of their dead infant, all Angkes and Tahuman found were a handful of fish scales and a hank of squirrel's fur. They were ashamed and ran away to live in the jungle.

Eventually Antang Taui and Tapih produced a son. They named him Rasan. Unbeknownst to them, Angkes and Tahuman had also had another child, a daughter named Lusuh. After Rasan had reached adolescence, he decided to go on a hunting trip to a part of the jungle his father had forbidden him to visit. There he met Angkes, Tahuman, and their daughter, Lusuh, about whom he had never been warned. They acted very kindly toward him, though what they actually wanted was revenge for their humiliation at Antang Taui's hands. Soon the two young people, Rasan and Lusuh, were wed.

Oddly, however, after they were married Lusuh refused to obey *hadat* and bathe together with her husband for the first seven days following their marriage. To see why, Rasan decided to follow his bride and secretly watch her bathe. To his horror, when Lusuh took off her clothing her head also came loose. Blood poured out of her throat, and her intestines swung from her neck. Lusuh's head began to fly around in a circle over her body. Rasan, terrified, ran far away to a village in the direction of the setting sun. Although he remarried, Lusuh continued to follow Rasan. She eventually even went so far as to attach her head to his body. After that happened, Rasan was ashamed to be seen and wandered ceaselessly through the jungle. One day as he and Lusuh walked, they came upon a fruit tree. Lusuh demanded to eat, and her head perched on a nearby stump while Rasan climbed the tree and appeared to pick fruit. But instead of feeding Lusuh, Rasan threw the heavy branches of the fruit tree at her head. The head finally shattered. With her dying breath, Lusuh cursed her husband and his entire family.

The legend of Angkes and Tahuman illustrates a number of important points concerning *hadat* and concerning the relationship of humans to their kin and to the two categories of supernatural beings discussed earlier. First, contrary to *hadat,* Antang Taui left to find the owner of the mysterious hat without waiting for an omen about the outcome of his journey. The implication is that if he had waited, an Upperworld being would have indicated that he should cancel his trip. Second, the story emphasizes that the effects of *hadat* may be postponed and visited upon the transgressor's descendants. Third, it makes the point that children should never anger or disobey their parents as did Angkes, Tahuman, and Rasan. Fourth, as Angkes and Tahuman were the adopted children of Antang Taui and Tapih, their offspring's marriage to their adoptive parents' natural child was both incestuous and intergenerational. Fifth, one should never marry strangers, especially from other rivers, as they may not be human.

The importance of avoiding miscegenation with descendants of *hantuen* is a key factor in Kahayan people's concern with genealogy *(jereh).* Yet, at the same time, the concern is often offset by the desire to amass large reserves of kin. The result is that villagers broadly classify society into two categories, kin and non-kin, the former being most assuredly human, the latter perhaps not. Although this generalization simplifies many issues and raises many questions, it can nevertheless be argued that at the level of ideal conceptualizations of society and cosmology, the boundaries of kinship are conceived of as coterminous with the boundaries of humanity. These conceptualizations of kin and non-kin relations are rooted firmly in the notion of *hadat.*

Hadat and Conceptualizations of Kinship

This section offers a short introduction to conceptualizations of kinship, drawn specifically from data gathered among Kahayan villagers in the upriver districts, particularly in the area known as Bara Dia. Though not intended to be an exhaustive study of the mechanics of kinship, the discussion nevertheless suggests a relationship between the maintenance of order within the family, as depicted through marriage preferences, and the maintenance of order throughout the cosmos, as depicted in beliefs about the nature of human and nonhuman relations.

As is generally true for Bornean societies, Kahayan villagers reckon kinship bilaterally. Solidarity is felt with individuals to whom one has cognatic or affinal linkages. Kinship imposes certain moral obligations, and loyalty and trust among family members are cultural ideals. Among Kahayan villagers, people meeting for the first time—fellow passengers on a river taxi, for example—might quickly compare their geographic origins and apparently relevant genealogical information to ascertain whether a kinship link exists between them. If such a linkage is found, its discovery is greeted with much mutual satisfaction.

Despite the existence of this "moral bond," as Victor King has pointed out in his study of the Maloh of West Kalimantan, "obligations attached to kinship are generally not supported by strong jural sanctions" (1985a, 22–23). Likewise, Douglas Miles writes of the Mentaya River Ngaju:

> Recognition of kinship implies that two people may ask for temporary shelter and food from each other, but not that they are obliged to comply with the request or that they have a jural right to each other's property and services. This is not to say that Ngadju Dayaks never engage in more binding obligatory relationships with their relatives, but simply that they may choose the cognates with whom they have such dealings according to criteria other than kinship status. (1976, 59)

This analysis raises an important point. The fact that a kinship linkage can be presumed to exist between two individuals is generally of greater importance than identifying the precise degree of the relationship. Miles, for example, persuasively argues that kin groups are voluntary associations: "By far the most important function of kinship is that it serves as a catalyst for establishing social relations. . . . The Dayaks may *choose* to accentuate ties with some relatives and neglect those with others" (1976, 61).

Miles appears to be correct in his assessment of the desirability of amassing large reserves of kin or even of treating non-kin as if they were cognates, under certain circumstances. He even goes so far as to claim that "Ngadju Dayaks show little interest in genealogies; for them, one of the most significant aspects of kinship is that it classifies people into broad categories" (59). Yet, at the same time, in order to represent Ngaju conceptualizations of kinship correctly, it is necessary to point out that these normally informal attitudes may, in particular contexts, be superseded by more acute concerns. Among Kahayan villagers, for example, the fact that the same kin terms are extended to cognates and affines, and even to non-kin, does not guarantee that distinctions, perhaps unverbalized, are not made between those individuals at some other level. In fact, many Ngaju villagers are very much concerned with genealogy and its implications. The presence or absence of cognatic linkages are of utmost importance in the arrangement of marriages and the enactment of mortuary ritual, as we shall see.

Key terms generally used by villagers to refer to their kin are *kula* and *babuhan*. These terms can be glossed as "field of cognates" and "field of cognates and affines," respectively.[7] Neither term refers to discrete or corporate groups but rather to two expanding spheres of kin with ego at their center. The *kula* of any individual includes all of his or her cognates from and including lineal and lateral kin of the fourth ascending generation. Terms of address within the *kula* are generational. An adult will address the offspring of a grandparent's sibling as "aunt" or "uncle" even if, for example, that person is considerably younger. One's own parents are distinguished by specific terms of reference and address. After a couple has produced a child, they assume teknonyms to which generational terms of reference are appended. A teknonym is a name that refers to a person according to his or her relationship with a descendent. Even after grandchildren are born, teknonyms based on the name of the individual's eldest child continue to be used. In the case of childless couples or of the newly married, the generational referent plus personal name is sometimes used. Nevertheless, it is also the case that childless couples may take pseudo-teknonyms or even teknonyms incorporating the name of some common object to avoid the stigma of being childless. The use of pseudo-teknonyms also enables others to avoid *pali* associated with using the personal names of relatives in ascendant generations. Behavior toward one's *kula* is hedged with prohibitions, particularly toward members in ascendant generations. A parent's or grandparent's oath against a descendant, accompanied by slashing rattan, scattering kitchen ash, cutting off a hank of hair or hurling a stone irretrievably into the river, harbingers terrible misfortune for a child or grandchild and seven generations of its descendants.

Does the *kula* constitute a kindred? Readers familiar with the ethnography of Borneo will be aware of controversy within Bornean studies concerning whether the term "kindred" can be applied to cognatic societies.[8] George Appell, whose insightful observations on isolates can be applied to many Dayak groups, concludes that among the Rungus, the kindred, as the term is usually understood, does not exist (1967, 204). Appell warns, for example, against disregarding treatment of spouses of cognates in determining the existence of meaningful structural isolates. Many villagers, too, refer to spouses of particular cognates as members of their *kula*. Furthermore, after the marriages of oneself, one's siblings, and one's children, nephews, and nieces, persons in ten affinal categories are incorporated into one's *kula*. The term "kindred" therefore seems ill suited here.[9] A guarded distinction can perhaps be made between "branch *kula*" (*kula rinting*; see figure 1) and "carried *kula*" (*kula lumpat* or *tamput*; see figure 2) in distinguishing between one's cognates and affines. Yet this distinction is similarly labored. To most villagers, emphasizing a difference between two types of *kula* would be to suggest that someone was marginally kin and not truly entitled to the moral bonds, mentioned earlier, that obtain between *kula*. Normally, it is only in determining who has the right to be placed in particular bone repositories that the unspoken distinction between affines and cognates makes itself felt. This is a point I will return to shortly.

The term *babuhan* refers to a broader group of kin than *kula*. *Babuhan* includes one's own *kula* as well as one's affines' *kula*. The term connotes an amorphous group of hundreds of persons united by kinship linkages and there-

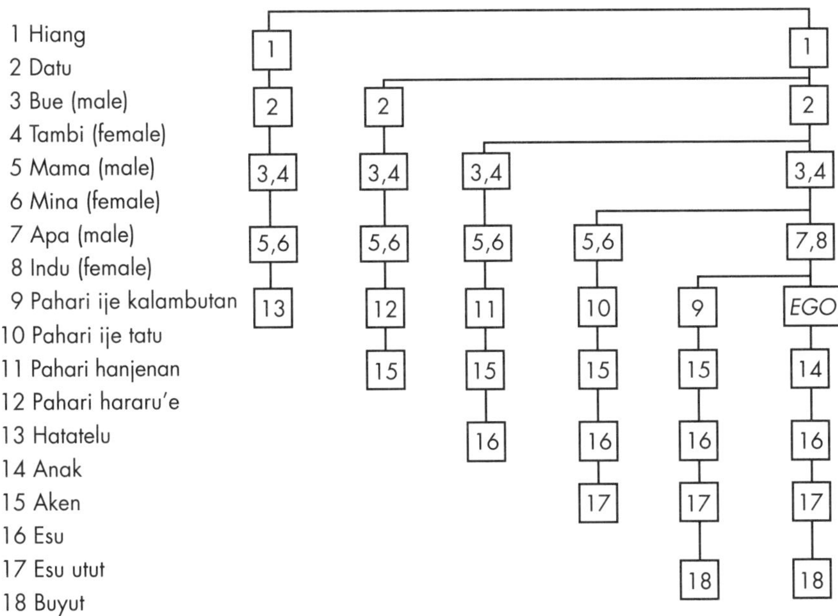

FIGURE 1. Terms of Reference for Members of Ego's *Kula Rinting*

fore by affective ties. A parent's *babuhan,* in the sense of one side of the family, is called the mother's or father's "net" *(jalahan bapa, jalahan indu).* Both cognates and affines are included in the net. Ideally, marriages take place among individuals who are *kula* or *babuhan.*

Marriage and Avoidance

Understanding Ngaju conceptualizations of kinship calls for a consideration of marriage preferences and proscriptions. Most village marriages are arranged by the parents, aunts, and uncles of a prospective pair. Discreet inquiries are made to ascertain that a prospective spouse is the descendant neither of *hantuen* nor of slaves. Such an inquiry is easiest, obviously, if marriage takes place within the *kula.*

Much important work has been done on systems of social stratification in Borneo generally. It is clear that in southern Borneo local peoples formerly practiced a system of social ranking, reflected in the use of the different styles of bone repositories and decorative poles described in chapter 3 as well as in levying fines in "slaves." It is clear that ranking was of concern in the arrangement of marriages. Schärer, for example, writes that "membership in the superior group can be lost by marriage into a lower one" (1963, 41). Contemporary

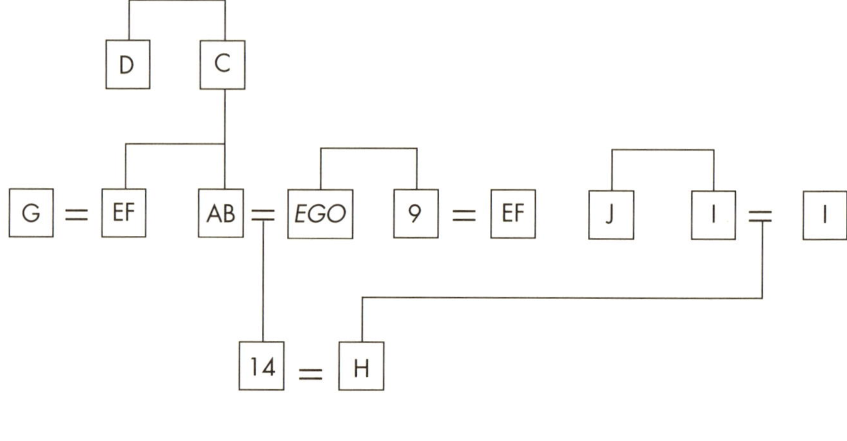

FIGURE 2. Terms of Reference for Ego's *Kula Tamput*

villagers speak of two broad social ranks, but it is only with great difficulty that any further information regarding ranking can be extracted. This distinction between "high" and "low" groups undoubtedly conflates differentiations of past importance even within those categories, particularly with regard to slavery. As Anthony Reid (1983) has suggested, the nature of slavery across various Southeast Asian contexts is not necessarily comparable. It is difficult to surmise the former limits of local slavery or to know how the institution might have functioned differently among peoples on various rivers. Evidence exists that there were several different types of slaves, even within a single area. Schärer, for example, makes a distinction between serfs (*rewar*) and debt-slaves (*jipen*) (43). It is clear that slaves of some sort were available for use in ritual purposes. Reports of missionaries (Harrisson 1959) and eyewitness accounts of older villagers today confirm that slaves were previously among the sacrifices at some *tiwah*.

Several stories are bandied about regarding celebrated instances in which slaves tried, successfully or not, to escape their fate. One such anecdote concerns a slave who was dropped into a deep hole to await being crushed to death by an ironwood post the next morning. During the night, the desperate woman dug a small niche for herself in the side of the hole. When the post dropped, she was able to huddle in the niche. Although one of her ears and part of her face were torn off in the process, she was able to escape the next night. There seems to have been an assumption that at least some kinds of slaves were without the souls possessed by other men. It is said that slaves could only ascend to the Prosperous Village at their master's bidding.

Slavery was officially abolished in 1894 during a meeting between representatives of the colonial government and various Dayak leaders at the Kahayan River village of Tumbang Anoi (Ilun et al. 1983b). Although today villagers unanimously decry slavery, echoes of attitudes that may have informed the thinking of earlier generations linger in the age when "slaves own their masters," a reference to the financial success of many families thought to be descended from slaves. Fines and marriage prestations continue to be paid in goods or monies equivalent to certain numbers of slaves. Parents chastise children by comparing them to slaves in dress, manner, or intellect. The chance of being ridiculed as slavish continues to dampen enthusiasm for public works. One villager explained the deteriorated condition of his surroundings by confiding that cleaning village paths and repairing bridges were formerly the domain of slaves and not of free men such as himself.

At the same time a family determines that a candidate for marriage is not of slave descent, efforts are made to ensure that he or she is also not the descendant of *hantuen*. A study of marriage *hadat* published by Palangka Raya University reiterates the view, expressed in the myth of Angkes and Tahuman, that villagers conceive of marriage with *hantuen* as an ever-present danger: "Upon every marriage, genealogy is usually enquired after. If it happens that one is the descendant of a *hantuen* or vampire, the marriage is usually canceled immediately" (Mihing et al. 1978/79, 91).

It is not my intention here to detail marriage rules but rather to note that marriages preferably take place between cousins. Cousin marriage, which occurs from the first to the fourth degree but is most common among second cousins, is said to play an important role in strengthening the family. The study just cited corroborates the popular view of the role of cousin marriage in contributing to the autonomy of families:

> Marriage also often has the aim of once again making close a relation that has already begun to become distant. In the Ngaju Dayak system of kinship relations, if the distance between two persons descended from the same ancestor has already reached the degree of third cousin or each constitutes the fourth generation, if in the fifth generation the kinship relation is not tightened and made close once again by means of marriage, it can be said that they who constitute the fifth generation are not related. Because of this matter, for the sake of making close and guarding the wholeness of the family, children of the third generation are usually married to each other, and if that is not possible, the children of the fourth generation are married to each other. (Mihing et al. 1978/79, 89–90)

Finally, the careful checking of a prospective couple's respective genealogies assures their kin that the bride and groom are not of different generations.

Partners in intergenerational marriage, their kin, and even their village are said to be endangered by the gravity of this transgression of *hadat.* It is said that in the past lightning would strike villages where incestuous marriages occurred. Unusual rock formations, including the infamous Tangkiling Hill outside Palangka Raya, are said to bear mute testament to the consequences of incest. In the unlikely event that an incestuous couple remains in their village, they are subject to a ritual of purification. Offerings to the *pali* are set up in the middle of the village path. A black pig is sacrificed, its blood mixed with rice and scattered. In the past the guilty couple then proceeded toward crawl toward the offerings on their hands and knees from opposite ends of the village. They would eat from a pig trough without using their hands, for it is said that "like pigs, they do not care with whom they mate." When circumstances necessitate performing this ritual today, however, it is usually held indoors, and the couple is allowed to eat with their hands.

A related problem with less serious consequences is a marriage between two persons that makes it impossible for a third party to use normal terms of address toward one of the pair. (This situation is diagrammed in figure 3.) The wronged party is entitled to receive a fine "to turn the tongue" from the bride and groom on their wedding day.

The celebration of marriage ideally involves the ritual re-creation of the wed-

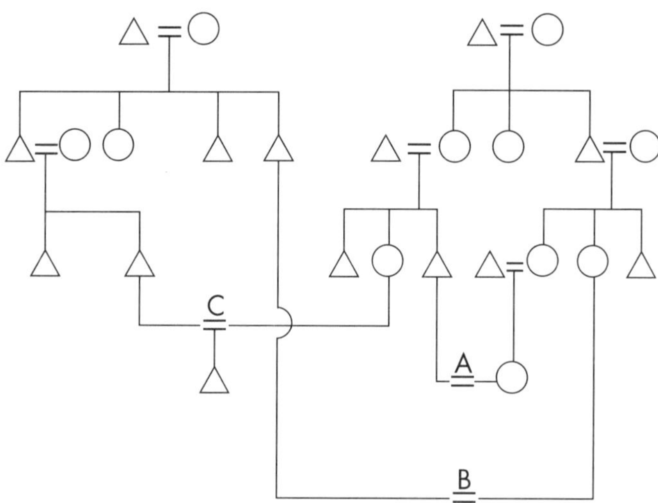

A Kawin tulah

B/C If couple B weds before C, C will be fined *singer tambalik jela* or vice versa.

FIGURE 3. Marriage Proscriptions: *Kawin Tulah/Singer Tambalik Jela*

ding of the grandparents of humankind, Manyamei Tunggul Garing Jajahunan Laut and Kameluh Putak Bulau Janjulen Karangan Limut Batu Kamasan Tambun. Today nearly all marriages between Hindu Kaharingan are performed in this way. The climax of the celebration—sanctification of the marriage—is preceded by a host of prefatory rituals of great interest. During these rituals, the groom and his entourage are depicted as threatening, potentially dangerous intruders. Stylized struggles between the bride's and groom's families occur at several points in the celebration. First, when the boat bringing the groom to the bride's village attempts to tie up, the bride's male relatives repeatedly try to cast it away. Moments later in the courtyard of the bride's home, representatives of the groom's family must defeat the bride's in a display of traditional martial arts, as they break through a string "fence," festooned with flowers in order to enable the groom to proceed to the house. The fence is vigorously defended by the uncles, cousins, and brothers of the bride. Although the groom's entourage is ultimately destined to win the encounter, it is not uncommon for members of both sides to stagger away with a bruise or two. At the bride's doorway, the groom's entrance is blocked by a row of expensive Chinese jars covered by yellow cloth. The groom is allowed to roll back the cloth and pass by the jars only after extensive interrogation by the bride's father. The final drama unfolds within the bride's house later that evening. The groom's family sits separated from the bride's by a curtain hung across the room. His relatives are interrogated in jest once more, with both parties sending envoys armed with daggers to deliver questions and answers around the screen. These dramas are eventually resolved with the young man's incorporation into the bride's household, in the sense that he is invited to store his personal belongings there. Whether the new couple remain at the bride's parents' home and for how long depends on personal factors; they are not obliged to live there permanently. Then seven kings of the Upperworld, as well as other supernatural beings, are summoned to officiate at an anointment, during which the bride and groom are seated on gongs and grasp a *sawang* branch together.

Maintaining Order in Natural and Supernatural Worlds

The importance that Kahayan villagers attach to distinctions between kin and non-kin, coupled with their marriage preferences and views of the extended family, suggests that their manner of conceptualizing human relationships parallels their understanding of order in the supernatural world.

To summarize briefly, I have so far proposed that villagers' social relationships take place in a field divided into safe versus potentially perilous zones. One's own kin are safe: one's non-kin perhaps are not. The former, at least, are assuredly human. Endogamous marriage is preferable to marriage outside the family because the genealogies of the parties involved can be checked and because a moral bond uniting the parties is already given.

Although safe versus perilous zones as structures characterizing human relationships do not correspond to an explicit model, a parallel view is discernible in villagers' understanding of their pantheon/pandaemon. This explains why adherents of the indigenous religion emphasize similarities rather than differences between supernatural beings. Only in the course of interviews that focused specifically on qualities and characteristics of particular beings did diacritical distinctions between inhabitants of the Upper- and Lowerworlds and Unclean Ones emerge. Villagers consistently described the former as anthropomorphic, similar to humans in their appearance and general way of life. The inhabitants of the Upperworld and Lowerworld constitute a vast, benevolent pool of potential allies. Although no human can achieve extensive knowledge of these beings, one can still feel confident that they intend no harm and can even be a resource in moments of need. And, as the origin myth makes clear, these beings are in fact distant cousins of humankind.

Just as villagers fail to make distinctions between supernatural beings, they also tend to use idioms of kinship toward non-kin and do not distinguish between cognates and noncognatic affines in most situations. Among Kahayan peoples, *kula* and *babuhan* constitute a vast network of associates and potential spouses. No one is acquainted with all of his of her *babuhan*. People are content to know that their nets of kin extend widely.

Just as it may prove advantageous to initiate relationships with specific Upperworld or Lowerworld beings when dealing with the supernatural, an individual may actualize linkages with any member of his or her *babuhan*. Petitioners of supernatural tutelaries trust that no harm will befall themselves or their families so long as they fulfill their obligation to provide a celebration on the tutelary's behalf. Similarly, when engaged in an enterprise based on kinship, villagers expect that neither party will attempt to take unfair advantage of the other.

Unclean Ones, mercenaries of the supernatural, are distinct from Upperworld and Lowerworld beings in many respects. Unclean Ones are inhuman, feral jungle dwellers, socially and geographically beyond the safe zone. They are dangerous and unpredictable. In this they are like non-kin. Hence the ambiguity of marriage with a man or woman from the perilous zone of social relationships. By marrying non-kin, one potentially enlarges the family's kin group and thus its allies. Yet such a marriage risks introducing a *hantuen* into the family. The in-marrying spouse may be a malignant being in disguise whose loyalty can never be relied on and whose presence may occasion disaster or death. The force of this perceived threat is popularized in the legend of Angkes and Tahuman, dramatized during marriage *hadat,* and concretized in the celebration of mortuary rituals. Thus, it becomes apparent why women in childbirth and the newly dead are thought of as being in the most immediate danger from *hantuen*. Childbirth is ideally the result of a marriage between members of the same *kula:* only unions between cognatic kin should lead to the birth of a child. Similarly, death offers an opportunity to incorporate the soul into a realm where it is beyond reach of any save its cognatic kin. In *Ngaju Religion* (1963), Schärer did not venture to explain why suspected *hantuen* were compelled to dance around bone repositories to ascertain whether they were human. From the analysis presented here, it is clear why *hantuen* must dance and why men and women circumambulating bone repositories before they place their kin's remains inside are carefully observed. The bone repository is, literally and symbolically, the place where the concentrated life force of the family is contained. It follows that it is the very place where *hantuen* could be expected to reveal the awful secret of their dual nature.

How does marriage articulate with the performance of death rituals? According to my informants, marriage should endure until one spouse cradles the other's bones. The bones of a husband and wife should ideally be wrapped together in a single cloth and entombed in the same ossuary ("ije kakandin tulang, ije sandung mantang"). The surviving spouse's family must share in the cost of providing *tiwah.* Schärer insinuated that among the Ngaju, a husband is a stranger in his bride's home (1963, 182). In the Kahayan case, if the husband and wife are not cognatically related, they will remain "strangers" even after death. Noncognatic affines have no right to be placed in a family's bone repository. The final determination of where bones will be placed is based on many considerations, including residence, affection, and coincidence.[10] Whenever necessary, however, villagers build small repositories suitable for the remains of lone individuals. That such repositories are rarely erected perhaps provides some evidence of the infrequency with which nonendogamous marriages take place. By means of mortuary ritual, Kahayan villagers ultimately protect their kin in the Prosperous Village from harassment by the minions of Angui Bungai and perpetuate the social and cosmological order which people are compelled to maintain by their *hadat.*

Tiwah as a Template for Social Relations

Once one recognizes how villagers' cosmological beliefs find parallels in their conceptualizations of the family and attitudes toward kin and non-kin, the role of *tiwah* and associated rituals as templates for social and moral order becomes more apprehensible. Mortuary rituals can be fully understood only within the broader context of social organization.

In the preceding chapters, secondary mortuary rituals have been described as lengthy performances that may involve hundreds of participants. Theoretically the cooperation of the deceased's entire extended family is necessary to complete the ritual cycle. Sponsors' willingness to work together to enact *tiwah* itself fulfills a social ideal. Large numbers of participants contributing goods and money are usually necessary to amass sufficient resources to provide lavish celebrations. Why are elaborate *tiwah* desirable? Three explanations have been proposed. First, it was suggested that through participation in *tiwah,* sponsors protect themselves from the hazardous consequences of ignoring *hadat,* of offending or transgressing the *pali,* and of disappointing the deceased. *Tiwah* are therefore scheduled to afford maximum participation by survivors. Even infants are carried to bone repositories to join in the ritual processing of ancestral remains. Just as proper performance of death ritual benefits the family, its improper performance places the entire extended family at risk of supernatural reprisal. The *pali* respond to individuals or families remiss in fulfilling their ritual obligations by inflicting punishment. If a sponsor of *tiwah* dies during or soon after the celebration, the death is often blamed on a transgression of *hadat* in which the victim may or may not have been personally involved. The second reason why elaborate *tiwah* are desirable is that by provisioning the deceased with ample goods, animals, and slaves for use in the Upperworld, survivors try to court their ancestors' favor. It is hoped that the ancestors will feel obliged to reciprocate this generosity. Third, mourners themselves ultimately derive benefit from ensuring that their deceased kin enjoy comfortable surroundings in the afterlife, as the extended family is said to dwell together in the repository.

Death rituals accentuate family solidarity. They also perpetuate it into another realm of existence. The sense of moral obligation between kin in this life and the next is enhanced through their joint sponsorship of ritual. To apply Victor Turner's notion of liminality in ritual contexts to the case of the bereaved family, participation in activities associated with *tiwah* leads to a submerging of self in the *communitas* engendered by the event. During *tiwah,* an irrevocable distinction between kin and outsiders is internalized by participants. Internalization of this message strengthens the bond that unites sponsors.

At the climax of death ritual, the living, the dead, and the inhabitants of supernatural realms revel in a momentary revisitation of the prelapsarian condition, the cosmos as it was before Maharaja Bunu lost immortality for himself and his descendants. A village in the midst of *tiwah* is no longer considered part of the human world, but rather it occupies an intermediate location between earth and the Upperworld. Its special status as a realm apart is symbolically expressed by erection of a long fence that runs parallel to the river. Outsiders must pass through this fence to gain entry to the celebration. The temporality of the fence, as well as all other mortuary edifices save bone repositories and sacrificial posts, is itself telling. It manifests the village's special position vis-à-vis space and time. Conversely, proscriptions imposed upon sponsors of *tiwah* serve as barriers theoretically preventing them from venturing out of the village before the celebration is complete. In this setting, bounded from inside as well as out, the *tukang hanteran*'s recitation of the origin myth assumes heightened significance. His chants re-create the cosmos purified, untainted by transgressions of *hadat* and the pollution of death.

The theme of death ritual is the re-creation of the cosmos, and it speaks to the association of death with fertility. In writing about death rituals generally, Maurice Bloch and Jonathan Parry pointed out that in many cultures death is associated with a renewal of fertility, though that which is renewed may be the fecundity of people, animals, or crops or of all three (1982, 7). In the Kalimantan case, mortuary rituals are more powerful still, leading to a regeneration of life and, therefore, of *hadat* in the broadest sense. At the same time, death ritual is also a celebration of procreative sexuality (Metcalf and Huntington 1991). The apposition of symbolic representations of maleness and femaleness and of life and death figure prominently throughout all stages of the celebration. Male and female ritual elements must be constantly balanced to produce a procreative effect. These symbols of maleness and femaleness permeate mortuary celebrations. When a man dies, for example, it is often his female relatives who cut the animal sacrificed at his funeral, and when a woman dies, it is the men who do so. A man's coffin is carved in the shape of a water snake, a woman's in the shape of a bird. Doorways of bone repositories are guarded by two figurines, one male, the other female. A male sacrificial post is usually carved to honor a deceased female at *tiwah,* and vice versa. The apposition between male and female is also dramatized during dances preceding sacrifice. The dance around the sacrificial post is unique among villagers' dances, for it is solely on this occasion that men and women dance in separate concentric circles. During the popular social dance, *manasai,* they dance in one large ring.

The dictum that marriage should endure until one spouse cradles the other's bones finds its literal expression at *tiwah.* Couples about to marry are reminded of the myth of Nyai Endas Bulau Lisang Tingang, who asked her Upperworld husband Raja Garing Hatungku for a coffin and a bone repository as her bridewealth. Ideally the celebration of *tiwah* should be initiated by the surviving spouse. In fact, however, the deceased's children usually shoulder most of the responsibility for its performance. By providing *tiwah,* descendants repay a debt. Parents give life to their children. Consequently, it is the child's duty to bestow immortality on his or her parents by sponsoring a secondary mortuary ritual on their behalf.

Repayment of this gift begins in the early stages of the ritual processing of the dead. For example, we have seen that when mourners prepare to transport the coffin to the graveyard, one of the deceased's descendants is obliged to sit astride the coffin as it is carried in and out of the doorway of the house in a manner reminiscent of an act of penetration. Rituals suggestive of birth become increasingly explicit as the mortuary cycle moves toward culmination. Exhumed remains are kept near lighted oil lamps beside the repository. As I pointed out in chapter 2, light is associated with life. When transporting their parents' bones, children cradle them in the manner in which, as infants, they themselves were carried by their parents. An association between death ritual and birth is also apparent in the eschatological beliefs associated with the final stages of the ritual performance. According to ritual specialists, souls revisiting their grieving kin before the final ascent to the Prosperous Village travel in the cloth in which they were swung as infants. It is said that the last bridge souls must cross before joining their predecessors is composed of the animate essence of their own umbilicus.

In chapter 3 I described the bone repository as a house for souls. Repositories can also be thought of as symbolic of the womb. Descendants straddle ossuaries as they emplace their parents' bones, often in a posture reminiscent of giving birth. Mourners descend from the repository in the direction of the sunrise, associated with life. Shortly after the repository is closed, a wooden or cement phallus, ranging from a foot to over thirty feet in height, may be placed alongside it. Here, too, symbols of maleness and femaleness strike a procreative balance. The energetic, chaotic play between men and women that follows final placement of the bones celebrates and generates vitality.

In emphasizing the solidarity of the extended family, *tiwah* also conveys a concomitant message, namely, that the family exists in opposition to its social other. That other is composed of non-kin. Distinctions between kin and non-kin are underscored at several points in the ritual. Once the *sangkaraya* is under construction, for example, sponsors have the right to demand money or goods from the boats of passers-by, non-kin by definition. The opposition between kin and non-kin is most dramatically portrayed with the arrival of the decorated ship bearing an unrelated family's contribution to *tiwah*. The mock "attack" of the wildly gesticulating dancers who make up the ship's crew is a veritable onslaught of non-kin, a mob of strangers displaying grossly exaggerated ferocity and sexuality. In a spirited defense, sponsors overcome these marauders. The crew's inhuman aspect, achieved through the use of fantastic costumes and masks, recalls characteristics of the dangerous Unclean Ones. Turner has suggested that masks depicting distorted human features with especial grotesqueness and monstrosity may be intended less to frighten participants in rituals than to make them more cognizant of their culture. Turner writes:

> Much of the grotesqueness and monstrosity of liminal sacra may be seen to be aimed not so much at terrorizing or bemusing neophytes into submission or out of their wits as at making them vividly and rapidly aware of what may be called the "factors" of their culture. . . . Monsters startle neophytes into thinking about objects, persons, relationships, and features of their environment they have hitherto taken for granted. (1967, 105)

I would argue similarly that the arrival at the village gate of "manufactured monsters" that lead to associations with *hantuen* provokes participants in *tiwah* to reflect on the certainty and essence of their own humanity. The essence of their humanity lies in their adherence to *hadat,* in this instance demonstrated by their "correct" performance of *tiwah.* The certainty of their humanity is revealed through a genealogy that does not include alliances with questionable outsiders who may not be human. Defeating "monsters" results in the acquisition of sizable largesse for the souls' enjoyment in the Prosperous Village. In the creation or repayment of a ship, a symbolic attack or revenge between families is also effected. Nonetheless, that the ship, while desirable, is an entirely optional adjunct to the celebration underscores the point that the bereaved family is actually self-sufficient when it comes to sponsoring death rituals. They do not need the help of non-kin in any capacity, except perhaps *basir* to process their own dead.[11]

It can thus be said that *tiwah* reveals tensions both within and beyond the extended family that are an integral part of villagers' conceptualizations of kinship and their view of society. Much of this tension surrounds the normally unspoken distinction between cognatic kin and noncognatic affines. Although it is the deceased's cognatic kin who initiate preparations for *tiwah*—that is, by tying a strip of shroud around the surviving spouse's head during the wake and deciding what the minimally acceptable sacrificial animal will be—it is the spouse, even a noncognatically related one, who is responsible for organizing the ritual. If *tiwah* seems unreasonably postponed, cognatic kin may ask that their complaint be settled by a specialist in local tradition.[12] On the one hand, *tiwah* educates participants that solidarity within the extended family is prerequisite to prosperity and insulation from supernatural reprisal. On the other, however, it teaches them that possibilities exist for distinctions even within the family. Spouses may not be placed in the same repository if they are not cognatically related; in this life and the next, an in-marrying spouse is said to pose a potential threat.

I offer one illustrative example in this regard. In a poignant case, the father of a young widow who was planning to carry out *tiwah* on her husband's behalf denied his daughter permission to place her husband's remains in the family repository. The massive *sandung* had been erected five generations before. According to legend, seventeen slaves were sacrificed to consecrate the handsome repository, a legacy of which the family was tremendously proud. But the deceased was not cognatically related to his widow; they had met while attending high school in a village downriver. The widow's father based his decision to refuse access to the repository on the grounds that his son-in-law had been born on the Katingan River, which the father insisted was a notorious origin place of *hantuen.*

I visited the widow's village more than two decades after her husband had

Large *sandung*. Note the smaller *sandung* on the left erected for a nonconsanguineal affine. Kahayan River, 1983. Photo by author.

died. The tiny ossuary built for the man's remains had crumbled long before. Most of his bones lay scattered on the earth beside the handsome repository where his obstinate father-in-law's remains now reposed alongside those of his recently deceased daughter. The Katingan River man's grandchildren assured me, however, that it would not be long before their grandfather's bones would also find their way into the large *sandung*. They claimed that after his *tiwah*, they had discovered that their grandfather had actually been their grandmother's distant cousin. At an upcoming *tiwah*, they planned to move the remains to the other repository and thereby reunite for eternity their long and unfairly estranged ancestors.

5 | Hindu Kaharingan in the New Order

Tiwah is the ritual form that villagers and townspeople most often characterize as expressing the essence of their indigenous culture. People ardently declare, "*Tiwah* tell us who we are." In the preceding chapter, I made a case for the way such pronouncements speak to genealogical issues. People also claim that the celebration's format has remained constant throughout generations. Yet *tiwah* and the eschatological beliefs and attitudes surrounding its performance are clearly changing. For many indigenous inhabitants of Central Kalimantan, their sense of who they are is also changing. A host of variables have conspicuously influenced the contours and contexts of *tiwah.* These include the colonial experience, the independence revolution, and a guerrilla campaign that culminated in the creation of the province of Central Kalimantan. The past sixty years have brought widespread conversion to Christianity and a growing Islamic presence, and those two faiths have affected the indigenous religion in very direct ways. In the 1970s and 1980s the expansion of Indonesia's transmigration program introduced thousands of Balinese, adherents of yet another religion, Hinduism, to the region. Exposure to the hegemonic discourse of religion or *agama* and emplacement of an institutional infrastructure whose authority extends deep into praxis and belief have also had enormous effect.[1] It is within these parameters that a range of dialogues concerning cultural and religious identity and their representation are presently being conducted. Villagers' dramatic pronouncement that death rituals tell them who they are demands further examination in light of these changes.

The recent official recognition of Hindu Kaharingan figures importantly in these debates, not only among adherents of the indigenous religion but also among their counterparts who have converted to other faiths. Hailed by some as a vindication of Kalimantan's indigenous peoples, decried by others as a portent of the evisceration of local practice and belief, Kaharingan's newly won consolidation with Hinduism has focused local attention even more closely on the problematic relationship between religious affiliation and "being Ngaju." Negotiating identities in the face of these concerns is at the root of what Chairman Lewis described to me in 1983 as "the greatest struggle within Ngaju culture today." More than a decade later, his position remains unchanged.

In order to understand why these negotiations are deemed a struggle, it is important to contextualize consolidation as part of a larger process by which Indonesian religions have gradually been restructured at the national and local levels. The Ngaju are not the only Indonesian minority people to have been affected by religious reform. A growing body of anthropological scholarship, much of it prefigured by Geertz's essay on Balinese "internal conversion," documents the efforts of various groups to confront the complex relationship between traditional religions and their "political" identities. These include accounts of the Tengger of Java (Hefner 1985), the Toraja of Sulawesi (Volkman 1984; Adams 1993), the Wana of Sulawesi (Atkinson 1989), the Meratus (Tsing 1993), and others. Several anthropologists have found it useful to approach the topic through a focus on ritual change. Susan Russell and Clark Cunningham, for example, have suggested that as vehicles to communicate the cultural experience of social groups, rituals can often serve as barometers of changing political and economic relations with the wider society (1989, 2). A rich understanding of complex cultural dynamics can be achieved through the investigation of the conditions under which societies revise rituals in response to new political and economic ideas (4). It is to a focus on these kinds of wider sociocontextual features of the celebration of *tiwah* and other Hindu Kaharingan ritual events that I now turn.

Rationalization of Hindu Kaharingan

> In the past we were referred to as the dark religion. It was true, because at that time we never held meetings for worship, we never listened to religious lessons, we didn't have a book. At that time we had not been consolidated with Hindu religion.
> —Testimony by a Palangka Rayan youth, 1983

> Don't be embarrassed to be Kaharingan. Don't be embarassed. Don't be embarrassed. People come from all over the world to write about our culture.
> —Testimony by the same man, now a Hindu Kaharingan *basir*, 1995

Two sociological models that have addressed the social implications of religious practice are those of Émile Durkheim and Max Weber. Both are now regarded as classic. And both are largely evolutionary, although they are characterized by very different emphases. Durkheim primarily addressed the symbolic character of religious systems. Weber was more concerned with the developmental path of religions. Both approaches provide starting points from which to consider the place of "traditional" versus contemporary religious beliefs and practices in Borneo societies.

A Durkheimian-style analysis of Ngaju mortuary rituals has, in fact, been available for some time, published by Durkheim's student Robert Hertz (1960 [1907]). Hertz found in missionaries and travelers' accounts of secondary burial among the "Olo Ngaju" a rich source of descriptive data with which to argue the point that society becomes conscious of itself and of the phenomena that constitute its life in an indirect way, as reflected in the material world by the treatment of mourners, souls, and physical remains. In treating Ngaju rituals as social facts, Hertz wrote, "if the physical phenomena which constitute or follow death do not in themselves determine the collective representations and emotions, they nevertheless help to give them the particular form that they present, and lend them a degree of material support" (83).

The explanatory power of this model falters when called upon to speak to the relationship between religious practice and social change. Unlike Durkheim, who sought to explore and explain the social underpinnings of transcendental concepts, Weber dealt largely with the relationship between religion and the more particular interests of individuals involved in social change. To elucidate this relationship, Weber attempted to ascertain the directional paths along which religious systems differentiate and to identify situations in which populations become most susceptible to religious "breakthroughs." By "breakthrough," he meant those occasions when a change in established order occurs rather than a reinforcement of the traditional order. Prophets often figure instrumentally in this regard. When breakthroughs come to pass, argued Weber, a process of religious rationalization commences. Characteristics of rationalization include intellectual clarification and systematization, as well as the internalization of a normative code and a motivational commitment. Over time, the religious community takes a more defined shape and the cultivation of a written tradition ensues, allowing the breakthrough to become institutionalized and persevere.

Contemporary social scientists have developed this trajectory in various ways. Robert N. Bellah, an anthropologist, focused on changes in symbolization that occur as part of the evolution of religious forms and the implications of these changes for social practice. Bellah (1964) suggested that religions move toward increasing differentiation and complexity of organization. In time the sphere of the religious is likely to become more autonomous relative to other spheres of life. As a result, individuals become increasingly conscious of themselves as religious actors. Types of religious symbol systems, Bellah continued, are closely linked to types of social organization, to religious action, and to social action. He proposed three corollaries to his hypothesis: that as religions evolve, symbolization becomes more comprehensive and rationalized; that the place of religion in society and the nature of an actor in that religion change in related ways; and that religious change is connected to a variety of other dimensions of social change (360). He posited five stages in the development of religious systems, but cautioned that these are ideal types and not necessarily inevitable nor sharply distinguishable (361).

Bellah's paradigm can be used to isolate several important characteristics of religious belief and practice among Central Kalimantan villagers, past and present. In its transition from *hadat* to Kaharingan to Hindu Kaharingan, Ngaju religion is moving toward a more differentiated system of symbolization. Although this process is only beginning, some of its effects can already be identified through examination of variant conceptualizations of what constitutes the "religious," what it means to "be religious," and the creation or denial of social bonds on religious grounds. For example, three characteristics of villagers' religious practices and beliefs situate the system in the category Bellah termed "primitive religion." The first is the adherents' sense that the enactment of ritual constitutes direct participation in sacred mysteries with a minimum of mediation (363). The second characteristic is the close congruency that adherents conceptualize as existing between mythological and actual worlds (362). The third is the free-associational nature of mythological belief (363).

According to the Hindu Kaharingan villagers, the world of supernatural beings mirrors the world of humans to a high degree. Sponsors of *tiwah* identify closely with supernatural beings summoned to take part in the ritual. It is said that even the village itself participates in this identification through the elevation of its own animate essence to an intermediate status between the human realm and the Upperworld. Ritual specialists do not mediate this experience of the supernatural; rather they interpret and facilitate it. Also, Upperworld and Lowerworld beings are said to resemble humans both in aspect and in their general manner of life. The primary distinction between the two groups is that the former are immortal. Even mortality can be mediated to some extent, however, by the performance of secondary mortuary rituals. Similarly, the supernatural beings known as Unclean Ones are said to have the ability to become "humanlike" and therefore pose an ever-present threat to the arrangement of marriages.

The free-associational nature of Ngaju belief helps to maintain what Bellah calls a "hovering closeness" between mythic and experiential worlds. Adherents of Hindu Kaharingan can turn to whichever beings they feel might assist them in their particular circumstances. When *tiwah* is enacted, for example, a *nenung* is held first to ascertain which *sangiang* are available to lend support. The sphere of the supernatural is conceptualized as flexible and accommodating;

for this reason, indigenous cosmological beliefs can be widely and disparately characterized. For example, Miles reported that when he attempted to read sections of Schärer's *Ngaju Religion* to his Mentaya River informants, they professed to having only a general familiarity with the ideas described in the myth (1976, 76). Indeed, based on the fixedness he ascribed to indigenous belief, I found Schärer criticized roundly by intellectuals in Central Kalimantan for presenting an "inaccurate" portrayal of Ngaju religion. Two factors figure here. First, as I noted earlier, the understandings of ritual specialists differ significantly from those of lay practitioners, and beliefs current in one region may be absent in a neighboring region. Second, the beliefs themselves are constantly transforming. For example, as the version of the origin myth presented in chapter 4 details, Hatalla-Jata is generally considered the creator(s) of the cosmos. After creation, it appears that Hatalla-Jata no longer occupied an active place in the affairs of supernatural beings or of mortals. Nevertheless, some adherents of Hindu Kaharingan claim to have initiated a personal relationship with Hatalla as their supernatural guardian. Others, however, claim that such a relationship is impossible. Saililah, Schärer's key informant, insisted to me that Schärer had misrendered adherents' relationship to the creator(s) by suggesting that they make offerings to "Jata the Creator." To corroborate his argument, he proceeded to cite the names of twenty-five other Lowerworld beings, also known as Jata, to whom offerings could be made.

Strikingly diverse versions of the origin myth, too, exist. One young *basir* adamantly insisted to me that the elephant, which some specialists describe as the fruit of premarital sexual relations between Manyamei Tunggal Garing and Kameluh Putak Bulau and sister to Maharaja Bunu, was created by Ranying Hatalla Langit under different circumstances (Simpei and Hanyi 1996, 76). Another offered a lengthy account of how the earth had been created from the stub of a cigarette cast down by a supernatural being. I would suggest that to "fix" the myths, to deny their capacity for transformation, is to misrepresent the traditional dynamics of this belief system.

This capacity for accommodation does not operate only in the realm of belief. A related characteristic is the plasticity of indigenous ritual forms. The vitality of the death ritual lies in the fact that it is constantly revised and altered to suit the peculiar circumstances of its performance. Thus, a paradox, first pointed out in the introduction to this volume, reemerges here as a distinctive characteristic of indigenous ritual forms: that is, although "acceptable" mortuary rituals are said to conform to the origin myth, the origin myth does not make the format of the death ritual explicit.

To return to Bellah's paradigm, specifically his account of the "archaic" period, widespread accounts of human sacrifice and headtaking at *tiwah* intimate that, at some point in the region's history, there was a relationship between hierarchy and religion, though it is now unclear. As Bellah suggests, "The emergence of a two-class system . . . has its religious aspect. The upper-status group, which tends to monopolize political and military power, usually claims a superior religious status as well" (364). I recall one old man's account of preparations for his grandparents' *tiwah:* his grandfather bore the title *harimaung,* "tiger." When his grandmother was dying, she called her descendents together. She squeezed her right breast, then cut off a hank of her hair. As she threw the gray locks at her children and grandchildren, she cried: "You who drank from my breasts, obey my request. After I am dead, encircle the earth around my *sandung* with the heads of my slaves and enemies. Only then will I be satisfied." Relevant too in this regard is the former practice of erecting a *pantar sanggaran* or *pantar panjang* alongside the bone repository of an illustrious individual, although villagers today are unsure as to the grounds upon which these people qualified for such unusual recognition. Bellah's paradigm continues with the inauguration of the "historical" period in the evolution of religion. Diacritic in this regard is the emergence of a notion of salvation (366) and differentiated religious collectives (367), both of which change radically the manner in which people relate to one another. In Central Kalimantan today, these characteristics are well in evidence; there is an emerging consciousness of the self as a religious actor as well as a member of a religious congregation.

How have movements toward the "modernization" of "traditional" religion affected the aforementioned resilient qualities of belief and ritual? Can changes be detected in religious and social action or in conceptualizations of such action that correspond to changes in patterns of symbolization occasioned by official religious reform? Much of the responsibility for the current reform movement lies in the hands of the Supreme Council of Hindu Kaharingan Religion. To understand the council's overall agenda and the effect of its activities on religion in Central Kalimantan, it is necessary to consider not only how the council itself came into existence but also the broader processes of religious change that have affected all Indonesians at the national and local levels. Although it is not a "new" religious movement, Hindu Kaharingan, like many Asian NRMs (Keyes et al. 1994, 9), has lately exhibited a considerable degree of religious innovation. Innovation within Hindu Kaharingan is shaped by the dominant state discourse on religion. Much of this innovation follows the pattern DiMaggio and Powell (1983) have termed "institutional isomorphism," particularly of the coercive and mimetic varieties. Innovations include the strategic positioning of an extensive bureaucracy that oversees religious activities throughout the province, the production of religious tracts, the introduction of new forms of worship, and the propagation of a notion of religious legitimacy rooted in legal mandate rather than divine inspiration. It is to an examination of these processes of change and their implications that I now turn.

The Rise of the National Religious Bureaucracy

Jurisdiction over religious affairs and policies throughout Indonesia is handled through an administrative body known as the Department of Religion (Departemen Agama). The Department of Religion, established on 3 January 1946, is headed by a minister *(menteri agama)* appointed by the president.[2] Also at the highest reaches of the department's bureaucratic echelon are the secretary general whose ambit encompasses administrative operations including finances and supplies, and the following director generals whose supervisory authority extends over the affairs of specific religious congregations: the director general of leadership to the Islamic community *(bimbingan masyarakat Islam* or BIMAS Islam), the director general of the Islamic Organization *(bimbingan kelembagaan agama Islam),* the director general of leadership to the Catholic community" (BIMAS Katolik), the director general of leadership to the Protestant community" (BIMAS Kristen Protestant), and the director general of leadership to the Hindu-Buddha community" (BIMAS Hindu-Budha). Below the minister, the secretary general, and the director generals extends a vast network of functionaries that stretches into the country's hinterlands.

The bureaucratic model established at the national level is replicated at the provincial level. Supervising each provincial Office of Religious Affairs (Kantor Wilayah Agama) is an office head *(kepala kantor),* who is assisted in turn by division heads *(kepala bagian sekretariat)* in charge of administrative affairs and field heads *(kepala bidang)* in charge of operational affairs for each congregation. If a particular congregation is not considered large enough to warrant a field head—for example, the Islamic and Catholic congregations in Bali—the office is instead administered by a counselor *(pembimbing),* whose staff is smaller than that of a field head.

Given these bureaucratic networks, one might expect that the needs of Central Kalimantan's Kaharingan population would be addressed through the auspices of a Kaharingan field head or counselor. Until quite recently, however, the Kaharingan faithful qualified for no such consideration, nor were they officially entitled to any facilities whatsoever at the Department of Religion's Central Kalimantan headquarters. The beliefs and practices of Central Kalimantan's indigenous peoples, like those of many other Indonesian minority groups, were relegated to the catchall category of "tribal religion" *(agama suku)* or "belief sect" *(aliran kepercayaan).* Tribal religions and belief sects are not officially religions at all. Instead, they are deemed aspects of customary law (Ind. *adat;* Ngaju *hadat)* and, therefore, fall under the administrative auspices of the Department of Education and Culture (Departemen Pendidikan dan Kebudayaan or DEPDIKBUD) rather than the Department of Religion.

In order to qualify as an official religion, certain requirements must be met.

One is belief in a single supreme being (ketuhanan yang maha esa), coterminous with the first principle of Indonesia's Five Principles of State. Rita Kipp
and Susan Rodgers explain:

> The first of the Pancasila tenets is elaborated in two statements in the Indonesian
> constitution, sections one and two of Article 29. Section one merely elaborates
> earlier parts by stating "The State shall be based upon belief in the all-embracing
> God." Section two adds that "The State shall guarantee the freedom of the people to
> profess and exercise their own religion." These official pronouncements, and the gov-
> ernment structures and policies that grew out of them, have become part of the con-
> text in which the religious life of all Indonesians must be understood. (1987, 17)

Although five official religions provide structures within which most Indonesians worship, many localized belief systems lack explicitly monotheistic doctrines and, for this and other reasons, do not qualify as religions. Kipp and
Rodgers have pointed out that individuals unaffiliated with official religions
may be viewed by some factions as unpatriotic (19). They may also be considered dangerous. During my 1991 visit, a member of the staff of the Department
of Religion showed me a government statement published in 1986 that warned:
"Lately there has been a rise in *aliran/organisasi kepercayaan,* that are contrary
to religious lessons and laws. This endangers existing religions. . . . *Aliran kepercayaan* should be directed toward [absorption into] healthy religion."

Given the bureaucratic support that religious recognition confers, one won-
ders why adherents of Kaharingan did not request it some time ago. In fact,
they did. Recognition, however, is not easily won, and it is extremely unlikely
that any more "new" faiths will be recognized. This stance was made explicit
in a government directive titled "Broad Outlines of the Direction of the State"
("Garis-Garis Besar Haluan Negara"), ratified in 1965: "A belief sect does not
constitute religion. Guidance toward belief sects must be carried out . . . so as
not to head toward the establishment of a new religion. . . . Necessary steps
must be taken so that belief sects are truly in accordance with the principle of
Divinity on the basis of a just and civilized humanity" (657/CI–7/IV/7 April
1988, 61). An alternative is for adherents of a localized religion to seek consolidation with a religion already recognized by the state. This path was eventually
chosen by some adherents of Kaharingan when they decided to pursue integration with Hinduism. This decision, and the campaign that followed, ultimately
had a tremendous impact on life within and beyond the religious arena.

The Rise of an Indigenous Religious Bureaucracy

To put this campaign into perspective, it should be noted that until quite recently, despite its lack of acknowledgment at the national level, Kaharingan has

long been informally recognized by successive regional administrations as a political as well as a religious force.[3] In the past, several explicitly Kaharingan political parties achieved regional prominence. Most successful was the Union of Kaharingan Dayaks of Indonesia (Sarikat Kaharingan Dayak Indonesia or SKDI). SKDI's members included a number of well-known *basir* and *damang*.[4] In the 1951 election, Adji Bahen of the Kapuas Regency won a seat in the Provincial Assembly on the SKDI ticket. In the 1961 election, Itar Ilas, a prominent *basir*, won his seat campaigning as a Kaharingan religious scholar (Alim Ulama Kaharingan), as did Simal Penyang, later the head of Central Kalimantan's association of *damang*, in 1966.

In 1967 SKDI relinquished its nonaffiliated status when its members decided to consolidate with a rising new national party or "functionary group," the Work Group (Golongan Karya, or GOLKAR).[5] In the 1971 election, three former SKDI supporters—Sahari Andung, Simal Penyang, and Liber Sigai—won appointment to the Provincial Assembly on the GOLKAR ticket. Four SKDI/GOLKAR candidates were elected to regency-level councils (Dewan Perwakilan Rakyat Daerah Tingkat II) at that same time. In the 1977 election, a younger SKDI/GOLKAR member, referred to throughout this volume as Chairman Lewis, secured a spot in the Provincial Assembly that he has continued to hold.

Since their organization's inception, SKDI members pushed for installation of a representative of Kaharingan in the Department of Religious Affairs. In 1965 Unget Djunas, a *basir*, was appointed to the provincial office of the Department of Religion's clerical staff. Although he did not serve in an official capacity, Unget was nevertheless able to assist adherents of the traditional religion informally and to advise the head of the provincial Department of Religion on matters pertaining to Kaharingan ritual and belief. In the early 1970s, in a move that will forever affect the local religion and regional politics, Lewis, Simal Penyang, and Liber Sigai decided to organize a "nonpolitical" synod to oversee the administration of matters related to Kaharingan. They founded the Council of Religious Scholars of Kaharingan Indonesia (Majelis Alim Ulama Kaharingan Indonesia, or MAUKI) on 20 January 1972. Lewis assumed the post of general chairman, Simal Penyang that of first chairman, and Liber Sigai that of general secretary.[6] The following year, MAUKI's leaders voted to establish regional councils patterned after the Department of Religion model. These included 10 regency councils (*majelis daerah*, or MAUKI-MD), 50 subdistrict councils (*majelis resort*, or MAUKI-MR), and 159 village councils (*majelis kelompok*, or MAUKI-MK). It was anticipated that the number of subdistrict and village councils would gradually increase as the need arose and administrative expertise became available. Indeed, the number of village councils has already grown to 300. MAUKI also redoubled long-standing local efforts to prepare texts pertaining to Kaharingan worship and doctrine. Funds to help carry out these activities were made available to MAUKI by the then-governor of Central Kalimantan, W. A. Gara.

Despite MAUKI's gains in terms of organizational visibility, the lack of official government recognition for Kaharingan continued to inconvenience and even anger many adherents. The situation was characterized by extreme tension between representatives of the government bureaucracy and the Kaharingan faithful. For example, all adult citizens of Indonesia are expected to carry identity cards stating, in addition to their name and place of residence, their marital status and religion. Village and subdistrict heads refused to register as married those individuals who had "only" participated in a Kaharingan wedding or even to enter "Kaharingan" on identity cards. Thus, with regard to self-identification of religious preference, individuals were presented with two options, both regarded as extremely unattractive. On the one hand, they could claim to embrace an officially sanctioned religion. On the other, they could leave the religion category blank. In Indonesia the inability to ally oneself with a specific religion has repercussions reaching into the political sphere. Adherents of particular religions tend to back particular political parties. Some adherents of Kaharingan grumbled that it remained unclear whom they should vote for in elections.

Toward Consolidation with Agama Hindu

In 1979, in the midst of growing anxiety over their faith's status vis-à-vis Indonesia's formal religious bureaucracy, the leaders of MAUKI convened a meeting to air their plans for Kaharingan's future. Invitations were extended to the counselor of the Palangka Raya's Hindu-Buddhist community, I Wayan Madu; to the head of Central Kalimantan's provincial branch of the Hindu Duty Council, Oka Swastika; to the secretary of the province; and to the national secretary to the director general of Hindu-Buddhist affairs. Speaking on behalf of MAUKI, Lewis proposed the official affiliation of Kaharingan with Hinduism. After some limited initial discussion, the issue was tabled until such time as a formal petition could be made to the Department of Religion in Jakarta. Attendees decided to submit the petition with as little publicity as possible in order to, as one of them told me in 1991, "protect regional security."

Lewis subsequently sent a letter to the minister of religion in which he asked for religious training for Central Kalimantan's Kaharingan population, to be offered through the auspices of the BIMAS Hindu-Buddha in Palangka Raya. It was thoroughly understood, of course, that an affirmative response was unlikely, given that Kaharingan was not "really" a religion. In 1980 Lewis went on to compose a second, more explicit letter, which he delivered in person. Together with Oka Swastika, Lewis flew to Bali. There he met with the national head of the Hindu Duty Council, Ida Bagus Oka Puniatmadja, as well as with Ida Bagus Mantra, then-governor of Bali. Afterward Lewis and Oka traveled to Jakarta, where they met with the director general of the Hindu-Buddhist congregation, Gde Pudja. Their letter, submitted on 1 January 1980, read in part:

> With complete awareness, without any outside pressure . . . a request is made to the Leaders of The Hindu Duty Council that . . .
>
> 1. The Supreme Council of Religious Scholars of Indonesian Kaharingan is permitted to affiliate/integrate with the Hindu Duty Council.
>
> 2. That Kaharingan religion is permitted to affiliate/integrate with Hinduism, and that the books/doctrine of Hinduism also become the doctrine of adherents of Kaharingan in addition to the books that already exist. (MBAUKI No. 5/KU-KP/ MB-AUKI/I/1980)

Jakarta's response arrived swiftly. In a letter dated 12 January, Willy Surya, writing on behalf of Gde Sandhi and I Wayan Surpha, second in command at the Hindu Duty Council, conveyed that in a meeting held on 9 January the council had decided to approve the integration of the Kaharingan and Hindu congregations "because the book/doctrines of Hindu dharma are also the doctrine of the Kaharingan congregation" (Dirjen BIMAS HB H II/10/1980). A copy of the letter was forwarded to the governor of Central Kalimantan, who subsequently notified the commanders of the local armed forces, police, and all subdistrict heads, that "AGAMA HINDU should hereafter be noted in the religion column on all identity cards and other official documents prepared on behalf of adherents of the traditional religion" (GUB KALTENG PEM/43/1/3).

On 30 March 1980 a ceremony was held at Palangka Raya's Balai Kaharingan, a large meeting hall erected in 1978 with funds from the local government, to mark the integration of Kaharingan and Hinduism. The national headquarters of the Department of Religion was represented by Willy Surya, with I Wayan Madu representing the provincial office. The director general of the Hindu Duty Council, Ida Bagus Oka Puniatmadja, attended, as did Gde Surpha and the head of the council's local office, Pak I. D. M. Gereh Putra. A priest from Bali, Pak Ida Pedanda Gde Putra, arrived to bless the observances. In his address, the director general emphasized that, given the discovery of ancient Hindu relics in Kutei in East Kalimantan, it was entirely possible that the adherents of Kaharingan were in fact the oldest followers of Hinduism in the archipelago. He pointed out as well similarities between ritual practices in Bali and in "Kaharinganism *[sic]*." He focused particularly on the format of mortuary celebrations, which he referred to by the Balinese term *ngaben* rather than the Ngaju word *tiwah*. Also on this occasion, twelve notables, including the governor of Bali (who was not present but sent a congratulatory telegram), were honored with commemorative citations as being "benefactors" of Hindu Kaharingan.[7]

The next day, 31 March, was the first full moon after the Hindu New Year celebration of *nyepi*. It was marked by a ritual purification of Palangka Raya's Hindu temple, Puri Pita Maha. The Hindu Kaharingan congregation was officially invited to attend. The holy water used in the ceremony was obtained from a local source, Tangkiling Hill, well known among adherents of Hindu Kaharingan for its supernatural properties.

Two weeks later, the leadership of MAUKI voted to rename their organization the Supreme Council of Hindu Kaharingan Religion (MBAHK) and informed the Department of Religion to that effect. In a letter of response, the minister congratulated the MBAHK leaders on their efforts to "raise themselves" from the status of "belief sect" yet warned that as the adherents of Kaharingan were now considered Hindu, MBAHK should in turn be absorbed into the Hindu Duty Council, the latter being the sole organization sanctioned to provide leadership to the Hindu congregations of Indonesia. The minister also emphasized that this integration should be handled as diplomatically as possible so as not to invite friction or discord that might in turn threaten national security interests (MA/203/1980). In response to the minister's request, members of MBAHK were inducted into the provincial-level office of the Hindu Duty Council on 8 June. One of the first actions of the newly restructured council was to issue an announcement that the only persons qualified to comment on the integration of the Hindu and Kaharingan congregations were members of the Hindu Duty Council or of MBAHK.

Hindu Kaharingan Religious Education

Religious education is a required part of the school curriculum in Indonesia from primary through secondary school. According to the curriculum approved in 1994, every student should receive two class hours of religious education a week. In the past, during hours of religious instruction, Kaharingan students were encouraged to attend lessons on other religious traditions, such as Christianity or Islam, or were simply excused from school. Although the consolidation of Kaharingan and Hinduism has made it appropriate for Kaharingan children to receive religious education alongside their Hindu counterparts, the problem remains of securing teachers and books. First, it has proven difficult to induce teachers from Bali to relocate to Central Kalimantan. Second, no curricular materials with Kaharingan content are currently available. The expansion of Hindu religious education in Central Kalimantan has therefore become a major focus of MBAHK's efforts.

In conjunction with efforts on the part of the provincial office of the Department of Religion, two advances have been made in this regard. On 15 August 1980, just months after the official recognition of Kaharingan, a private high school with a teacher's training program in religious studies for students pursuing a career in elementary education was established in Palangka Raya. This school, called the PGA Hindu Kaharingan Parentas, received much of its support from the Hindu organization Yayasan Dwijendra in Den Pasar, Bali. The school's first class graduated in 1983. By 1991 approximately 500 students had earned their degrees from PGA Parentas, and 182 students had already secured civil service positions as religious teachers.[8] In order to produce even more individuals qualified to provide primary and secondary religious education, MBAHK also founded a college, the Sekolah Tinggi Agama Hindu Kaharingan Tampung Penyang (STAHK), which opened its doors in 1986. The school currently offers two programs of study: teaching and religious education and philosophy. Many STAHK graduates have already secured civil service teaching appointments.

Following New Orders

Since the early 1970s, with the absorption of the SKDI into GOLKAR, the leadership of MBAHK has continued to ally itself with the government and has become increasingly outspoken in its support of the Suharto regime. MBAHK's 1981 coordinators' meeting is illustrative in this regard. The theme was "Coordinate the Full Potential and Raise the Spirituality of the Hindu Kaharingan Congregation in Order to Maintain P4 and Entrench Development," with the subtheme "Contribute to the Success of the New Order Government, and Keep the Leadership of the Government in the Hands of the New Order, with MBAHK as Partner to the Government."[9]

According to transcripts of speeches read on that occasion, the meeting was called, in part, to emphasize that MBAHK's goal in pursuing recognition for Kaharingan was not merely to change its status but also to provide the province's inhabitants with a vehicle to participate more fully in the election activities of 1982. Ironically, although the council had been established, in the words of its general chairman, with the support of "all the key personnel in Hindu Kaharingan *(basir) [sic]*," there were still those *basir* who did not recognize the council's authority or acknowledge that its leadership was "stabile" (stable). It was important, the chairman emphasized, to persuade the *basir* to recognize the council's legitimacy and primacy. As part of the meeting, the governor was invited to discuss the importance of persuading *basir* to encourage the Hindu Kaharingan faithful to support New Order programs. In his concluding remarks, Governor Gara warned that "it is only people without religion who refuse to support development," and "in the face of insufficient development, suffering surely ensues which makes it easier for new ideologies to enter." The general chairman followed up with the promise that this meeting would ensure that more people would ally themselves to the New Order in the 1982 election and closed with a comparison of the "many similarities between Hindu Kaharingan prayers and the Indonesian Constitution" (Undang-Undang Dasar). The head of the local police was invited to speak on the "communist threat," and the meeting adjourned soon after, closing with the Salam GOLKAR (GOLKAR chant).

Chairman Lewis's remarks on the importance of inducing all *basir* to recognize the authority of the Supreme Council suggest that the council has encountered resistance in its attempts to implement reforms. Indeed, I repeatedly met *basir* and lay practitioners who complained to me at length about council policies and priorities. Their complaints, and the form of their resistance, will be discussed shortly.

Spreading the Word

When Lewis, Simal Penyang, and Liber Sigai founded MAUKI in 1972, they considered the preparation of religious texts to be among their most pressing responsibilities. They sought to compile a written text of the creation story *(Buku Panaturan)*, a book on how to propitiate supernatural beings *(Buku Tawur)*, a Kaharingan hymnal *(Buku Kandayu)*, a prayer book *(Buku Do'a)*, a guide to performing marriages *(Buku Pemberkatan Perkawinan)*, a guide to performing funerals *(Buku Petunjuk Mangubur)*, a book of prayers appropriate for anointing celebrants in order to "cool their souls" on various supernaturally charged occasions *(Buku Kandayu Manyaki)*, a general volume on other types of religious ceremonies, and at least three Indonesian-language books explaining selected aspects of Kaharingan intended for the general public.[10] In 1973, the members of MAUKI produced the first widely circulated local-language volume pertaining to the form and content of Kaharingan religious worship. It was titled *Buku Ajar Agama Kaharingan* (Lesson Book of Kaharingan Religion). The *Lesson Book* was a landmark volume. It designated Kaharingan as a body of belief that must be taught, in contradistinction to *hadat,* which some people claim is "in the blood." The book was intended to efface personalistic understandings of cosmology. It presented a lengthy account of the creation myth *(panaturan)*. Its popularity attested to the growing acceptance of the religious bureaucracy and a corresponding devaluation of personal religious experience.[11]

The *Lesson Book* was revised by MBAHK in 1995 as *Talatah Basarah.* It continues to play a critical role in the teaching of Hindu Kaharingan doctrine. The primary forums of public religious instruction are Thursday evening worship services, instituted in 1981, which are held in towns and in many villages throughout Central Kalimantan. The services are known as *basarah,* which is usually translated into Indonesian as *meminta,* "to request." As noted in chapter 3, during the ritual interlude called *basarah* held at the conclusion of *tiwah,* ritual specialists travel from house to house collecting small offerings for later consecration to Mantir Mama Luhing, an important Upperworld being associated with life rituals. The offerings collected at these weekly *basarah,* however, are intended instead for Ranying Hatalla Langit, "Almighty God," and used to support the Hindu Kaharingan Youth Association. The council also claims that *basarah* is an acronym for three Ngaju phrases that, roughly translated, mean "enclosed in the commandments of Ranying Hatalla" *(basalupu auh* Ranying Hatalla), "protected by the love of Ranying Hatalla" *(basalungkem asin* Ranying Hatalla), and "based on the lessons of Ranying Hatalla" *(basalupu ajar* Ranying Hatalla).

Basarah provide opportunities for adherents to familiarize themselves with the contents of the creation story. Both the book and the weekly meetings have had a palpable impact in popularizing the belief that humans are accountable to a supreme being and that the supreme being is accessible to humans through prayer. In Palangka Raya *basarah* are usually led by students from the Hindu Kaharingan university in a public religious hall. *Basarah* are occasionally held in private homes. Wherever they are enacted, the format of *basarah* is similar.[12] They begin with passing of the *sangku tambak raja,* a brass bowl of offerings, including raw rice, areca nuts, cigarettes (tobacco), and a hornbill feather, over smoldering incense. The prayer that opens the *basarah* includes a recitation of the "five pillars of Hindu Kaharingan faith" *(lima sarahan).* These are *Ranying Hatalla katamparan* (God is the source of everything that exists); *langit katambuan* ([all men are] below the heavens with God above them); *petak tapajakan* ([God created the] Earth for men to live upon); *nyalung kepanduian* (water of life with which men can purify themselves); and *kalata padadukan* ([there is an] order to the universe). The recitation is followed with a hymn in praise of the *sangku tambak raja,* a reading from the creation story, another hymn, a sermon concerning the text, another hymn, a closing prayer, and a communion during which worshipers are sprinkled with coconut oil and perfume. A coin is dipped into raw egg and touched to participants' foreheads. Uncooked rice is strewn upon their heads.

Worship services emphasize the direct and private relationship of an individual worshiper with Ranying Hatalla Langit. They also familiarize the concept of appealing to the deity for forgiveness of transgressions rather than making restitution through ritual. To refer to transgressions, an Indonesian word, *dosa* or "sin," is used rather than the Ngaju word *pali.* An Indonesian-language report on the meaning of *tiwah,* prepared for general circulation by Chairman Lewis, is illustrative in this regard. On the subject of why *tiwah* are performed, Lewis writes: "*Tiwah* is carried out to erase or liberate *pali* from the individuals/family/village that perform it. In addition, the man or woman who has died is freed from all the *dosa* the person has committed during life." Adherents sometimes remarked to me "off the record" that, not long ago, their religion did not include a notion of sin.

The Indonesian language is also used at *basarah* to explicate the characteristics of nonhuman entities that figure in Hindu Kaharingan. Thus, although services are conducted largely in Ngaju, words used to refer to supernatural beings are borrowed from the national language (or from Sanskrit or Arabic). The supernatural is presented as a bureaucracy headed by Tuhan Yang Maha Esa, or "Almighty God." "God" is also often compared to the "president" *(presiden)*. Upperworld beings who play important roles in the processing of souls and in life rituals are referred to as *nabi* (prophets) or *malaikat* (angels). *Sangiang* are also often compared to the *anggota* DPR (national parliament members), each with an appointed post. Suggestions of parallels between the organization of a heavenly cabinet and Indonesia's administrative elite lead one to wonder whether Kaharingan heaven is indeed like a bureaucracy or whether, at least for reformers, a bureaucracy is like heaven.

During sermons, which occasionally focus explicitly on the celebration of religious rituals, adherents of Hindu Kaharingan are urged toward parsimony in fulfilling their obligations. As one council member said, "It is no longer necessary to perform costly sacrifices. We live in an era of small sacrifices. It is enough to place a coin in a *sangku tambak raja* and let the *sangiang* attend to the rest. Hindu Kaharingan need not be an expensive religion."

Worship services are held in specially constructed halls (balai Hindu Kaharingan), which the council hopes will eventually replace the home as the setting for many types of ritual performance. *Basarah* are therefore the first Kaharingan religious meetings focused entirely outside the family. Participants are related not necessarily by kinship but rather by their desire to be part of an established religious community, a congregation, with activities focused on a "church." Not surprisingly, secret personal sources of power that are said to provide protection from the Unclean Ones and other dangers are repudiated or relegated to an earlier phase of the religion's development. In this regard, one council spokesperson remarked that such arcane knowledge leads to unrest and has outgrown its usefulness now that the Ngaju recognize a common identity. Yet efforts to revise the version of the origin myth published in 1983 were attributed by some adherents to the need to restrict access to the potential sources of power contained therein. The complete names of various supernatural beings, for example, could be catastrophic if misused.

Organizers of *basarah* claim that the meetings are vehicles for regional development. Many adherents, particularly young people, attend regularly. They enjoy the opportunity to engage in structured worship, like their Christian and Islamic counterparts. They value the "answers" about how to live within the tenets of their religion that they claim sermons provide. In fact, the desire for answers is the factor that numbers of young people claim persuaded them to convert to other religions and abandon their Kaharingan faith. For many, answers have become synonymous with books. The fact that mythologies, confessions of faith, and hymns are published in vernacular rather than ritual languages and sometimes even in Indonesian, signal that the council intends some degree of religious understanding to become accessible to all adherents, not merely the learned *basir,* and that they hope to disseminate this knowledge quickly.

The enthusiasm of Palangka Raya's young people notwithstanding, critics of the direction in which Hindu Kaharingan is moving are still to be found. Many villagers and some ritual specialists express concern that Kaharingan has become etiolated in the reform process. Trends toward parsimony within the context of ritual, such as minimizing sacrifice and shortening the length of celebrations, are condemned as risking the supernatural displeasure of the *pali* and as not taking ritual obligations seriously. There appears to be particular concern over consequences of the parsimonious performance of death ritual.

Ritual Standardization and Mortuary Practice

Many of MBAHK's publications focus on the mechanics of ritual, including weddings, name-giving ceremonies, and funerals. In 1982 guidelines for rituals of primary interment, the *Burial Book (Buku Mangubur),* were distributed in a number of Kahayan villages. It is widely recognized that the guidelines prescribing innovations in ritual formulas presented therein echo local Christian practice. In the past, for example, villagers claimed that no prayers accompanied primary interment. Yet the *Burial Book* counsels mourners to perform a graveside prayer that beseeches Ranying Hatalla Langit to pity the soul of the deceased and receive it into immortality. Little mention is made of secondary treatment or the fate of the other parts of the soul. The intimation is that the deceased's acceptance into the Upperworld is contingent on whether he or she has sinned, not whether *tiwah* is later performed on his or her behalf. In short, the prayer emphasizes the notion of individual salvation. In light of this new possibility for divine clemency, many younger participants evince little concern that they will be targeted for supernatural punishment as a result of transgressions occurring within the context of ritual. The importance of large numbers of kin providing sacrifices and observing ritual proscriptions to ensure the deceased's comfort in the afterlife is likewise diminished. Nevertheless, some remain hesitant to consult the Burial Book. The start of funerals is often delayed while bereaved kin search for someone willing to read the prayers. Indeed, I have seen quite literate persons with excellent vision claiming to have "misplaced their eyeglasses" when a neighbor attempts to pass the book into their hands.

Efforts to standardize *tiwah* are also under way. Control over the performance of *tiwah* is made possible by the necessity for participants to acquire the council's permission to sponsor the celebration before the local police agree to issue the now obligatory *surat ijin keramaian,* or "festivities permit." As part of their application, sponsors are required to prepare a timetable detailing ritual activity planned for each day, often to the hour. The council then makes suggestions for modification of the proposed format and provides participants with a list of foods proscribed for the duration of the celebration. Sponsors are asked to sign a document promising that behavior that does not conform to the Indonesian national character will not be tolerated at *tiwah.*[13] Finally, the council may also recommend particular specialists, with the result that *basir* already retained may be dismissed.

It is clear that rationalization has put in question the roles of both sponsors and specialists. For example, with the reform of Hindu Kaharingan has come a notion that not all adherents are equally "religious." Yet the grounds for developing a Hindu Kaharingan religious hierarchy remain vague. Specialists, for example, are not identifiably "religious figures" in the same sense as are leaders in other traditions. One Christian was quick to emphasize this distinction: "A *basir* is only a *basir* when he is performing *balian.* He cannot talk to you about religion. He cannot answer questions about God." The council is acutely sensitive to this criticism. It has introduced a three-month course on "how to participate in *balian*" into the Hindu Kaharingan University's curriculum. It is hoped that in the near future all *basir* will be university graduates and hold a certificate that qualifies them to be "traditional priests."

By assuming indirect control over the selection of specialists, obliging participants to script their performances of the death ritual, and issuing lists of proscriptions, the council has introduced new concepts of acceptability, accountability, and authority into ritual spheres. The council's directives may be inconsistent with local practice, for the council, composed primarily of nonspecialists from large towns, is often unfamiliar with the nuances of local tradition. According to one council spokesperson, the aim of *tiwah,* regardless of its form, is simply to return to God. Thus, the council chooses to remain unaware of local meanings that inform ritual practices.

Participants, however, feeling that they must privilege official directives in order to hold *tiwah* and discharge the responsibilities imposed by bereavement, blame mishaps and tragedies associated with misperformance on the council. At one *tiwah* in which the specialists originally engaged were replaced, the new head specialist delayed the start of sacrifice for one day beyond the customary practice in that region. During the night, two of the water buffaloes destined for sacrifice died from inexplicable causes while tethered to their poles. Their untimely demise decreased the soul's largesse and threw sponsors into a panic. On another occasion, the festooned bamboo pole that informs inhabitants of the supernatural world that *tiwah* is in progress was placed at the river's edge in the manner of primary interment by a council-recommended *basir* rather than at the sponsor's doorway as is usual at *tiwah.* On the day of the sacrifice, one sponsor died. Having deduced the cause of death, a local specialist moved the pole to the side of the house. At another Kahayan *tiwah,* the illness of several sponsors was attributed to their having eaten a type of monkey meat said to be traditionally proscribed during death ritual. Because the council had failed to note it on a list of foods and activities that were prohibited for the duration of the celebration posted next to the head sponsor's house, the participants claimed that they had thought it was safe to partake of the food.

Despite situations such as these—word of which may or may not reach the council—in the council's view, only *tiwah* performed entirely under its supervision is truly correct. A *basir* associated with a subdistrict branch of the council once called me away from a ritual in order to examine what he referred to as the only "correct" *sandung* in the village. He solicited me to photograph him standing alongside the *sandung* and then requested that I deliver the photograph to the council when I returned downriver. The sole characteristic that distinguished this *sandung* from the many others I had photographed was that on this one, Hindu swastikas had been painted squarely above the repository's door.

From the preceding remarks, anecdotes, and observations, it is clear that many adherents of Hindu Kaharingan today share a common concern. Although the council standardizes ritual, the brunt of supernatural reprisal for modifications in its format still apparently falls on them. To some adherents, therefore, ritual standardization is unacceptable. Some of the sharpest critics of rationalization complained to me that Kaharingan is now *kekeringan* (all dried up), a play on the phrase *air Kaharingan,* usually translated as "water of life." Some specialists unaligned with the council do not recognize the legitimacy of standardization. They demonstrate their disapproval by refusing to attend rituals or other activities such as *basarah* with "official" overtones. In one case, a traditionalist *basir* told me he was unable to conduct a *basarah* in his village per the council's request because he had misplaced the key to the village's Hindu Kaharingan meeting hall some time ago. I noticed, as I walked by the hall, that the window of the building had never been secured. Even a very large person could easily pass through it. Some adherents consider it only a matter of time before the council members themselves will be "eaten by their own *pali.*" Rumors of illness or of personal tragedies that befall members are taken as evidence of supernatural retribution.

Ritual Change in Central Kalimantan

In implementing programs of religious education, codification of belief, and standardization of ritual, the council claims to avoid privileging the ritual practices of any specific area, thereby contributing to regional integration. As one council member described it to me, differences in death rituals can be compared to the differences between taking the flights that various airlines operate from Palangka Raya to Jakarta. One airline may be more comfortable than another. One flight may take longer than another. One ticket may cost more than another. Ultimately, however, all the planes end up on the same landing strip. So, too, all of the Hindu Kaharingan dead eventually find themselves in the Prosperous Village. And yet local responses to ritual standardization suggest that differences in ritual practice and the bearing that these differences have on broader issues of identity may not be so glibly dismissed.

As I argued in chapter 4, for example, plasticity in the construction of death ritual belies a sense of religiosity that is strongly rooted in details of practice. Overall similarities in ritual forms can mask minute yet meaningful differences. These variations may reveal themselves to be structural permutations with important implications for the content of the ritual. During Kahayan *tiwah*, for example, the practice of placing the bones of the dead in repositories with the remains of their cognatic kin points to a desire to reunite the extended family in the Upperworld. On the Katingan River, however, I observed a preponderance of small repositories and few of the massive structures that are so characteristic of Kahayan peoples. Many other examples of seemingly insignificant variations in practice could be cited. Among practitioners of Kaharingan, however, such differences are important. Even minor variations in ritual have, at the very least, traditionally served as boundary markers between peoples on different rivers of the region (Miles 1976, 77–78). Kahayan villagers sometimes recounted invidious comparisons between their own death rituals and those of neighbors, suggesting that the latter's rituals were incorrect. They hinted darkly at the sponsors' supposedly inhuman attributes and conjured images of *hantuen*. Today, ritual hybridization is often blamed on the council. It is said to be symptomatic of its privileging of "other people's religion." Local *basir* are sometimes surreptitiously asked to identify the "foreign" elements of ritual and to excise them in hope of averting disaster.

Concern with identifying distinctive regional traditions parallels a situation now emerging between Christians and adherents of Hindu Kaharingan that became apparent to me on my very first opportunity to observe *tiwah*. My host, a Christian, explained that he was serving as head sponsor of *tiwah* on his Hindu Kaharingan father's behalf. He situated the occasion in a tradition stretching far back in time. "*Tiwah* is our *hadat*. This *tiwah* is no different than those performed by my ancestors. My children and grandchildren know who they are because they have participated in *tiwah*. They feel proud that they were born on the Kahayan River." I took his remarks to mean that his family would confirm their personal and collective identities through participation in this compelling celebration. As he continued his explanation, however, I realized that there were additional dimensions of ritual performance to be explored:

> This will be the final *tiwah* held in my village. The only Hindu Kaharingan present are ritual specialists and members of the Supreme Council of the Hindu Kaharingan Religion. I personally don't believe that my father's soul needs this *tiwah* in order to ascend to heaven. To me this is custom, not religion. Participating in *tiwah* is merely a way of expressing pride in our traditional way of life. *Tiwah* is a part of Ngaju culture. The council planned this celebration and advised me how to carry it out. I requested their assistance because I am a law-abiding Indonesian citizen.

That conversation helped me to recognize the configuration of issues facing participants in *tiwah*. Three elements in my host's declaration became avenues for further investigation. How does it happen that Christians often serve as head sponsors of secondary mortuary rituals? How do villagers conceptualize the relationship between tradition and religious practice? And on what grounds had the responsibility for planning *tiwah*, traditionally the privilege of sponsors and ritual specialists, been relegated to an administrative council?

Christian Participation in Secondary Mortuary Ritual

Christian participation in secondary mortuary celebrations is a widespread, though reportedly recent, phenomenon. In the past, missionaries discouraged converts to Christianity from taking part in *tiwah*. Villagers, in response, either repudiated traditional rituals or delayed conversion until after they had performed *tiwah* for their parents.

Today the majority of Kahayan villagers are nominal Christians. As conversion was formerly contingent on abjuring traditional ritual practices, particularly the obligation to *tiwah,* it is necessary to seek an explanation for Christian villagers' current enthusiasm for secondary mortuary ritual. Two explanations for Christian participation in *tiwah* since the departure of most of the missionaries from Central Kalimantan seem compelling. The first is the continued importance of secondary treatment as a model of and for reality, illustrated by the development of a uniquely Christian mode of secondary mortuary celebration. The second is the potential for secondary mortuary ritual to serve as an emblem of Ngaju culture.

Unlike children of adherents of Hindu Kaharingan, the children of Christians are not obligated to perform secondary mortuary rituals for their deceased parents. Primary interment occurs within a few days of death; and on the fifth or seventh evening thereafter, the congregation gathers at the deceased's home to offer prayers for the soul. Lately, however, a subsequent celebration, highly reminiscent of *tiwah,* has gained popularity. The ritual, usually performed several years after death, is called "raising a cross" *(mampendeng sampalaki).* On this occasion, survivors gather in the cemetery to clean and cement the grave. The slab is often decorated with stones or inlaid with expensive tiles. After the cross is emplaced, the grave is roofed and fenced and the headstone sprayed with perfume. As in the performance of other indigenous rituals, pungent woods are burned throughout the celebration. A feast follows in the head sponsor's home.

Christians claim that until they have cemented their parents' graves, they feel indebted. They emphasize that cementing a grave is a duty God intended when he commanded us to honor our parents. Christians stress that it is not a prerequisite for the soul's ascent to heaven yet maintain the belief that the dead can observe the living cementing their graves. Parents, they say, feel content when they look down from heaven and see their children and grandchildren attending to their final resting place.

Hindu Kaharingan villagers describe cementing graves as "Christian *tiwah.*" Their close identification of the two celebrations was evident at a *tiwah* held for the mother of a renowned ritual specialist. The specialist, head sponsor of the *tiwah,* had also lost a son about a year earlier who had converted to Christianity before his death. The specialist decided that it would be appropriate to raise a cross on his son's grave during the secondary mortuary ritual held on his mother's behalf.

The sponsor himself planned to assume the role of head specialist at the *tiwah.* Yet it was necessary to obtain the services of a Christian to lead the prayers over his son's grave. Beginning with the elder of the village's Christian congregation, he went from person to person trying to find someone who would agree to perform the prayers. Those whom he asked refused, claiming that they were confused as to whether it was proper to carry out two different observances, one Christian, one indigenous, simultaneously. Frustrated by his lack of success, he announced that he was simply going to exhume his son's remains and put them in the bone repository along with those of the boy's grandmother. Soon afterward, word reached him that a cleric from a large village several hours away had offered to recite the prayers. The churchman later explained to me: "We have realized that it is not wrong to be associated with *tiwah.* It is just Kahayan *hadat* to show respect for the dead in this way." Since that event, other Christian graves have been cemented during *tiwah.* On one occasion, I observed sponsors placing a handful of earth inside the repository, although the deceased's remains were buried nearby. It was probably significant that in this case the deceased was the only non-Christian in the family and that Christians do not exhume their dead.

It seems telling that although Christians are unfailingly invited to participate in *tiwah,* adherents of Hindu Kaharingan are seldom asked to contribute to raising a cross. The notion of *tiwah* as Kahayan custom rather than Hindu Kaharingan religious ritual suggests a second reason why Christian participation in *tiwah* has increased: the emerging sense of *tiwah* as a cultural performance, a readily recognizable emblem of Ngaju tradition. It is this latter theme to which I now turn.

6 | Religions and Identities

Writing of the Sipirok Batak peoples of Sumatra, Susan Rodgers Siregar suggested that without losing their local culture *(adat),* the Sipirok Batak had managed to absorb the influence of two pan-ethnic religions, Islam and Christianity. In assimilating these belief systems, the Sipirok hybridized their symbolic complexes until they "worked." By way of illustration, she directed attention to the case of Batak students who, upon returning from universities where they had completed degrees in law or engineering, paid tribute to their ancestors in a traditional manner, then concluded their celebrations by offering up Islamic prayers (1981, 2).

The data presented in this book also include examples of assimilation among the Ngaju. In chapter 5 I cited an instance of a Christian who, in organizing a *tiwah* on behalf of his deceased Kaharingan father, had relegated responsibility for supervising the rituals to representatives of the Supreme Council. By so doing he claimed to demonstrate that he was a law-abiding citizen. For this sponsor, however, more than religion was clearly at stake. He had assimilated, as well, a political ideology; that is, he felt that this *tiwah* made a statement not only about his religious beliefs vis-à-vis his father's but also about his political identity as a citizen of the modern Indonesian state.

Indeed, religion often figures importantly among the "gross actualities" within which "peoples' sense of self remains bound up" and with which the state must come to terms (Geertz 1973c, 258). Nevertheless, religious, ethnic, and nationalist dimensions of identity are not always easily reconciled. Some citizens of new states are confronted with new dilemmas. Amid their search for their own identity and in the course of promoting their own goals, they recognize the potential of the state to serve as an instrument for realizing larger, collective aims (259). As Richard Handler points out, "However individual members of the nation may differ, they share essential attributes that constitute their national identity; sameness overrides difference" (1988, 6).

In this regard, several recent studies of Southeast Asian societies have focused on either how "the faithful" reconcile their religious, ethnic, and national loyalties in an age of growing secularization (Russell and Cunningham 1989) or, alternatively, how these compromises complement or undermine official state religious policies (Kessler 1980; Nagata 1978). As to the latter, it has been suggested that whether the state is viewed as an ally or as an adversary depends, to a large extent, on religious factors (Ackerman and Lee 1988, 1–9). In some cases, as states have modernized, religion appears to have become more significant by offering adherents a vision of authority other than that advanced by the state (Keyes et al. 1994, 1–2).

Modernization, then, does not necessarily lead to disenchantment. Confrontations with state demands in the religious sphere may also evoke a period of religious dynamism. That this dynamism itself may have important consequences for the construction and reformulation of identity has become exceedingly clear in Central Kalimantan, where religion figures prominently, and problematically, in a burgeoning sense of cultural awareness. The Ngaju case is especially intriguing as, despite the importance of the traditional religion in the formulation of identity, only a minority of Ngaju-speaking peoples actually claim to adhere to it.[1]

Religion and Tribal Identity

The most sustained of the early discussions of Ngaju-speaking peoples focuses on the articulation of religious belief with tribal organization. When I began fieldwork, my expectations concerning how this belief system contributed to the maintenance of tribal identity were shaped largely by Schärer's *Ngaju Religion*, originally published some forty years earlier. Schärer portrayed Ngaju "traditional" religion as the major unifying force among the peoples of southern Borneo. He argued that Ngaju religious beliefs, particularly those pertaining to the supreme deity, Ranying Hatalla Langit–Jata Balawang Bulau, constituted a conceptual model that shaped most aspects of primordial Ngaju society. Schärer proposed that the deity's twin aspects, male and female, were lent discernible form by the organization of the Ngaju tribe into moieties. Relations between moieties were tempered through the performance of rituals that affected the final processing of the dead: "When the Watersnake [Jata Balawang Bulau] emerges and Mahatala [Ranying Hatalla Langit] leans down to conduct the sacred service *[tiwah]*, the total community prepares to take part in the sacred ceremonies and to celebrate in common" (1963, 137). He continued:

"The words 'total community' here require some explanation. We may take it for granted that the whole tribe formerly gathered for the great religious/cosmic ceremonies—or, more probably, that it took part in the persons of its most important representatives" (137–38). To explain variances in custom, Schärer proposed that the Ngaju tribe and its religion were disintegrating:

> It can no longer be said that the Ngaju Dayak are amalgamated into a coherent tribal organisation, but they still form a linguistically and culturally homogenous unity. The organisation has long since broken down, and when this process of disintegration began is beyond our knowledge. But there are nevertheless clues to be found. In this society there are differentiated groups, socially distinguished from each other, which are developing into classes, though it is too early to speak of a class-organisation. (39)

The richness of Schärer's accounts notwithstanding, my own observations led me to treat his notions of the Ngaju tribe with reserve. For example, questions I posed to ascertain the extent of Kaharingan's role in confederating local peoples yielded remarkably disparate reactions. Whereas some respondents insisted "that to be Ngaju" was to embrace the old religion, others took a different stance and decried the backwardness of the ancestral rituals, declaring them unworthy of the name "religion." Still others applauded what they considered the positive changes Kaharingan was undergoing as it "modernized," although they often disagreed about precisely what form these changes should take. Their arguments did not necessarily break down along "traditionalist" versus "reformist" lines.

As my research progressed and my proficiency in the local language increased, I also collected myths and legends, including the story of Angkes and Tahuman and chilling accounts of *hantuen,* that seemed to suggest there was little about Kaharingan belief, at least in terms of its popular doctrine, that could easily foster a broad-based sense of community. In fact, it seemed rather to militate against the development of suprafamilial bonds. For many adherents of Kaharingan, the notion of belonging to any community—beyond one defined on the basis of kin relations—was highly controversial. Most chose to be identified by reference to the particular river on which they lived or to an even more delimited geographic locale: "Yes, I'm Ngaju, but I'm really a person of Bara Dia [region]." I was reminded of Douglas Miles's assertion that "the . . . Ngaju have never looked upon themselves as a cultural sub-group" (1976, 75). Indeed, I was struck by the sheer numbers of people who openly expressed their aversion to the appellation "Ngaju," for in the local language, *ngaju* means "upriver" and carries associations of arrant ignorance and lack of sophistication. This signification is underscored by many stories, perhaps largely apocryphal, about the travails of unfortunate upriver rubes. In a typical one, a *ngaju* fellow, on his first visit to Palangka Raya, discovers ice in the fruit drink sold to him by a roadside vendor. Delighted with this find, he pours the beverage out and slips the cubes into his pocket in anticipation of sharing them when he returns upriver the next week. "Hai! *Uluh ngaju!*" (an upriver person), listeners guffaw.

Ngaju Cultural Iconology

Yet, although the name "Ngaju" has been slow to gain currency in some quarters, in others it has not. Its growing popularity is particularly apparent in Palangka Raya, where many locals, regardless of religious affiliation, openly express pride in the customs of their forebears and favor publicization of "Ngaju" traditions. For example, in 1991 friends were pleased to invite me to visit the spacious "model longhouse" built in downtown Palangka Raya five years earlier. Replete with its own shrine for a village guardian and a variety of stylized sacrificial posts, the longhouse is a conference facility and venue for entertainments for visiting dignitaries. On that trip, too, the staff of the provincial museum escorted me to the newly renovated exhibit on "Ngaju *tiwah*" that will remain a key display in its permanent collection. I also met with several local university faculty who claimed that their expertise lies in "Ngajuology." Finally, I went to see a clock that tells more than the time. Built with funds from the governor's office, Palangka Raya's town clock is located close to the main harbor, where it can easily be seen by travelers who wander ashore to stretch their legs or by townspeople on their way to market. It was built in the style of a *pantar guci,* the large post usually decorated with a Chinese porcelain jar (although this one happened to be made of cement) formerly erected at the *tiwah* of some prominent individuals. Alongside the *pantar guci* stands a *sapundu.* Atop this post, where the representation of a servant for the deceased would normally be featured, is an electric lamp. A bone repository of a local hero stands nearby, as does a bronze statue of a Ngaju family attired in "traditional" garb.

The prominence now accorded to representations of indigenous traditions is important. As Handler suggests, the objectification of culture entails "seeing culture as a thing: a natural object made up of objects and entities ('traits')" (1988, 14). Once "objectified," culture can be managed, regulated, and to some degree controlled. The Ngaju case is thus in some ways reminiscent of the situation faced by the Toraja of Sulawesi, another Indonesian minority with a tradition of elaborate mortuary rites. Toby Volkman (1984) has suggested that, among the Toraja, there is a growing tendency to reify Toraja culture as ritual. Ngaju cultural identity, too, is grounded in and expressed through reference to ritual. Emergence of this sense of Ngaju culture as ritual can be traced, I would suggest, to emerging structural conditions that have enhanced some existing bonds, encouraged the rise of others, and submerged certain long-standing animosities and prejudices. Indonesian politics continues to contribute to its genesis.

Isen Mulung—"Never Retreat"

In Central Kalimantan today, local leaders cry out for "strength through unity" *(penyang hinje simpei)* for Central Kalimantan's peoples. Sensitive to their position vis-à-vis many hundreds of culture groups in Indonesia, some local citizens have come to defend vociferously a "traditional" way of life they quite rightly believe has been subject to contumely and derision. They demand, too, that the pace of "development" quicken in their long-neglected province. Concerning the quality of life in the region, the important national daily, *Kompas,* reported, for example, that "in 1991 the average expenditures of a village household in Central Kalimantan was 152,023 rupiah monthly [approximately $72]. Ninety-five percent of households have an income below the minimum physical requirement of 182,960 rupiah (for a laborer with a wife and two children). Of 82 subdistricts in 5 regencies and 1 municipality, there are 41 subdistricts that fall in the category of backward, critical, and minus" *(Kompas,* 23 October 1992). *Suara Pembaruan,* another newspaper, noted even more recently that despite the allocation of World Bank monies for road improvements between Palangka Raya and Pulang Pisau, a small town hard by the entrance to the canal connecting the Kahayan and Kapuas rivers, no progress had been made. Although the contract was to expire in September 1995, the project had not even commenced because the road path remained under water *(Suara Pembaruan,* 20 March 1995). Four months later, *Suara Pembaruan* ran another article on Central Kalimantan that remarked, "If there is a provincial capital in this country that doesn't have a People's Entertainment Park *[taman hiburan rakyat],* it's Palangka Raya" *(Suara Pembaruan,* 10 July 1995). The column bewailed the provincial capital's Saturday night scene, or rather its lack of one. It described a bored populace milling aimlessly around a large traffic circle.

Local citizens' appeals to the national government to speed up the region's "development" have, on at least two occasions, spawned public demonstrations and sporadic violence. These periods of marked unrest took place forty years apart. The first occurred throughout most of the 1950s. At that time, tens of thousands of Dayaks mobilized to lay claim to provincial autonomy. Despite the central government's initial resistance, it eventually acceded to their demand. The second period of unrest was more recent, commencing during the final months of 1993 and continuing through the first half of 1994. The proximate cause was dissatisfaction with Jakarta's appointment of yet another non-Dayak governor. Thousands of citizens took to the streets. They marched on the headquarters of the Provincial Assembly in Palangka Raya, and they milled around the large traffic circle for reasons other than boredom. This time, however, their demands were disregarded.

Concerning the 1950s struggle for provincial autonomy, according to the terms of the Linggadjati Agreement, the former Dutch Borneo was to be divided into several administrative units, one of which was the "Great Dayak." Its area was roughly coterminous with the region where most Ngaju-speaking peoples live. Although the Great Dayak survived the territorial reorganization that accompanied the 1949 Round Table Conference held at The Hague, federalism soon disintegrated (Miles 1976, 112–14). In 1950 the Great Dayak, like West, East, and Southeast Borneo and Banjar, was absorbed into a single administrative unit known as Kalimantan. The province's capital was Banjarmasin, the strongly Islamic city in the southeast.

Inhabitants of the former Great Dayak soon began to demand greater government representation. To this end, several new political parties were founded. Most active among them was the Sarikat Kaharingan Dayak Indonesia (SKDI), or Union of Kaharingan Dayaks of Indonesia. It was formed in July 1950 by Sahari Andung, son of a farmer from Tewah Pajangan, Kahayan. Various underground movements also took shape at this time. The latter included the Gerakan Pembela Keadilan or Movement To Defend Justice; the Pasukan Sumpit Kanyawung, or Kanyawung Blowpipe Forces; and, most notorious of all, the Gerakan Mandau Talawang Pancasila (GMTPS), or Movement of the Cutlass and Shield pro Pancasila, founded in 1952. GMTPS maintained three sectors: a Barito sector, headed by Charles Simbar, a Kotawaringan sector, led by William Embang, and a Kahayan-Kapuas sector, allegedly under the leadership of Sahari Andung himself.[2] GMTPS's rank and file included Muslims, Christians, and Buddhists, as well as adherents of Kaharingan. By all accounts, it was vast. At the height of its activity, GMTPS was estimated to have a membership of more than 42,000 members, or about 10 percent of Ngaju-speaking Dayaks. GMTPS exerted pressure through indirect threats and occasional terrorist acts. Its first major action took place in 1953 in Buntok, on the Barito River, when the rebels attacked a government post. That incident claimed the lives of several members of the government forces.

As a registered political party, SKDI operated openly and directly. At its third conference, held in July 1953 in Bahu Palawa, Kahayan, SKDI passed a motion demanding that a "Province of Central Kalimantan" be established prior to the 1955 elections. The Jakarta government denied that petition, ostensibly on the grounds that the regional economy was too weak and the local intelligentsia too few. SKDI members responded, to the contrary, that the strong economy of Banjarmasin was based on the exploitation of interior forests. A Dayak province could indeed support itself, and well. In 1955 a Central Kalimantan Peoples' Congress (Dewan Rakyat/Kongres Rakyat Kalimantan Tengah), headed by

Mahir Mahar, also formed to pursue the issue of regional autonomy. It quickly released a document, "Statement of the Wishes of Central Kalimantan Peoples," that stated:

> Awarding the status of Province of Central Kalimantan will increase opportunities for, along with the faith and trust of, a group that suffers much in Central Kalimantan; it would provide proof that their fate is given more attention than [it was] during the colonial period, in accordance with the wishes of our country and national government; and [demonstrate] that [Dayak peoples'] fate will be given as much attention as their backwardness warrants.

The committee members awaited Jakarta's reaction.

The central government's response again proved disheartening. In 1956 it decreed that Kalimantan would be divided into three provinces: West, South, and East. It mentioned the possibility that a fourth province might be established at the end of three years. The decision was deemed entirely unacceptable by Dayak leaders. After a November meeting in Tangkahen, on the Kahayan River, GMTPS commenced a series of armed raids and demonstrations in Dayu, Tangkahen, Tumbang Samba, Kasongan, Masaran, and elsewhere. One of the most celebrated took place at the Kahayan village of Panhandut (now Palangka Raya), in which two civil servants and one GMTPS rebel died. While these disturbances were occurring upriver, the Peoples' Committee held a plenary session in Banjarmasin from 2 to 5 December 1956. On 5 December, it approved the following motion: "[We] urge the Government of the Republic of Indonesia that in the shortest time possible, that is, before the upcoming regional parliamentary elections, Central Kalimantan be established as an autonomous province." Congress representatives presented their demands to Kalimantan's then-governor, R. T. A. Milono. In an interview conducted in 1995, Sahari Andung described that meeting to me:

> I told Milono, if this petition fails, we will all carry out a simultaneous action. Everyone, everywhere, we will just strike out. The way it turns out, yes, well, we'll see. I am very moved by emotion, and full of regret if Central Kalimantan isn't established immediately. This situation is very difficult. The people will not possibly remain still. Not possibly, not possibly. I asked [Milono], Is it the intention of the government of Indonesia that all Dayak peoples be wiped out? If that's the case, let the government decide. For us, it's better to die in an underground movement than to live our lives as powerless as corpses. Yes, things are getting desperate. And we're not backing down.

Milono indicated to the delegates that he would pass along their petition to President Soekarno, and that they could expect some word by 1 January. Sahari Andung, in turn, wrote to Simbar requesting that the GMTPS not initiate any further actions pending the results of Milono's meeting with Soekarno. On 23 December Sahari Andung was arrested in Banjarmasin and charged with leading the GMTPS revolt. Although he denied the charges of subversion, he later recalled: "At that time I explained that our plan was not to establish a country within a country. We understood the government's position. But we insisted, if Central Kalimantan isn't awarded [provincial autonomy], beginning right now, we will attack and destroy with all the strength we possess. Until we're all dead, *isen mulung,* we will never retreat."[3]

One week later, while still in custody, Sahari Andung learned of the president's New Year's Day announcement that Central Kalimantan would be granted provincial status. The GMTPS officially surrendered on 5 March in Madara, a remote village on a Barito River tributary in the vicinity of Buntok. At its disbandment, the group was renamed the Ranks of Youth for the Development of Central Kalimantan. Small commemorations marked the cessation of hostilities between government forces and the GMTPS. One was held in Tehang, near Sampit, on 11 May, another in Pahandut on 18 May, and a third in Dayu Barito on 23 May. Upon his release from custody, Sahari Andung was appointed head of the Committee to Relocate the Victims of Regional Unrest. That committee was charged with resettling former GMTPS guerrillas, hundreds of whom had been living in the jungle for years.

On 23 May 1957 the province of Central Kalimantan was officially established. Tjilik Riwut, war hero and Ngaju Dayak, was appointed its first governor just over a month later and served in that capacity until 1966. The two governors who succeeded him were also Dayaks. In 1983 Central Kalimantan's first non-Dayak governor was installed. He was followed by two more. By 1993 the local citizenry was eager to see a "putra daerah Kalteng" (son of Central Kalimantan region,) appointed to their province's highest office again. Jakarta, apparently, was not.

"Let Us Follow in the Footsteps of the Late Tjilik Riwut"

> In *Surya Karya*'s interviews last week with several regional leaders, they conveyed they would like to see a *putra daerah* be given the opportunity to serve as governor. One reason to hope for a *putra daerah* as governor is that a *putra daerah* will have a greater understanding of the area and be more committed to it.
>
> —*Suara Karya,* 13 August 1993

On 20 July 1993 Central Kalimantan's then-governor, Soeparmanto, tendered his resignation after four and a half years of service. Speculation was rife concerning who would be designated to replace him when he officially stepped down in January 1994. In speaking with the national press, local leaders insisted that the selection of a governor must be made *sesuai aspirasi rakyat* (in accordance with the people's wishes). "Kita tidak mau drop-dropan" (We don't want someone dropped on us), one commented (*Suara Karya,* 15 September 1993).

This sentiment was echoed by another who said, "Social organizations and youth groups in Central Kalimantan strongly reject the 'depositing' of an [outsider] candidate" (*Suara Karya,* 10 November 1993), and "although it's still a rumor [that an outsider might be picked for the post], it's enough to upset the people of Central Kalimantan. If the individual that the center is plotting to install actually takes charge of Central Kalimantan, it will be a setback, because up to now we've always been led by a son of Indonesia born in Central Kalimantan" (*Media Indonesia,* 23 October 1993). It was also acknowledged that the GOLKAR members of the DPRD, the provincial branch of the People's Constitutive Assembly, wanted a *putra daerah* to assume the next five-year term.

By the end of the two-month registration period for gubernatorial candidates, twenty-four organizations in Central Kalimantan had submitted fourteen names for the DPRD's consideration. Nearly all were Dayaks. Following the DPRD's initial vote, the names of five candidates were passed to Minister of the Interior, Yogie, for review. The list included two subdistrict officers, two assistant district secretaries, and the assistant head of the GOLKAR development faction. When the list came back from Jakarta, however, one of the local candidates had been replaced. The top five contenders for the post now included Karna Suwanda, the deputy governor of West Java. It was widely noted that the interior minister himself was a West Javanese *(Orang Jawa Barat)* and reputedly Karna's close friend. Pundits circulated the following anecdote. At the time of his appointment as minister of the interior, President Suharto allegedly charged Yogie with the task of "*menjabarkan*" points of the "Broad Outlines of the Direction of State" (GBHN) in the ministry. Roughly translated, *menjabarkan* means "to clarify." *Jabar,* however, is also an acronym for "Jawa Barat" or West Java. Owing to alleged regional chauvinism, the new minister supposedly assumed that the president expected him to "*meng-Jawa-Barat-kan*" the ministry right down to the provincial level—in other words, to "West Javanize" it.

In Central Kalimantan, however, few people were laughing. Several delegations traveled to Jakarta to protest Karna's candidacy.[4] On 18 December demonstrators marched on the DPRD headquarters in Palangka Raya. According to newspaper estimates, between 1,000 and 3,000 citizens took part. (Brigadier General Walman Narang, founder of the Gerakan Aspirasi Rakyat, or People's Aspiration Movement, and head of the local branch of the military's Council of the Generation of '45, or Dewan Harian Angkatan '45, suggested that the actual number was closer to 10,000.) Some protesters carried signs demanding, "Human Rights in Central Kalimantan." Others wore T-shirts proclaiming, "Let Us Follow in the Footsteps of the Late Tjilik Riwut." The demonstrators sang songs dating from the independence struggle of 1945. Although three platoons of riot police were deployed to "guard against undesirable things" *(untuk menjaga hal-hal yang tidak diinginkan),* then-governor Soeparmanto, as well as most of the members of the DPRD, were "imprisoned" in DPRD headquarters for nearly two and a half hours.[5] At least one rock-throwing incident was reported—a window was smashed—and demonstrators bolted the building's doors from the outside. The next day, a large faction of DPRD delegates who came to be known as the Group of 21 (Kelompok 21) threatened to resign in response to the interior minister's actions. Several accompanied Brigadier General Narang on a hastily arranged trip to Jakarta, where he lodged a protest directly with President Suharto. The ten GOLKAR delegates who had voted for Karna were labeled turncoats. Security officers were sent to guard their homes.

On 24 December Karna asked to have his name withdrawn from consideration for the governorship. Yogie accepted the letter on 30 December. The search for governor resumed, the first time in Indonesia's history that a gubernatorial election had to be repeated. On 22 January Warsito Rasman, the Ministry of Home Affairs' director general for public administration and regional autonomy, was appointed the province's temporary caretaker. The new election was scheduled for 22 June.

After a brief period of calm, the situation in Palangka Raya again became unsettled. Warsito, who citizens had been assured was only a temporary appointee, appeared on the final list of gubernatorial candidates after it returned from the minister of the interior's office. Representatives of forty-two social organizations, along with various local leaders including the head of Central Kalimantan's Association of Customary Law Experts, visited Warsito's office on 6 June. They urged him to withdraw his name from consideration for the permanent post. Chairman Lewis of MBAHK, commenting on his role in organizing the meeting, stated:

> There are many underdeveloped villages in Central Kalimantan—where the majority of the population are members of the Hindu Kaharingan population—whose conditions never improve as a result of decisions which reflect a lack of understanding of the Dayak tribe's situation and social conditions. Up to now the tribe has been ignored and given few opportunities. It would therefore be very wise if the central government and the DPRD of Central Kalimantan offered the opportunity to serve as governor to the best *putra daerah* in Central Kalimantan.[6]

Public outcry notwithstanding, Warsito Rasman remained on the ballot and eventually secured thirty-nine out of a possible forty-four votes. On 19 July he was installed as governor. Security was tight. Anti-riot police lined the streets. Roads leading to DPRD headquarters, where the swearing-in was to take place, were closed to public traffic. Local citizens could only watch the ceremony on a few closed-circuit televisions. Dissatisfaction was rampant. A delegation representing sixty-five *demang* left immediately for Jakarta to file a complaint against the interior minister with the State Administrative Court (Pengadilan Tata Usaha Negara).[7] Commission V of the National Office of the People's

Constitutive Assembly recommended that the new governor be removed, citing questionable dealings with operators of timber concessions as a reason.[8] Yogie issued a statement in response that portrayed the election in Central Kalimantan as progress toward the development of "Pancasila democracy." He noted, "Democracy doesn't drop from the sky just like that; instead, we must seize it with various means of struggle and sacrifice."[9] He invited Dayak leaders to "sue him" if they were unhappy with his role in the elections.[10] In the end, however, the State Administrative Court refused to hear the customary law experts' petition, stating that "the *demangs*' loss was not material, but immaterial."[11] The new governor remained in office.

One year later, in reviewing these events with me in his office at armed forces headquarters in Palangka Raya, Brigadier General Narang remarked:

> Actually, we did achieve our goal. We were seeking more consideration from the government. It's like this. Once again, the spirit of the Dayak people awakened. It didn't awaken to fight the government, but rather to defend Pancasila and our nation's constitution. [This protest] wasn't an isolated incident, it was part of a process. In 1894 we Dayaks used the conference at Tumbang Anoi as an opportunity to unite. The Dutch had their own agenda, but Dayaks did it for the sake of our tribe. Also, the establishment of the province of Central Kalimantan wasn't like the establishment of any other province. [The province] wasn't given to us; we struggled for it physically and politically. The people of Central Kalimantan want development. Our goal has always been to make right that which wasn't right, in accordance with Pancasila. That is what we did last year, and will always continue to do.

Hindu Kaharingan Ritual as Cultural Performance

Throughout the painful process of "electing" a new governor, citizens of Central Kalimantan were united by what was variously termed "Dayak" or "tribal" identity. In seeking the appointment of a *putra daerah,* local leaders appealed to their constituency's sense of place and to values rooted in the local culture. That the indigenous religion is a source of many of these values is widely acknowledged. This has not always been the case, however.

In the past, for example, conversion to another religion was usually accompanied by rejection of traditional rituals and an accompanying shift in "ethnic allegiance." Villagers who became Christian might identify themselves as "Bakumpai," while those who converted to Islam might characterize themselves as "Malays" (Riwut 1963, 180; Schärer 1963, 3). The fact that Kaharingan was not accepted as a religion when Central Kalimantan won provincial status in 1957 was apparently of little concern to some Dayaks, who while campaigning alongside their Kaharingan neighbors for political autonomy had been promoting "ethnic" songs, dances, and rituals that, in their opinion, "had absolutely no connection with Kaharingan religion" (Ukur 1960, 121).

Unlike their predecessors, many contemporary converts participate in Hindu Kaharingan rituals and even create celebrations such as "raising a cross," described in chapter 5, that are rooted in what they refer to as the "ethic of Kaharingan." Just a few decades ago, attempts to introduce traditional music into church services were vigorously resisted by local clergy. Today some Christians who occasionally participate in *balian* claim that they are performing "folk music." They point to their participation in ritual forms inspired by regional tradition as diacritic of Ngaju identity. The format of weddings also comes under scrutiny in this regard. Now, one wedding is no longer sufficient for many couples. Young people often undergo multiple nuptials as a means of coping with the perceived demands of the state, of religion(s), and of tradition or *hadat*. Printed wedding announcements, increasingly popular among urban families, inform guests of the time and place of a *hadat* ceremony involving the transference of bride wealth, of the civil service held in a government office, and of a church service if at least one of the partners is Christian. Particulars of the *hadat* ceremony are usually written in Ngaju, whereas Indonesian is used on the rest of the invitation.

Many Christians and Muslims also espouse a feeling that *tiwah* should be perpetuated as a kind of *acara kebudayaan,* or "cultural performance." Their usage of the term calls to mind Sherry Ortner's anthropological definition of cultural performances as "rituals or other culturally formalized events that the people themselves see as embodying in some way the essence of their culture, as dramatizing the basic myths and visions of reality, the basic values and moral truths, upon which they feel their world rests" (1978, 1).[12]

Enthusiasm for promoting *tiwah* as a vehicle to express generic cultural pride is not universally shared, however. As one adherent of Hindu Kaharingan remarked concerning the etiolation of belief, "If a *sapundu* is just a carving, if a *balian* is just a song, it isn't Kaharingan any longer." Chairman Lewis himself noted, in a pamphlet prepared for general circulation, that "*tiwah* contains within it lofty values and advanced culture, and it is not *adat,* it is *Religion*" (emphasis in original).

As Hindu Kaharingan has now become "official," many Christians seek to pinpoint differences between "folkways" and the elements of ritual that are "religious." They claim that participation is appropriate once substitutions for the religious elements have been made. An example is the refusal of many nonadherents of Hindu Kaharingan to be anointed with the blood of sacrificial animals during *tiwah*. They demand that ritual specialists use water instead. Yet the attempts of Christians and others to appropriate selected aspects of indigenous religion are increasingly contested. In the pamphlet just quoted, for example, Chairman Lewis took aim at such efforts. Many Hindu Kaharingan voice concerns that without the observation of proscriptions that originally framed their performance, these ritual events are sacrilegious. Some interpret the use of water rather than blood as *pali*. Others decry Christian participation out-right. As one exclaimed: "How can Christians say that *tiwah* is not a religious ritual? If they truly understood what we have been through, they would quit their new religion and become fanatic Hindu Kaharingan."

In fact, conversions to Hindu Kaharingan are indeed taking place. Rather than referring to these experiences as "to become Kaharingan," or *"masuk Kaharingan"*, as other people *"masuk Kristin"* or *"masuk Islam"*, conversion to Hindu Kaharingan is called a "return" or *"kembali Kaharingan."* As the rector of the Hindu Kaharingan University Tampung Penyang explained to me, "We say 'kembali Kaharingan' because the first religion in the world was Hindu Kaharingan."

The emphasis on declaring religious affiliation through participation or non-participation in ritual is becoming acute, even within nuclear families. In one village, for example, the head of the only remaining Hindu Kaharingan family subjected his son to an "indigenous baptism" that involved bathing the son in pig's blood. He did so in order to "wash away the blood of Christ" when he learned that the boy had converted to Christianity while attending university in Palangka Raya. The baptism was a ritual created for the occasion, although its roots were in other types of indigenous celebration.[13] While going along with the ritual, the boy nonetheless refused to renounce Christianity. The father disowned him. The young man then returned to Palangka Raya to live with his future in-laws, a couple active in a local Protestant church. Since that ill-fated baptism, the boy's mother has claimed to suffer from a serious illness brought on by her son's obstinacy, in other words, *pali.*

It is not only in this life that religion is potentially divisive. A high school teacher in Palangka Raya boasted to me that he had persuaded his aged mother to convert to Christianity by offering this ultimatum: he asked whether she would prefer to be in the Hindu Kaharingan Upperworld, surrounded by "dead people" whom she had never met, possibly having been sent there by a *tukang hanteran* who did not know the "old way" (and thereby intimating that her souls might become lost en route), or wait for him, her grandchildren, and their friendly neighbors in the Christian heaven, where they would all enjoy eternal life. The old woman opted for the latter and converted to Christianity one week before her death. Such deathbed conversions are not infrequent. I recall the telling epitaph of a former ritual specialist on a tombstone proudly erected by his Christian children. Below the deceased's name was inscribed: "A former Kaharingan *basir* who, at the very end of his life, admitted/accepted that Jesus is Lord." Hindu Kaharingan often refer to these alleged intimidations as "Politik Kristin," or "Christian politics." Other examples include Christian school principals who allegedly force children to become Christians before allowing them to register for instruction, the sponsorship of lavish *tiwah* by Christians in villages where Hindu Kaharingan could not afford to host such extravagant events, or the Christians' purported insistence that water buffaloes be sacrificed at *tiwah* despite their knowledge that not all Hindu Kaharingan can afford them.

How can these concerns, oriented around religion, be reconciled with the emergence of Ngaju cultural identity today? It is obvious, of course, that the individuals involved in the campaign for the creation of the Dayak province and in the more recent protests over the governor's election were united by a Dayak identity regardless of their particular religious affiliation. Nevertheless, a strong solidarity cannot be assumed. Religious cleavages clearly figure here in a number of ways. With regard to Kaharingan only, the natural environment, which precluded frequent interaction between inhabitants of distant villages, probably contributed to the rise of mythologies about the importance of maintaining physical and social distance from non-kin. Even today villagers evince little feeling of being one in spirit with people who live on other rivers, often employing supernatural means to protect themselves from them. Hence older *basir* often warned me not to reveal that I was from the Kahayan area when I visited villages on neighboring rivers, lest I come to harm.

It is intriguing to reflect on how this emergent cultural identity might articulate with the conceptualizations of society presented in previous chapters. On the one hand, divisiveness appears to be arising at precisely the point where *tiwah* and other Hindu Kaharingan rituals seek to integrate and strengthen— that is, the extended family. On the other hand, new varieties of community are emerging that are at least partly contingent on the objectification of elements of Ngaju culture. A more explicit formulation of identity will require that the Ngaju continue grappling with the relationship between culture and the indigenous religion in its past and present forms.

Some students of Borneo once assumed that the Ngaju formed a tribe held together by a "primitive" religion. Citizens of Central Kalimantan today have begun to identify themselves as members of a tribe for their own ends.[14] They borrow selectively from indigenous traditions to reap benefits from a state system that offers incentives for being "ethnic" in particular ways. On this point, I turn one final time to the rich ethnographic legacy left behind by Johannes Saililah, the consummate cultural broker and translator of indigenous thought for three generations of anthropologists who sought to render the lives of his people intelligible to the world beyond the jungle, beyond mission posts, beyond Borneo. In a collection of reminiscences and commentaries recorded by his own hand, "Bue," or "grandfather" (a term of endearment and respect that I used to address him), struggled to convey the urgency with which he felt that the inhabitants of his region must forge new solidarities in the face of rapid social change. He asked the reader to consider the similarities between our people's circumstances and the old amulet belts, *penyang*. *Penyang* must be cared for as they are characteristic of the religion and culture of the Ngaju Dayak tribe of Central Kalimantan. *Penyang* are mirrors that reflect the problem of what is valuable today, in the age of independence, of the New Order . . . because if the items making up the *penyang* are not tied together to become one, they have no strength and no use. They are strong because they are made one. If they were carried into battle in the past, the Dayak would win. Today it is we ourselves who must become a *penyang*. In the past, if there was no unity within the village, an enemy could easily enter. We citizens of Indonesia in Central Kalimantan must become a *penyang* that will be useful to our province. (Saililah, unpublished manuscript)

Although Hindu Kaharingan may not serve as the cord that fastens together this new human *penyang*, the manner in which interpretations of religion are insinuated into the genesis and expression of Ngaju cultural consciousness will remain an evolving phenomenon of interest. In this respect, what is likely to happen to *tiwah*? Will it become streamlined or perhaps disappear entirely, a small sacrifice on the road to development? Will it evolve into a pan-religious festival of local culture? Members of the Supreme Council describe *tiwah* as an "asset" to Indonesian national culture. Chairman Lewis himself has publicly asserted his hope that the government will take a more active role in the administration of religion and promote *tiwah* as a *daya tarik pariwisata,* or "tourism attraction." Meanwhile, as friends in Central Kalimantan say, "Death rituals tell us who we are." For now, at least, mortuary practices will remain a crucible for their identity.

Epilogue:
Basir Muka and Religious Reformulations

This volume has offered an exploration of rituals, beliefs, and attitudes associated with treatment of the dead among an indigenous rain forest people of Indonesia. I have sought to relate the rituals to their changing social contexts and, in so doing, probe the relationship between religious and social transformation. To this end, I have focused attention on the changing form and content of *tiwah* as understood by lay people as well as priests.

Writing about ritual analysis generally, Victor Turner proposed that ritual provides a setting or frame for symbols, which include objects, activities, relationships, events, gestures, and spatial units (1967, 1). By focusing participants' attention on the meanings the symbols convey, ritual makes it difficult for actors to perceive situations from other vantage points or to solve problems in different ways: "It may be said that any major ritual that stresses the importance of a single principle of social organization does so only by blocking the expression of other important principles. Sometimes the submerged principles, and the norms and customs through which they become effective, are given veiled and disguised representation in the symbolic pattern of the ritual" (40–41). Clifford Geertz set forth a similar though even more dynamic argument, suggesting that the demonstration of a meaningful relationship between the existential reality of the world and values that inform the affective quality of people's lives is an essential element in religion (1973a, 127). By synthesizing ethos and worldview, religious ritual delimits the boundaries of the participants' world, communicates to them how they should live in that world, and compels them to feel a particular way about their lives.

Is there a point, however, at which the adaptive capacity of a ritual is exhausted? Can worldview and ethos become so disparate as to be beyond articulation through established ritual forms? If the source of religion's moral vitality is the fidelity with which it is perceived to express the fundamental nature of reality (Geertz 1973a, 126), what is likely to happen in Central Kalimantan, where religious beliefs, ritual practices, and society are in the midst of rapid change? In a world of increased mobility and education, where children convert to other religions and marry outside the family and transmigrants pour into the region at what many locals consider an alarming rate, can *tiwah* continue to render "old" values intellectually convincing and a Kahayan, Ngaju, or even Dayak worldview emotionally satisfying? If *tiwah* cannot do this in its present form, how much can it change? What will it become? How will changes affect social action? Thus, the death rituals of the Ngaju once again submit to scrutiny, this time from within. If this scrutiny is not always overt, if participants cannot explicitly formulate all of their concerns, symptoms of the search for meaning can still be recognized in the vague discomfiture that surrounds ritual performance. This is expressed in various ways: in the vociferous belittling or celebrating of the "old" or "new" way, in participants' anxiety concerning which standards of acceptability should be applied, and in debates over who knows best, what must be done, and even who may participate in the celebration.

The power of entrenched beliefs to affect social action continues to have implications that reach far beyond the ritual arena. For example, one day in August 1986 thousands of Palangka Rayans thronged before a building in the capital city with the avowed intention of tearing it down. They reportedly refused to leave the site until an army officer had searched the building and declared it to be vacant. The citizens had assembled in order to expose a *hantuen* supposedly hiding inside. The building itself belonged to the regional branch of the Office of Transmigration. Under the auspices of that office, tens of thousands of outsiders have been, and will continue to be, settled in the environs of Palangka Raya and other "Ngaju" areas. The tone of the event recalled suspicions, voiced by many, that non-kin, no matter how pleasant they appear, may potentially be *hantuen* intent on destroying lives. In this regard, too, I might note that on several occasions townspeople have expressed to me that most of the Chinese shopowners in Palangka Raya are *hantuen.*

The changing realities of life in Central Kalimantan notwithstanding, this work has demonstrated that men and women still feel compelled to unearth and weep over their family members' bones, to gore cattle and oxen with a ferocity similar to that with which Maharaja Bunu impaled his elephant sister and subsequently lost his immortality. They smear powder, perfume, and ordure on loved ones and don horrific costumes so that they may dance at a neighbor's gateway. Hindu Kaharingan parents fervently bathe errant children in pig's blood and claim to become physically ill if the child refuses to rescind conversion to another religion. Christians, refusing to disinter their dead yet feeling the need to do something, delve into a repertoire of indigenous ritual forms to create appropriate commemorations and then, more often than not, forget to invite their Hindu Kaharingan kin. Do these actions represent a way of life ideally adapted to a state of affairs described by a worldview? To answer their own questions, villagers cast about for signs: a Christian becomes possessed by her traditionalist mother's soul when she decides to inter the deceased in a Christian cemetery; a local scholar, known for disparaging his ancestors' religion, dies of cancer; *Tempo* magazine, once accused of spreading falsehoods about the Kaharingan faithful in 1991, loses its publishing license in 1994.

"Ritual," Turner wrote, "converts the obligatory into the desirable" (1967, 30). Geertz has powerfully argued that the reverse is also true. The compelling quality of the Kaharingan ethos continues to find vehicles for expression, ritual or otherwise. No expression, however, is more poignantly eloquent than that of the ritual specialist Basir Muka. Basir Muka, with sixty years' experience as a religious functionary, served as the representative of the Hindu Kaharingan administrative council in his village. He accepted certain changes, ignored others, and insisted that life and ritual must continue to be informed by the values of the "old" religion. Thus, when he applied for permission to hold *tiwah* and it seemed too long in coming, he held the celebration anyway, remarking that it was his responsibility to proceed.

Fifteen years ago, close to the time when Kaharingan was recognized as a Hindu sect, Basir Muka completed a carving that he claimed was both a sacred artifact (a *sangiang* came to him in a dream and commanded him to create it) and his attempt to preserve the esoteric mythology as a guide for living. He called his sculpture the *hampatung karuhei. Hampatung* means sculpture. *Karuhei* has two meanings. On the one hand, it refers to an object such as a piece of wood, a stone, or a tiny vase filled with a particular oil said to be imbued with the power to attract riches or good fortune to whoever possesses it. On the other hand, *karuhei* is a quality or a kind of knowledge that brings prosperity. The elaborateness of Basir Muka's sculpture, and its unique role in ritual, distinguishes it from other types of religious carving. The dozens of figures on it represent humans, Upperworld and Lowerworld beings, geographic features of other realms, flora and fauna, all of which figure prominently in local legend and myth. Basir Muka displayed the carving during harvest and healing rituals, when it was said to have a remarkable influence over participants. Possessed, they seized the figures that are removable from the top of the carving and danced with them enfolded in their arms. On those occasions, Basir Muka "fed" the animate essence of the carving with blood from animal sacrifices. Most of the time, however, the carving merely rested on a table in a corner of his house. Underneath the table, he stored his other sacred artifacts: stencil copies of Hindu Kaharingan ritual guides, letters of instruction from MBAHK headquarters in Palangka Raya, and a calendar detailing the phases of the moon published by the Hindu Duty Council. In our conversations, he compared his carving to the *Lesson Book* of the Kaharingan religion.

Not surprisingly, many of the detailed carvings spiraling up the sides of the *hampatung karuhei* depict the celebration of *tiwah*. In an explication of the meaning of the carvings, Basir Muka emphasized that although particular elements of secondary mortuary rituals may seem "like a game," they are not. Instead they are "requirements." Although this book has suggested that from the point of view of ritual analysis the requirements themselves are somewhat arbitrary, grounded in personal interpretations of correctness, the motivation to provide them is quite real. For individuals who share Basir Muka's view of religion, the requirements are exacting, if not exact. He explained:

> [It seems during *tiwah*] that our resources are depleted, but we are depleted only in the goods of mankind. We prosper after carrying out such a work. In the affairs

Basir Muka and the *hampatung karuhei*. 1984. Photo by author.

of men there can be profit and loss, but souls [*liau*] know nothing of such things. Many people feel they are in difficulty after *tiwah* because of the goods. But everything in the old religion must be done according to specific requirements. Not in any other manner. We who perform *balian* feel that it cannot be carried out using fewer goods. The goods are proof of our devotion. These are the requirements of the old religion. Many are not capable of carrying them out. They want to be clever and not take a loss; they choose the easiest way. But I believe it is better to take a loss than not to take a loss. Think about my words. We are a defeated people, yet we will achieve another victory. If we lose, how can we go on losing forever? After a long dry season, there will certainly be rain. That is the way of our old religion.

In view of the relationship between religion and society discussed in this book, along with recent political developments in Central Kalimantan, one cannot help but note that Basir Muka's explication, born of his meditations on the relationship between affection and responsibility, religion and tradition, and the circumstances of the world in which he lives, rings at once of celebration, accusation, and perhaps premonition.

Notes

Chapter 1

1. Unless otherwise noted, all translations are my own.

2. The warning orginally appeared in a book published several decades earlier. See Riwut 1963.

3. On the creation of an Indonesian national culture, Virginia Hooker and Howard Dick have written: "Modern Indonesian culture is still young, and the concept of a national culture which would encompass the existing cultures of the various provinces of the Republic—founded only in 1945—has had to be carefully formulated. Enshrined in Article 32 of the 1945 Constitution is the statement that the government will develop a national culture as an expression of the personality and vitality of all the peoples of Indonesia. As in other new nation-states, the construction of this concept of a national culture is now considered an essential part of nation-building" (Hooker 1993, 4).

4. Eventually two members of *Tempo*'s editorial board were selected to represent the magazine. One was a Hindu from Bali. Members of the Supreme Council resented what they claimed was the choice of a "token" Hindu and refused to carry out the *hambai*. A lesser ritual, known as *mamapas*, was performed to "sweep away" the pollution wrought by *Tempo*'s remarks. For more on this notion of supernatural pollution, see chapter 4.

5. The missionaries' efforts are chronicled in several publications. See Fridolin Ukur's 1971 study, *Tantang-Djawab Suku Dajak, 1835–1945* (Challenge-response of the Dayak tribe), and Johannes Garang's 1974 volume, *Adat und Gessellschaft* (Custom and society).

6. Saililah eventually converted to Islam. He lived until 1986. At the end of his life he asked for, and received, a Christian burial service.

7. Martin Baier is another anthropologist indebted to Saililah. On Ngaju customary law, see Baier 1977.

8. I. H. N. Evans (1953, 70–79), for example, published an elaborate account of the fate of the seven parts of the soul given to him by the senior religious specialist of a

Dusun village. Several years later, he could elicit only an outline of the same idea from specialists in another Dusun village not thirty miles away.

9. I am indebted to Abby Ruddick for bringing this case to my attention. See *IQRA*, 16 (25 April 1991).

10. PHDI has been criticized by some Hindus, primarily non-Balinese, for its intransigence in refusing to move the organization's headquarters to Jakarta. Also, its leaders' religious expertise has sometimes been called into question by members of the congregation (anonymous *Sinar Harapan*, 10, 12 February 1986).

11. One teacher at the Hindu Kaharingan religious university made this point to me by citing the case of his uncle, a Christian cleric. When his uncle had finished building a new house, he arranged for another minister to officiate at a thanksgiving service in the front room. At one point in the celebration, the Hindu Kaharingan teacher went to explore the rest of the house. In a back room he found offerings of rice, tobacco, areca nuts, and cooked chicken, obviously set out for *sangiang* to enjoy.

Chapter 2

1. In the ritual language, the Prosperous Village is known by many names. The one cited in this chapter is Lewu Tatau Habaras Bulau, Habusung Hintan, Hasahep Bati Lantimpung, Hakarangan Bawak Lamiang, Hapasir Manas Marajan Bulau–Lewu Tatau Dia Rumpung Tulang Rundung Raja Isin, Dia Kamalesu Uhat. It should be noted that the word "village" does not convey the exact sense of *lewu* which can mean "place" or "country" depending on context.

2. Although this discussion follows common anthropological practice in referring to *tiwah* as a form of secondary treatment, it is important to note that the designation itself is rather imprecise. *Tiwah* is the second set of rituals that involve manipulation of the deceased's physical remains, but it is actually the third stage of the mortuary cycle. The second stage of the cycle provides preliminary treatment for the souls only.

3. According to some early sources (Schärer 1963, 53–59), male specialists are known as *basir*, female specialists as *balian*. The latter term of reference is no longer used to apply to female specialists, however.

4. On the ritual language, see Baier, Hardeland, and Schärer 1987.

5. The specific varieties of supernatural being said to seek out the newly dead are discussed in chapter 4.

6. This order is not absolute. In practice, the first several thrusts at the sacrificial animal are sometimes offered to honored non-kin guests.

Chapter 3

1. Another more permanent variety of *pasah patahu* is discussed in chapter 4.

2. Katingan villagers have also described this representation to me as the face of the Kambe Rawit, a variety of supernatural being known as an "Unclean One." As the

Kambe Rawit is carved on the post that supports the ossuary, the implication is that the sponsors of *tiwah* have defeated the "Unclean Ones." On the notion of "Unclean Ones," see chapter 4.

3. On areca as a symbol of sociality, see Reid 1985.

4. Although I never observed faux genitalia of this type, several older ritual specialists insisted that the crews of the ships should wear them. In Katingan villages, the masks are called *habukung*. Two masked dancers stand on the bow of each *lanting laluhan*.

5. Occasionally sponsors don similar masks they have prepared to greet the arrivals, though I was told that this practice was an innovation.

6. The first ship is called *banama ruhung ajung pulang*. The representation of the village is called *bintik lewu huma*. I saw such a mural used only once in a Kahayan death ritual. Ritual specialists claimed that it was actually characteristic of Kapuas River ritual. For a photograph of the drawing as it appears along the Kapuas River, see Schärer 1963, pl. 8, ill. 6.

7. The *lauk pahi* was described to me by Kapuas River *basir*. I never observed one at a Kahayan or Katingan river *tiwah* and suspect that these "fish" are rarely made.

Chapter 4

1. Readers who are interested in discovering more examples of Ngaju *singer* are referred to Martin Baier's 1977 doctoral dissertation, which offers a translation of a manuscript by Saililah as well as a useful descriptive introduction.

2. For an alternate version of this myth, see Simpei and Hanyi 1996.

3. The weapon they requested was the iron dagger, or *duhung*, mentioned in connection with the *tukang hanteran*'s costume and chant in chapter 3.

4. Although it is possible that in the past inhabitants of the Upperworld and the Lowerworld were conceptualized differently, contemporary adherents and specialists of Hindu Kaharingan characterize them as much the same, adding that Jata dwells in the Lowerworld and Hatalla in the Upperworld.

5. Many readers will presumably be familiar with the "Beautiful Indonesia" theme park, Taman Mini Indonesia Indah, located in Jakarta. A *pasah patahu* is located alongside the Central Kalimantan longhouse exhibit, and coins, soft drinks, and tobacco are sometimes left inside the *pasah patahu* by Kaharingan visitors to the park.

6. For a discussion of *tukang sangiang*, see Jay 1993. Contrary to her report, however, these mediums are not only "women who achieved their position by transcending a relationship with inferior, ill-disposed spirits belonging to the underworld" (165). I have met both male and female *tukang sangiang* who are possessed by a range of "highly placed" Upperworld beings. In fact, the *tukang sangiang* described in chapter 3 was male. Three of the *sangiang* who possessed him that night were female.

7. I am grateful to George Appell for this suggestion.

8. Much of the debate concerning kindred in Borneo was generated in response to Derek Freeman's influential essay (1961) on the Iban of Sarawak. For a discussion on procedures for recognizing kindred, see Appell 1967.

9. For a different interpretation, see Miles 1976, 59–67.

10. Kahayan villagers do not have isolates comparable to the *tambak* bone repository groups described by Alfred Hudson for the Ma'anyan (1972, 91–99).

11. I would note that a few individuals have mentioned to me that they plan to pay for and decorate offering ships and send them to their own village in order to add to the festivities and fun of the *tiwah* they intend to sponsor. I suspect this practice is a recent innovation.

12. See Miles 1976, 50–52.

Chapter 5

1. For a useful discussion of "civil religion" and *agama* in Indonesia, see Atkinson 1983.

2. At the time Kaharingan was declared a variety of Hinduism, the office was occupied by H. Alamsyah Ratu Perwiranegara.

3. For example, the use of the term "Kaharingan" can be traced back to at least the 1940s, and one of my informants claimed to have invented it during the Japanese occupation.

4. Representatives of at least one other Kaharingan party, the United Kaharingan Religion Party (Persatuan Agama Kaharingan), also ran in that election (Miles 1976, 122).

5. For a discussion of the "New Order" government, see Vatikiotis 1994.

6. The complete slate included Rangga Akup as second chairman, Djanatan Timbang as third chairman, Dugon Ginther as fourth chairman, Ranan Baut as secretary, Minan D. Sawung as first treasurer, and Nekan Sangkal as second treasurer. The following year, Walter Penyang replaced Ranan Baut as secretary, Kamerhan Djatrich replaced Djanatan Timbang as third chairman, and several other offices fell open owing to incumbents' personal circumstances.

7. These twelve individuals were Ida Pedanda Gde Putra, Ida Pedanda Istri Putra, Gde Pudja, Willy Surya, Ida Bagus Oka Puniatmadja, I Wayan Surpha, Ida Bagus Mantra, Anak Agung Kt Agung, Tjilik Riwut, W. A. Gara, R. Sylvanus, and Tjok Raka Dherana.

8. The program closed in 1993 as part of a Jakarta-led reorganization of private schools.

9. "P4" refers to the Pedoman Penghayatan dan Pengamalan Pancasila, or "Directive for the Comprehension and Implementation of Pancasila." Pancasila are the five principles of state, specifically: belief in one God; just and civilized humanitarianism; a united Indonesia; democracy guided by wisdom through consultation and representation; and social justice for all Indonesian people.

10. These books are not the first attempts at the codification of Kaharingan belief. Miles, for example, described the case of a Mentaya villager who was involved in the production of a "Kaharingan Bible" in 1955 (1976, 129). Nevertheless, the council-produced texts are by far the most influential and widely circulated.

11. The first revised version of the *panaturan* was published by the council in 1993. A second version was published in 1996. See Simpei and Hanyi 1996.

12. During services held outside Palangka Raya, participants in *basarah* sometimes

become possessed by other Upperworld beings. In Palangka Raya, I never witnessed a single incident of possession in the more than fifty services I attended.

13. When I inquired of one man what such behavior might be, he replied, "Manari disko" (disco dancing).

Chapter 6

1. Readers with an interest in the relationship between culture and ethnicity among other Bornean peoples will appreciate Jerome Rousseau's volume, *Central Borneo: Ethnic Identity and Social Life in a Stratified Society* (1990).

2. Sahari Andung maintains his innocence of having had any role in GMTPS's activities.

3. "Isen mulung," a phrase that Sahari Andung coined in 1962, is now the motto of Central Kalimantan province.

4. For an account of the delegation's activities, see "Masyarakat Dayak Kalteng Tolak Gubernur Titipan," *Media Indonesia*, 23 November 1993.

5. "1,000 Warga Kalteng Protes Karna Suwanda," *Merdeka*, 18 December 1993.

6. "Sejumlah Anggota DPRD Kalteng Tolak Warsito," *Kompas*, 15 June 1994.

7. "Demang Kepala Adat di Kalteng Gugat Menteri Dalam Negeri," *Kompas*, 4 July 1994.

8. "Komisi V DPR RI Mengusulkan Rekomendasi Warsito Dicabut," *Kompas*, 7 July 1994.

9. "Warsito Dilantik dengan Pengamanan Ketat, Mendagri: Berakhir, Perbedaan Soal Gubernur Kalteng," *Kompas*, 20 July 1994.

10. "Yogie Challenges Dayak Leaders to Sue Him," *Jakarta Post*, 5 July 1994.

11. "Gugatan Para Demang Kalteng Ditolak," *Kompas*, 25 July 1994.

12. Kreps offers another example of an attempt to balance "religion" and cultural identity. A visitor to Palangka Raya's Museum Balanga noted in the museum guest book that exhibits focused on "Dayak culture" and "Kaharingan" and inquired why the museum didn't exhibit old Bibles, too. Kreps remarks, "This comment was interesting in that it was the only reference made to the representation of religion in the entire survey, despite the fact that the majority (64%) of the individuals interviewed were Protestant Christians and only one was Kaharingan. . . . Although there is no overt reference to Kaharingan in Museum exhibitions, it is generally understood that Kaharingan is the inspiration for much traditional Dayak culture" (1994, 281–82).

13. In most cases, when someone converts to Hindu Kaharingan, the occasion is marked with a short ritual of purification called *hapalas*. During *hapalas* the convert is ritually swept with *sawang* leaves, and offerings are made to Upperworld beings.

14. This is not to suggest that "Ngaju" is synonymous with "Dayak," of course. On resistance as it is expressed by non-Ngaju visitors to the provincial museum, see Kreps 1994, 327–28.

Bibliography

Ackerman, Susan, and Raymond Lee
   1988   *Heaven in Transition: Non-Muslim Religious Innovation and Ethnic Identity in Malaysia.* Honolulu: University of Hawaii Press.

Adams, Kathleen
   1993   "Club Dead, Not Club Med: Staging Death in Contemporary Tana Toraja (Indonesia)." *Southeast Asian Journal of Social Sciences* 21(2):62–72.

Adicondro, George
   1979   "Perjuangan Kaharingan." *Tempo,* 27 January, 53–54.

Anderson, Benedict
   1991   *Imagined Communities: Reflections on the Origin and Spread of Nationalism.* London: Verso.

Anonymous
   1986   "Aparat Keamanan Membuyarkan Desas-desus Tentang 'Kuyung.'" *Kompas,* 7 August, 9.

Anonymous
   1986   "Ketua Parisada Hindu Dharma, Oka Puniatmadja: 'Ini Sepenuhnya Pengabdian.'" *Sinar Harapan,* 12 February, 1.

Anonymous
   1986   "Tentang Kepengurusan Parisada Hindu Dharma: Jangan Didudukan Karena Mereka Tokoh Legislatif Atau Eksekutif." *Sinar Harapan,* 10 February, 1.

Anonymous
   1993   "Memuja Kresna Sebagai Tuhan." *Tempo,* 27 February, 78.

Appadurai, Arjun, and Carol Breckenridge
   1988   "Why Public Culture?" *Public Culture Bulletin* 1(1):1–9.

Appell, George N.
   1967   "Observational Procedures for Identifying Kindreds: Social Isolates

among the Rungus of Borneo." *Southwestern Journal of Anthropology* 23(2):192–207.

1976a   *The Societies of Borneo: Explorations in the Theory of Cognatic Social Structure.* George Appell, ed. Washington, D.C.: American Anthropological Association Special Publication no. 6.

1976b   *Studies in Borneo Societies: Social Process and Anthropological Explanation.* George Appell, ed. DeKalb: Northern Illinois University Center for Southeast Asian Studies Special Report No. 12.

1983   "Methodological problems with the Concepts of Corporation, Corporate Social Grouping, and Cognatic Descent Group." *American Ethnologist* 10(2):302–11.

Atkinson, Jane Monnig

1983   "Religions in Dialogue: The Construction of an Indonesian Minority Religion." *American Ethnologist* 10(4):684–96.

1989   *The Art and Politics of Wana Shamanship.* Berkeley: University of California Press.

Avé, Jan B.

1972   "Ot Danum Dayaks." In *Ethnic Groups of Insular Southeast Asia.* Volume 1, *Indonesia, Andaman Islands, and Madagascar.* Frank LeBar, ed. and comp. New Haven: Human Relations Area File Press, 192–94.

1981   "The Dayak of Borneo: Their View of Life and Death and Their Art." In *Art of the Archaic Indonesians.* General introduction by W. Stohr. Geneva: Musée d'Art et d'Histoire, 94–117.

1982   "'Kaharingan' and 'Heathen': Some Additional Remarks." *Borneo Research Bulletin* 14(1):34–37.

Babcock, Barbara

1978   *The Reversible World: Symbolic Inversion in Art and Society.* Barbara Babcock, ed. Ithaca: Cornell University Press.

Baier, Martin

1977   "Das Adatbussrecht der Ngaju-Dayak." Ph.D. dissertation, Tübingen University.

Baier, Martin, August Hardeland, and Hans Schärer

1987   *Wörterbuch der Priestersprache der Ngaju-Dayak.* Verhandelingen van het Koninklijk Instituut Voor Taal-, Land- en Volkenkunde 128. Dordrecht: Foris Publications.

Barth, Fredrik

1969   *Ethnic Groups and Boundaries: The Social Organization of Cultural Differences.* Fredrick Barth, ed. Boston: Little, Brown.

Bateson, Gregory

1958   *Naven.* 2d ed. Stanford: Stanford University Press.

Bellah, Robert N.

1964   "Religious Evolution." *American Sociological Review* 29:358–74.

Bloch, Maurice

1971   *Placing the Dead.* London: Seminar Press.

1989   *Ritual, History, and Power: Selected Papers in Anthropology.* Monographs on Social Anthropology no. 58. London: Athlone Press.

Bloch, Maurice, and Jonathan Parry, eds.
1982   *Death and the Regeneration of Life.* Cambridge: Cambridge University Press.

Boas, Franz
1902   "The Ethnological Significance of Esoteric Doctrine." *Science* 16:872–74. Reprinted in *Race, Language, and Culture.* New York: Macmillan, 1949, 312–15.

Bock, Carl
1985 [1881]   *The Head-Hunters of Borneo.* Singapore: Oxford University Press.

Boon, James A.
1974   "The Progress of the Ancestors in a Balinese Temple-Group (pre–1906–1972)." *Journal of Asian Studies* 34(1):7–25.
1977   *The Anthropological Romance of Bali, 1597–1972: Dynamic Perspectives in Marriage and Caste, Politics, and Religion.* Cambridge: Cambridge University Press.

Bourdieu, Pierre
1977   *Outline of a Theory of Practice.* Richard Nice, trans. Cambridge: Cambridge: Cambridge University Press.

Bowen, John
1986   "On the Political Construction of Tradition: Gotong Royong in Indonesia." *Journal of Asian Studies* 45(3):545–61.

Cense, A. A., and E. M. Uhlenbeck
1958   *Critical Survey of Studies on the Languages of Borneo.* The Hague: M. Nijhoff.

Comaroff, Jean
1985   *Body of Power, Spirit of Resistance: The Culture and History of a South African People.* Chicago: University of Chicago Press.

Conley, William
1973   *The Kalimantan Kenyah: A Study of Tribal Conversion in Terms of Dynamic Cultural Themes.* Nutley, N.J.: Presbyterian and Reformed Publishing Company.

Crystal, Eric
1977   "Tourism in Toraja." In *Hosts and Guests: The Anthropology of Tourism.* V. Smith, ed. Philadelphia: University of Pennsylvania Press, 109–25.

Cunningham, Clark
1964   "Order in the Atoni House." *Bijdragen tot de Taal-, Land, en Volkenkunde* 120:34–68.

Danandjaya, James
1971a   "A Comparative Analysis of Peasant Kinship in Central Kalimantan and Nias." *Sarawak Museum Journal* 19(n.s. 38–39):237–52.
1971b   "Some Kahayan Legends." *Sarawak Museum Journal* 19(n.s.38–39):265–76.

Dentan, Robert

1979   *The Semai: A Nonviolent People of Malaya.* Chicago: Holt, Rinehart and Winston.

Departemen Agama Propinsi Kalimantan Tengah

1990/91   *Laporan Pembimbing Masyarakat Hindu/Budha Tahun 1990/1991.* Palangka Raya: Departemen Agama.

1994/95   *Laporan Pembimbing Masyarakat Hindu/Budha 1994/95.* Palangka Raya: Departemen Agama.

Departemen Pendidikan Dan Kebudayaan

1977   *Sejarah Daerah Kalimantan Tengah.* Jakarta: Proyek Penelitian dan Pencatatan Kebudayaan Daerah.

1978/79   *Sejarah Kebangkitan Nasional Daerah Kalimantan Tengah.* Jakarta: Proyek Penelitian dan Pencatatan Kebudayaan Daerah.

1979   *Monografi Daerah Kalimantan Tengah.* Jakarta: Proyek Media Kebudayaan.

1983   *Studi Kepustakaan Leksikon Tentang Kepercayaan Terhadap Tuhan Yang Maha Esa.* Jakarta: Proyek Inventarisasi Kepercayaan Terhadap Tuhan Yang Maha Esa.

1984   *Hasil Inventariasasi 3 Aspek Propinsi.* Bk. 8. Jakarta: Proyek Inventarisasi Kepercayaan Terhadap Tuhan Yang Maha Esa.

Dimaggio, Paul, and Walter Powell

1983   "The Iron Cage Revisited: Institutional Isomorphism and Collective Rationality in Organizational Fields." *American Sociological Review* 48:147–60.

Dinamika Pembangunan

1991a   "Upacara Tiwah Sakral, Mengandung Nilai dan Tujuan Hidup Tertinggi." 1 June, 6.

1991b   "Perdamaian Tempo—Kaharingan Masih Menunggu Waktu." 1 July, 1.

1991c   "Upacara Mengantar Roh Ke Alam Baka." 10 July, 3.

1991d   "Perbaikan Tulisan Upacara Tiwah." 21 July, 1.

Direktorat Jendral Pengerahan Dan Pembinaan

1985   *Mengenal Calon Lokasi Proyek Pemukiman Transmigrasi Pagatan SKP-A Kabupaten Kotawaringin Timur.* Jakarta: Departemen Transmigrasi.

Doko, Dominicus, et al.

1982/83   *Struktur Sastra Lisan Dayak Sangen.* Palangka Raya: Departemen Pendidikan dan Kebudayaan, Proyek Penelitian Bahasa Dan Sastra Indonesia dan Daerah Kalimantan Barat.

Douglas, Mary

1966   *Purity and Danger: An Analysis of the Concepts of Pollution and Taboo.* London: Routledge and Kegan Paul.

Douwes Dekker, Niels

1963   *Tanah Air Kita: A Book on the Country and People of Indonesia.* Special ed. Jakarta: BPU Perusahaan Pertjetakan dan Penerbitan Negara.

Durkheim, Émile

1965 [1915] *The Elementary Forms of Religious Life.* Joseph Swain, trans. New York: Free Press.

Dyen, Isidore
  1956   "The Ngaju-Dayak Old 'Speech Stratum.'" *Language* 32(1):83–87.
Dyson, Laurentius, and M. Asharini
  1980/81   *Tiwah: Upacara Kematian Pada Masyarakat Dayak Ngaju.* Jakarta: Pro-
                yek Media Kebudayaan, Direktorat Jendral Kebudayaan, Departemen
                Pendidikan dan Kebudayaan.
Elbaar, Lambertus, et al.
  1981/82   *Struktur Bahasa Sangen.* Palangka Raya: Departemen Pendidikan dan
                Kebudayaan, Proyek Penelitian Bahasa dan Sastra Indonesia dan
                Daerah Kalimantan Barat.
Emerson, Rupert
  1960   *From Empire to Nation.* Cambridge: Harvard University Press.
Epstein, Arnold
  1978   *Ethos and Identity.* London: Tavistock.
Evans, Ivor H. N.
  1953   *Religion of the Tempasak Dusun of North Borneo.* Cambridge: Cam-
                bridge University Press.
Fabian, Johannes
  1983   *Time and the Other: How Anthropology Makes Its Object.* New York:
                Columbia University Press.
Feldman, Jerome
  1985   *The Eloquent Dead: Ancestral Sculpture of Indonesia and Southeast
                Asia.* Los Angeles: UCLA Museum of Cultural History.
Fox, James
  1971a   "Semantic Parallelism in Rotinese Ritual Language." *Bijdragen tot de
                Taal-, Land, en Volkenkunde* 127:215–55.
  1971b   "Sister's Child as Plant: Metaphors in an Idiom of Consanguinity." In
                Rethinking Kinship and Marriage. Rodney Needham, ed. ASA Mono-
                graph no. 11. London: Tavistock, 219–52.
  1973   "On Bad Death and the Left Hand." In *Right and Left: Essays on Dual
                Symbolic Classification.* Rodney Needham, ed. Chicago: University of
                Chicago Press, 342–68.
Fox, Richard
  1990   *Nationalist Ideologies and the Production of National Cultures.* Ameri-
                can Ethnological Society Monograph no. 2. Washington, D.C.: Ameri-
                can Anthropological Association.
Freeman, J. D.
  1961   "On the Concept of the Kindred." *Journal of the Royal Anthropological
                Institute* 91:192–220.
Garang, Johannes E.
  1974   *Adat und Gesellschaft; Eine Sozio-Ethnologische Untersuchung Zur Dars-
                tellung Des Geistes- Und Kulturlebens Der Dajak In Kalimantan.* Wies-
                baden: Franz Steiner.
Geertz, Clifford
  1972   "Religious Change and Social Order in Soeharto's Indonesia." *Asia*
                27:62–84.

1973a   "Ethos, World View, and the Analysis of Sacred Symbols." In *The Interpretation of Cultures*, 126–41.

1973b   "The Impact of the Concept of Culture on the Concept of Man." In *The Interpretation of Cultures*, 33–54.

1973c   "The Integrative Revolution: Primordial Sentiments and Civil Politics in the New States." In *The Interpretation of Cultures*, 255–310.

1973d   "Internal Conversion in Contemporary Bali." In *The Interpretation of Cultures*, 170–89.

1973e   *The Interpretation of Cultures*. New York: Basic Books.

1973f   "Religion as a Cultural System." In *The Interpretation of Cultures*, 87–125.

1973g   "Ritual and Social Change: A Javanese Example." In *The Interpretation of Cultures*, 142–69.

George, Kenneth
1996   *Showing Signs of Violence: The Cultural Politics of a Twentieth-Century Headhunting Ritual*. Berkeley: University of California Press.

Goldman, Philip
1975   *The Divine Gifts: Dayak Sculpture from Kalimantan (Indonesian Borneo)*. London: Gallery 43.

Goody, Jack
1962   *Death, Property, and the Ancestors*. Stanford: Stanford University Press.

Grabowsky, F.
1889   "Der Tod das Begräbnis, das Tiwah oder Totenfest bei den Dajaken." *Internationales Archiv für Ethnographie* 2:177–204.

Handler, Richard
1985   "On Dialogue and Destructive Analysis: Problems in Narrating Nationalism and Ethnicity." *Journal of Anthropological Research* 41(2):171–82.

1988   *Nationalism and the Politics of Culture in Quebec*. Madison: University of Wisconsin Press.

Hardeland, August
1859   *Dajacksch-deutsches Wörterbuch*. Amsterdam: Muller.

Harris, Olivia
1982   "The Dead and the Devils among the Bolivian Laymi." In *Death and the Regeneration of Life*. Maurice Bloch and Jonathan Parry, eds., 45–73.

Harrisson, Barbara
1959   "Near to Ngaju: Rhinish Missionaries in South Borneo, 1836–1913." *Sarawak Museum Journal* 9(n.s. 13–14):121–31.

Harrisson, Tom
1962   "Borneo Death." *Bijdragen tot de Taal-, Land- en Volkenkunde* 118:1–41.

Harrisson, T., and B. Harrisson
1968   "Iban and Ngaju: A Significant Bird Folklore Parallel." *Sarawak Museum Journal* 16(n.s. 32–33):186–94.

Hefner, Robert
 1983   "Ritual and Cultural Reproduction in Non-Islamic Java." *American Eth-
         nologist* 10(4):665–83.
 1985   *Hindu Javanese: Tengger Tradition and Islam.* Princeton: Princeton Uni-
         versity Press.
Heider, Karl
 1991   *Indonesian Cinema: National Culture on Screen.* Honolulu: University
         of Hawaii Press.
Hertz, Robert
 1907   "Contribution à une étude sur la représentation collective de la mort."
         L'Année Sociologique 10:48–137.
 1960 [1907]   *Death and the Right Hand.* Rodney Needham and Claudia Needham,
         trans. Introduction by E. E. Evans-Pritchard. Glencoe, Ill.: Free
         Press.
Hocart, Arthur M.
 1952   *The Life-Giving Myth, and Other Essays.* Lord Raglan, ed. London:
         Methuen.
 1970 [1936]   *Kings and Councillors: An Essay in the Comparative Anatomy of Hu-
         man Society.* Rodney Needham, ed. Chicago: University of Chicago
         Press.
Hooker, Virginia, ed.
 1993   *Culture and Society in New Order Indonesia.* Kuala Lumpur: Oxford
         University Press.
Hubert, Henri, and Marcel Mauss
 1964 [1899]   *Sacrifice: Its Nature and Function.* W. D. Halls, trans. Chicago: Univer-
         sity of Chicago Press.
Hudson, Alfred B.
 1966   "Death Ceremonies of the Ma'anyan Dayaks." In *Borneo Writing and
         Related Matters,* special monograph of the *Sarawak Museum Journal.*
         Tom Harrisson and Benedict Sandin, eds., 1:339–416.
 1967   *The Barito Isolects of Borneo.* Ithaca: Cornell University Southeast Asia
         Program Data Paper no. 68.
 1972   *Padju Epat: The Ma'anyan of Indonesian Borneo.* New York: Holt, Rine-
         hart and Winston.
Ilun, Y. Nathan
 n.d.   "Batang Garing, Dandang Tingang & Bahasa Sangen." Unpublished
         manuscript.
Ilun, Y. Nathan, et al.
 1983a   *Kawin Adat Suku Dayak Ngaju.* Palangka Raya: Balai Pengabdian Pada
         Masyarakat Universitas Palangka Raya.
 1983b   *Rapat Damai Di Tumbang Anoi.* Palangka Raya: Balai Pengabdian
         Pada Masyarakat Universitas Palangka Raya.
Irwin, Graham
 1955   *Nineteenth-Century Borneo: A Study in Diplomatic Rivalry.* Singapore:
         Donald Moore.

Jay, Sian

1993   "Canoes for the Spirits: Two Types of Spirit Mediumship in Central Kalimantan." In *The Seen and the Unseen: Shamanism, Mediumship, and Possession in Borneo*. Robert L. Winzeler, ed. Borneo Research Council Monograph Series no. 2. Shanghai, Va.: Ashley Printing Services, 151–68.

Jensen, Eric

1974   *The Iban and Their Religion*. Oxford: Clarendon Press.

Kantor Statistik Kotamadya Palangka Raya

1980   *Kotamadya Palangka Raya Dalam Angka*. Palangka Raya.

Kantor Statistik Propinsi Kalimantan Tengah

1982   *Kalimantan Tengah Dalam Angka*. Palangka Raya.

1994/95   *Kalimantan Tengah Dalam Angka: 1994*. Palangka Raya.

Kapferer, Bruce

1983   *A Celebration of Demons*. Bloomington: Indiana University Press.

Kertodipoero, Sarwoto

1963   *Kaharingan: Religi Dan Penghidupan Di Penhuluan Kalimantan*. Bandung: Sumur Bandung.

Kertzer, David

1988   *Ritual, Politics, and Power*. New Haven: Yale University Press.

Kessler, Clive

1980   "Malaysia: Islamic Revivalism and Political Disaffection in a Divided Society." *SEA Chronicle* 75:3–11.

Keyes, Charles

1981   *Ethnic Change*. Seattle: University of Wahington Press.

Keyes, Charles, Laura Kendall, and Helen Hardacre, eds.

1994   *Asian Religions in Transition: Religion and the Modern States of East and Southeast Asia*. Honolulu: University of Hawaii Press.

King, Victor

1976   "Cursing, Special Death, and Spirits in Embaloh Society." *Bijdragen tot de Taal-, Land- en Volkenkunde* 132:124–45.

1985a   *The Maloh of West Kalimantan: An Ethnographic Study of Social Inequality and Social Change among an Indonesian Borneo People*. Leiden: KITLV 108.

1985b   "Symbols of Social Differentiation: A Comparative Investigation of Signs, the Signified, and Symbolic Meanings in Borneo." *Anthropos* 80:125–52.

Kipp, Rita

1993   *Dissociated Identities: Ethnicity, Religion, and Class in an Indonesian Society*. Ann Arbor: University of Michigan Press.

Kipp, Rita, and Susan Rodgers, eds.

1987   *Indonesian Religions in Transition*. Tucson: University of Arizona Press.

Kirsch, A. Thomas

1973   *Feasting and Social Oscillation: Religion and Society in Upland Southeast Asia*. Data paper no. 92. Ithaca: Southeast Asia Program, Cornell University.

Klokke-Coster, A.
1976   *De Slimme en de Domme: Ngadju-Dajakse Volksverhalen.* Collected by
            A. Klokke-Coster, A. H. Klokke, and M. Saha. Verhandelingen Van
            Het Koninklijt Instituut Voor Taal-, Land- en Volkenkunde no. 79.
            The Hague: Martinus Nijhoff.

Knauft, Bruce
1985   "Ritual Form and Permutation in New Guinea: Implications of Sym-
            bolic Process for Socio-Political Evolution." *American Ethnologist*
            12(2):321–40.

Kreps, Christina F.
1994   "On Becoming 'Museum-Minded': A Study in Museum Development
            and the Politics of Culture in Indonesia." Ph.D. disssertation, Univer-
            sity of Oregon.

Krober, Alfred L.
1927   "Disposal of the Dead." *American Anthropologist* 29:308–15.

Lévi-Strauss, Claude
1963   *Structural Anthropology.* C. Jacobson and B. Grundfest Schoepf, trans.
            New York: Doubleday Anchor Books.
1966   *The Savage Mind.* Chicago: University of Chicago Press.

Lowie, Robert
1970 [1924]   *Primitive Society.* New York: Boni and Liveright.

Magenda, Burhan
1988   *Ethnicity and State Building in Indonesia: Ethnicities and Nations—Pro-
            cesses of Interethnic Relations in Latin America, Southeast Asia, and the
            Pacific.* Austin: University of Texas Press.

Majelis Alim Ulama Kaharingan Indonesia
1973   *Buku Ajar Agama Kaharingan (Panaturan Tamparan Taloh Handiai).*
            Palangka Raya.

Majelis Besar Agama Hindu Kaharingan
1981a   *Buku Kandayu Basarah Agama Hindu Kaharingan.* Palangka Raya.
1981b   *Hasil Rapat Koordinasi Majelis Besar Agama Hindu Kaharingan.* Palan-
            gka Raya.
1993   *Panaturan.* Palangka Raya.
1995   *Talatah Basarah.* Palangka Raya.
n.d.   *Petunjuk Mangubur.* Palangka Raya.
n.d.   *Tawur.* Palangka Raya.

Majelis Permusyawaratan Rakyat Republic Indonesia
1988   *Ketetapan MPRI Nomor II/MPR/1988 Tentang Garis-garis Besar Ha-
            luan Negara.* Surabaya: Penerbit Indah.

Mallinckrodt, J.
1928   *Het Adatrecht Van Borneo.* 2 vols. Leiden.
1970 [1925]   *Gerakan Nyuli di Kalangan Suku Dayak Lawangan.* Indonesian transla-
            tion of the original Dutch. Jakarta: Bhratara.

Mallinckrodt, J., and L. Mallinckrodt-Djata
1928   "Het *magah liau,* een Dajaksche priesterzang." *Tijdschrift voor Indische
            Taal-, Land-, en Volkenkunde* 58:292–346.

Mauss, Marcel

1967   *The Gift: Forms and Functions of Exchange in Archaic Societies.* Ian Cunnison, trans., with an introduction by E. E. Evans-Pritchard. New York: W. W. Norton.

Metcalf, Peter

1981   "Meaning and Materialism: The Ritual Economy of Death." *Man* 16(4):563–78.

1982   *A Borneo Journey into Death: Berawan Eschatology from Its Rituals.* Philadelphia: University of Pennsylvania Press.

1989   *Where Are You/Spirits: Style and Theme in Berawan Prayer.* Washington, D.C.: Smithsonian Institution Press.

Metcalf, Peter, and Richard Huntington

1991   *Celebrations of Death: The Anthropology of Mortuary Ritual.* 2d ed. New York: Cambridge University Press.

Mihing, Teras

1976/77   *Penelitian Dialek Pulau Petak.* Palangka Raya: Proyek Pengembangan Bahasa Dan Sastra Indonesia Dan Daerah.

Mihing, Teras, et al.

1978/79   *Adat Dan Upacara Perkawinan Daerah Kalimantan Tengah.* Palangka Raya: Proyek Penelitian dan Pencatatan Kebudayaan Daerah.

Miles, Douglas

1964a   "The Funeral Rites of the Ngadju Dayaks of Central Borneo." *Australian Natural History* 14:331–33.

1964b   "The Ngadju Longhouse." *Oceania* 35(1):45–57.

1965   "Socio-Economic Aspects of Secondary Burial." *Oceania* 35(3):161–74.

1966   "Shamanism and the Conversion of Ngadju Dayaks." *Oceania* 37(1):1–12.

1971   "Ngadju Kinship and Social Change on the Upper Mentaya." In *Anthropology in Oceania: Essays Presented to Ian Hogbin.* R. Hiatt and C. Jayawardena, eds. Sydney: Angus & Robertson, 211–30.

1976   *Cutlass and Crescent Moon.* Sydney: Centre for Asian Studies, University of Sydney.

Nagata, Judith, ed.

1975   *Pluralism in Malaysia: Myth and Reality.* Leiden: Brill.

1978   "The Chinese Muslims of Malaysia: New Malays or New Associates?" In *The Past in Southeast Asia's Present.* George Means, ed. Ottawa: Canadian Council for SEA Studies.

Needham, Rodney

1961   Review of Stöhr's "Das Totenritual der Dajak." *American Anthropologist,* 63(3):600–602.

1967   "Percussion and Transition." *Man* n.s. 2(4):606–14.

1970   "Introduction." In Arthur M. Hocart, *Kings and Councillors.*

Ngindra, F.

1981   "'Ijambe' Di Ambung Kepunahan." In *Laporan Hasil Pertemuan Il-*

miah Tahunan Kalimantan Tahun 1980–81. Banjarmasin: Regional Scientific Development Center.

Nicolaisen, Ida
1976   "Form and Function of Punan Bah Ethnohistorical Tradition." *Sarawak Museum Journal* 24(n.s. 45):63–95.

O'Keefe, Daniel
1982   *Stolen Lighting: The Social Theory of Magic.* New York: Continuum.

Ortner, Sherry
1978   *Sherpas through Their Rituals.* Cambridge: Cambridge University Press.

Palgi, Phyllis, and Henry Abramovitch
1984   "Death: A Cross-Cultural Perspective." *Annual Review of Anthropology* 13:385–417.

Panjaitan, S., et al.
1983   *Penelitian Morfologi Dan Sintaksis Bahasa Dayak Ngaju.* Palangka Raya: Balai Penelitian Universitas Palangka Raya.

Patianom, Nang, et al.
1979   *Monografi Daerah Kalimantan Tengah.* Jakarta: Departemen Pendidikan dan Kebudayaan, Proyek Media Kebudayaan.

Peacock, James
1968   *Rites of Modernization: Symbolic and Social Aspects of Indonesian Proletarian Drama.* Chicago: University of Chicago Press

Peacock, James, and A. Thomas Kirsch
1973   *The Human Direction.* 2d ed. Englewood Cliffs, N.J.: Prentice Hall.

Pemberton, John
1994   *On the Subject of "Java."* Ithaca: Cornell University Press.

Peranio, Roger
1961   "Descent, Descent Line and Descent Group in Cognatic Social Systems." In *Symposium: Patterns of Land Utilization.* V. E. Garfield, ed. Seattle: American Ethnological Society, 93–113.

Perelaer, Michael T.
1887   *Ran away from the Dutch: or, Borneo from South to North.* New York: Dodd, Mead and Company.

Prasetyo, Ris
1981   "Tewah: Upacara Berdarah Bagi Sang Dewa." *Puteri Indonesia* 82:62–63.

Reid, Anthony
1985   "From Betel-Chewing to Tobacco-Smoking in Indonesia." *Journal of Asian Studies* 44(3):529–47.

———, ed.
1983   *Slavery, Bondage, and Dependency in Southeast Asia.* New York: St. Martin's.

Riwut, Tjilik
1962   *Memperkenalkan Kalimantan Tengah dan Pembangunan Kota "Palangka Raya."* Kalimantan Tengah: Pertjetakan Pemerintahan Daerah.

1963   *Kalimantan Memanggil.* Jakarta: Endang.

1979   *Kalimantan Membangun.* Jakarta: P. T. Jayakarta Agung Offset.

Robison, Richard

1981   "Culture, Politics, and Economy in the Political History of the New Order." *Indonesia* 31:1–29.

Rodgers, Susan

1985   "Symbolic Patterning in Angkola Batak Adat Ritual." *Journal of Asian Studies* 44(4):765–78.

Rosaldo, Michelle

1980   *Knowledge and Passion: Ilongot Notions of Self and Social Life.* Cambridge: Cambridge University Press.

Rosaldo, Renato

1980   *Ilongot Headhunting, 1883–1974: A Study in Society and History.* Stanford: Stanford University Press.

Rousseau, Jérôme

1979   "Kayan Stratification." *Man* n.s. 14(2):215–36.

1990   *Central Borneo: Ethnic Identity and Social Life in a Stratified Society.* Oxford: Clarendon Press.

Russell, Susan, and Clark Cunningham

1989   *Changing Lives, Changing Rites: Ritual and Social Dynamics in Philippine and Indonesian Uplands.* Ann Arbor: Center for South and Southeast Asian Studies, University of Michigan.

Saililah, Johannes

n.d.   Unpublished manuscripts.

Schärer, Hans

1946   *Die Gottesidee der Ngadju-Dajak in Süd-Borneo.* Leiden.

1963   *Ngaju Religion: The Conception of God among a South Borneo People.* Rodney Needham, trans. Preface by P. E. de Josselin de Jong. The Hague: Martinus Nijhoff.

1966   *Der Totenkult der Ngadju Dajak in Süd-Borneo.* 2 Vols. Verhandelingen Van Het Koninklijk Instituut Voor Taal-, Land-, en Volkenkunde, 51, 1, 51, 2. The Hague: Martinus Nijhoff.

Schiller, Anne

1989   "Shamans and Seminarians: Ngaju Dayak Ritual Specialists and Religious Change In Central Kalimantan." in *Contributions to Southeast Asian Ethnography* 8:5–24.

1991   "On 'The Watersnake Which Is Also a Hornbill': Male and Female in Ngaju Dayak Mortuary Symbology." In *Male and Female in Borneo. Contributions and Challenges to Gender Studies.* Vinson Sutlive, ed. Borneo Research Council Monograph Series no. 1. Shangai, Va.: Ashley Printing Service, 415–33.

Schophuys, H. J.

1985   "Transmigrasi di Kalimantan." In *Sepuluh Windhu Transmigrasi di Indonesia.* Sri-Edi Swasono and Masri Singarimbun, eds. Jakarta: Penerbit Universitas Indonesia, 43–69.

Sekretariat Dewan Perwakilan Rakyat Daerah

1986   *Sejarah Pembentukan Dewan Perwakilan Rakyat Daerah Propinsi Daerah Tingkat I Kalimantan Tengah.* Palangka Raya.

Setia, Putu, ed.

1992   *Cendekiawan Hindu Bicara.* Jakarta: Yayasan Dharma Naradha.

Sevin, Olivier

1983   *Les Dayak du Centre Kalimantan: Étude géographique du Pays ngaju de la Seruyan à la Kahayan.* Paris: Orstom.

Simpei, Bajik, and Mantikei Hanyi

1996   *Panaturan.* Palangka Raya: Litho Multi Warna.

Siregar, Susan Rodgers

1981   *Adat, Islam, and Christianity in a Batak Homeland.* Papers in International Studies, Southeast Asia No. 57. Athens: Ohio University Center for International Studies.

Smythies, B. E.

1981   *The Birds of Borneo.* 3d ed. Kuala Lumpur: Sabah Society with the Malayan Nature Society.

Stohr, W.

1959   "Das Totenritual der Dayak." *Ethnologica,* n.s., 1. Cologne: Brill.

Sumnik-Dekovich, Eugenia

1985   "Significance of Ancestors in the Arts of the Dayaks of Borneo." In *The Eloquent Dead.* Jerome Feldman, ed., 101–28.

Sutlive, Vinson

1976   "The Iban Manang: An Alternate Route to Normality." In *Studies in Borneo Societies.* George Appell, ed., 64–71.

1978   *The Iban of Sarawak.* Arlington Heights: AHM Publishing Corporation.

Tambiah, Stanley

1985   *Culture, Thought, and Social Action: An Anthropological Perspective.* Cambridge: Harvard University Press.

Tong, Chee-Kiong

1993   "The Inheritance of the Dead: Mortuary Rituals among the Chinese in Singapore." *Southeast Asian Journal of Social Sciences* 21(2):130–58.

Tsing, Anna

1993   *In the Realm of the Diamond Queen: Marginality in an Out-of-the-Way Place.* Princeton: Princeton University Press.

Turner, Victor

1967   *The Forest of Symbols.* Ithaca: Cornell University Press.

1969   *The Ritual Process.* Chicago: Aldine Publishing Company.

1974   *Dramas, Fields, and Metaphors: Symbolic Action in Human Society.* Ithaca: Cornell University Press.

Ukur, Fridolin

1960   *Tuaiannja Sungguh Banjak; Sedjarah 25 Tahun Geredja Kalimantan Evangelis Dan 125 Tahun Pekabaran Indjil Di Kalimantan.* Bandjarmasin: Geredja Kalimantan Evangelis.

1971   *Tantang-Djawab Suku Dajak; Suatu Penjelidikan Tentang Unsur2 Jang Menjeketari Penolakan dan Penerimaan Indjil Dikalangan Suku-Dayak Dalam Rangka Sedjarah Gereja Di Kalimantan (1835–1945).* Jakarta: BPK Gunung Mulia.

Ullmann, Kapitein

1868   "Het 'Tiwa' der Dayaks." *Tijdschrift Bataviaasch Genootschap,* 17.

Vatikiotis, Michael

1994   *Indonesian Politics under Suharto: Order, Development and Pressure for Change.* Rev. ed. Politics in Asia Series, Michael Leifer, ed. London: Routledge.

Volkman, Toby

1979   "The Riches of the Undertaker." *Indonesia* 28:1–16.

1984   "Great Performances: Toraja Cultural Identity in the 1970s." *American Ethnologist* 11(1):152–69.

1985   *Feasts of Honor: Ritual and Change in the Toraja Highlands.* Urbana: Illinois Studies in Anthropology no. 16. University of Illinois Free Press.

Vredenbreght, Jacob

1981   *Hampatong—Kebudayaan Material Suku Dayak Di Kalimantan: The Material Culture of the Dayak of Kalimantan.* Jakarta: Gramedia.

Wales, Quaritch

1959   "The Cosmological Aspect of Indonesian Religion." *Journal of The Royal Asiatic Society of Great Britain and Ireland* pts. 3 and 4:100–139.

Weber, Max

1948   *The Protestant Ethic and the Spirit of Capitalism.* Talcott Parsons, trans. New York: Scribner.

1968 [1956]   *Economy and Society.* Ephram Fischoff et al., trans. Guenther Roth and Claus Wittich, eds. Berkeley: University of California Press.

Weinstock, Joseph

1981   "Kaharingan: Borneo's 'Old Religion' Becomes Indonesia's Newest Religion." *Borneo Research Bulletin* 13(1):47–48.

1983   "Kaharingan and the Luangan Dayaks: Religion and Identity in Central-East Borneo." Ph.D. dissertation, Cornell University.

Whittier, Herbert

1973   "Social Organization and Symbols of Differentiation: An Ethnographic Study of the Kenyah Dayak of East Kalimantan." Ph.D. dissertation, University of Michigan.

Williams, Thomas

1965   *The Dusun.* New York: Holt, Rinehart and Winston.

Winzeler, Robert L.

1985   *Ethnic Relations in Kelantan.* Singapore: Oxford University Press.

———, ed.

1993   *The Seen and the Unseen: Shamanism, Mediumship, and Possession in Borneo.* Borneo Research Council Monograph Series no. 2. Shangai, Va.: Ashley Printing Service.

Witschi, H.
  1938   *Bedrohtes Volk.* Stuttgart: Evang. Missionverlag.
Wulff, Inger
  1960   "The So-Called Priests of the Ngadju Dayaks." *Folk* 2:121–32.
Yunus, A., and S. Sastrosuwondo
  1985   *Upacara Tradisional (Upacara Kematian) Daerah Kalimantan Tengah.*
                  Jakarta: Departemen Pendidikan dan Kebudayaan, Proyek Inventariasi
                  dan Dokumentasi Kebudayaan Daerah.

Index